TRANSISTORS: THEORY AND CIRCUITRY

TRANSISTORS
Theory and Circuitry

by

K. J. DEAN

*Head of the Department of Science
and Electrical Engineering
Letchworth College of Technology*

McGRAW-HILL PUBLISHING COMPANY LIMITED

NEW YORK   LONDON   TORONTO

1964

Published by
McGraw-Hill Publishing Company Limited
McGraw-Hill House, Maidenhead, England

94004

THIS BOOK HAS BEEN SET IN MONOPHOTO TIMES NEW ROMAN 10/12 PT
AND PRINTED AND BOUND IN GREAT BRITAIN BY
WILLIAM CLOWES AND SONS, LIMITED, LONDON AND BECCLES

To my wife
with my gratitude for her encouragement and forbearance

Table of Contents

Preface

This book was written as a result of experience in teaching electronics, and in particular, transistor circuitry. In it an attempt has been made to strike a balance between circuit analysis and circuit design. At the present time, there seems to be an increasing tendency in the universities and colleges of technology to concentrate on mathematical circuit analysis, often without much examination of practical circuits. The chief use of the careful analysis of equivalent circuits, for example, must surely be that it enables the designer to make the right approximations in the situation in which he is involved. He must face practical problems on the choice of operating point, the minimization of noise, and thermal stability.

In this book, the use of some powerful mathematical tools has been deliberately avoided so that the text might be of wider use. It is hoped that this book will be of help to students working for a degree or a diploma in technology in electrical engineering or for a higher national certificate or diploma in electrical engineering or applied physics. The book may also appeal to graduates concerned with the design of transistor circuits, or who find an increasing use for electronics in research and industry. The continued high attendance at transistor courses throughout the United Kingdom and the growing interest in tunnel diodes, silicon controlled rectifiers and field effect devices, amongst others, show the wide practical use of electronics.

The recent development of silicon epitaxial transistors and the trend to modular construction have found their place in this book. The use of "building bricks" and microminiaturized packaged circuits, particularly in the fields of computation, digital control and nuclear instrumentation may well be a foretaste of things to come. Their intelligent use must depend, in the last resort, not merely on rules or loading tables, but on both circuit analysis and a thorough understanding of the principles of circuit design.

I would like to offer my thanks to those people who have helped with the preparation of this book, and in particular to Mr. F. C. Evans of Kingston College of Technology.

K.J.D.

Glossary of Terms

a_i	current gain
a_v	voltage gain
a_w	power gain
A_v	voltage gain without negative feedback
α	current gain of transistor in the common base mode
α'	current gain of transistor in the common emitter mode
α''	current gain of transistor in the common collector mode
α'_o	current gain of transistor when $V_{cb}=0$
α'_s	"on demand" current gain of transistor in common emitter mode
c_o	output capacitance (using y parameters)
c_i	input capacitance (using y parameters)
D_n	diffusion coefficient for electrons
D_p	diffusion coefficient for holes
E_F	Fermi energy
ε	the fraction of possible energy levels at an energy E which is occupied at an absolute temperature T
f_α	the frequency at which the common base short-circuited current gain has fallen to 0·707 of its low frequency value
f_1	the frequency at which the common emitter short-circuited current gain has fallen to unity
f_T	the frequency at which the common emitter short-circuited current gain is calculated to fall to unity, on the assumption of a 6 dB per octave fall
g_i	the input conductance (using y parameters)
g_m	the mutual conductance, i.e. a small change in output current divided by the change in input voltage producing it at constant output voltage
g_o	the output conductance (using y parameters)
h_i	one of the general h parameters, $(\partial V_i/\partial I_i)_{V_o}$
h_{ib}	the h_i parameter referred to the common base mode
h_{ic}	the h_i parameter referred to the common collector mode
h_{ie}	the h_i parameter referred to the common emitter mode
h_f	one of the general h parameters, $(\partial I_o/\partial I_i)_{V_o}$

h_{fb} the h_f parameter referred to the common base mode
h_{fc} the h_f parameter referred to the common collector mode
h_{fe} the h_f parameter referred to the common emitter mode
h_r one of the general h parameters, $(\partial V_i/\partial V_o)_{I_i}$
h_{rb} the h_r parameter referred to the common base mode
h_{rc} the h_r parameter referred to the common collector mode
h_{re} the h_r parameter referred to the common emitter mode
h_o one of the general h parameters, $(\partial I_o/\partial V_o)_{I_i}$
h_{ob} the h_o parameter referred to the common base mode
h_{oc} the h_o parameter referred to the common collector mode
h_{oe} the h_o parameter referred to the common emitter mode
I_b direct base current
i_b alternating component of base current
I_c direct collector current
i_c alternating component of collector current
I_{cbo} leakage current of a common base circuit
I_{ceo} leakage current of a common emitter circuit
I_{cs} thermally stabilized collector current
I_e direct emitter current
i_e alternating component of emitter current
I_i direct input current
i_i alternating component of input current
I_o direct output current
i_o alternating component of output current
J current density
k thermal stability factor, dI_{cs}/dI_{ceo}
μ mobility
μ_n electron mobility
μ_p hole mobility
N number of minority carriers
n density of free carriers (in Chapter 1)
n turns ratio
ω pulsatance, $2\pi \times$ frequency
Q selectivity factor
Q_b base charge
Q_{bs} excess base charge due to saturation
Q_{on} base charge necessary to turn transistor on
Q_{off} base charge necessary to turn transistor off
Q_v charge which is necessary to charge the depletion layer capacitance

r_b	one of the T parameters $(=z_r)$
r_c	one of the T parameters $(=z_o-z_r)$
r_e	one of the T parameters $(=z_i-z_r)$
r_{eb}	r_e+r_b
r_{ee}	$r_e+(1-\alpha)r_b$
ρ	resistivity
R_L	load resistance
R_T	transresistance, $(\partial V_o/\partial I_i)_{V_i}$
s	thermal stability, dI_{cs}/dI_{cbo}
σ	conductivity
τ	lifetime
T	absolute temperature
T_{amb}	ambient temperature
T_c	collector time constant
T_{co}	collector time constant when $V_{cb}=0$
t_D	delay time
t_F	fall time
θ	thermal resistance
T_j	junction temperature
t_R	rise time
t_S	storage time
T_s	saturation time constant
V_{cb}	direct collector–base voltage
v_{cb}	alternating component of collector–base voltage
V_{eb}	direct base–emitter voltage
v_{eb}	alternating component of base–emitter voltage
V_{ce}	direct collector–emitter voltage
v_{ce}	alternating component of collector–emitter voltage
V_i	direct input voltage
v_i	alternating component of input voltage
V_f	forward voltage of tunnel diode
V_o	direct output voltage
v_o	alternating component of output voltage
V_p	peak voltage of tunnel diode
V_v	valley voltage of tunnel diode
y_f	one of the y parameters, $(\partial I_o/\partial V_i)_{V_o}$
y_i	one of the y parameters, $(\partial I_i/\partial V_i)_{V_o}$
Y_L	admittance of an amplifier load
y_o	one of the y parameters, $(\partial I_o/\partial V_o)_{V_i}$
y_r	one of the y parameters, $(\partial I_i/\partial V_o)_{V_i}$

z_f one of the z parameters, $(\partial V_o/\partial I_i)_{I_o}$

z_i one of the z parameters, $(\partial V_i/\partial I_i)_{I_o}$

z_{in} input impedance of a transistor stage

z_o one of the z parameters, $(\partial V_o/\partial I_o)_{I_i}$

z_r one of the z parameters, $(\partial V_i/\partial I_o)_{I_i}$

CHAPTER 1

Semiconductor Physics

Semiconductors are substances with electrical resistivities in the range between those of insulators and metals. The resistivity of glass, for example, is about 10^{12} ohm cm, and that of copper is 10^{-6} ohm cm. Semiconductors invariably have a negative temperature coefficient of resistance and they often exhibit some degree of rectifier action and photoconductivity. Typical semiconductors are the elements germanium and silicon and the compounds indium antimonide, indium arsenide and copper oxide. Their chief properties can be discussed successfully by reference to their atomic structure and the forces which are acting at intermolecular levels. The energy associated with the electrons can be illustrated in energy level diagrams and by using the band theory of solids. A brief treatment of conduction in semiconductors is given in this chapter.

It is known that the electrons in an isolated atomic structure can only have certain definite energy levels, transitions being made from one energy level to another accompanied by the emission or absorption of energy. Electrons possessing little energy orbit close to the nucleus, due to their high binding energy, while energy received due to, say, ultra-violet light, increases the orbit by discrete steps and not by a continuously variable amount. Alternatively, it may remove a high energy electron in an outer orbit completely from its atomic site.

The definite energy levels in the case of individual atoms, not influenced by interatomic forces, become a series of energy bands when applied to the regular structure of a crystal lattice. The lowest energy levels are all filled. One important energy band, corresponding to electrons furthest from the nucleus in the unexcited state, is the valence band. An electron when given energy is said to be excited. It may then leave the valence band by temporarily jumping to a conduction band at yet higher energy. Such bands are often empty or only partly filled. This is illustrated in Fig. 1.1. Conduction electrons, being far from the nucleus, may be easily made to drift under the action of a field. This drift is commonly known as a conduction current.

Conduction of electrons takes place, as might be expected, in the conduction bands and so the gap between the top of the valence

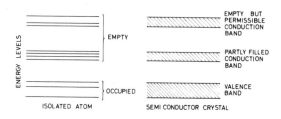

FIG. 1.1

band and the lowest energy level in the conduction band is an important characteristic of a substance. This band-gap is the minimum energy necessary to make a valence electron mobile within the crystal. Also the binding energy and the melting point of the crystal are related to the crystal structure, so that a high binding energy gives rise to a wide band-gap. Some examples are quoted in Table 1.1.

Table 1.1

substance	melting point (°C)	energy gap (eV)	mobilities (cm sec^{-1}/V cm^{-1}) electrons	holes
Gallium arsenide	1,233	1·5	4,000	400
Silicon	1,420	1·1	1,300	500
Germanium	937	0·65	3,800	1,800
Indium arsenide	940	0·36	20,000	250
Indium antimonide	525	0·2	78,000	4,000

Fermi Level

As shown in Fig. 1.1, the energy of an electron in a crystal may take one of a number of closely spaced values within these bands, and it may not take any value which lies within the non-permitted bands between them. At 0°K the lowest energy levels are filled by the electrons, so that these levels are completely occupied up to a certain level, and completely unoccupied above it. At higher temperatures, the thermal energies which the electrons possess lift them to higher energy levels. By using Fermi–Dirac statistics it is possible to calculate the fraction, ε, of possible levels at any energy E which is occupied at a temperature T:

$$\varepsilon = \frac{1}{\exp(E - E_F)/kT + 1}$$

This relationship involves the Fermi level, E_F, which is such that, at any temperature, the number of electrons with greater energy than the Fermi energy is equal to the number of unoccupied energy levels lower than this. The permitted energy band immediately above the Fermi level is the conduction band and that below it is the valence band. In conductors, the Fermi level occurs in a permitted band and, in insulators, it is in the centre of a large forbidden band. In semiconductors, the Fermi level lies in the relatively small energy gap.

Mobility

Electrical conductivity depends both on the number of charge carriers in the conduction bands and on the rate at which these charges move under the influence of an electric field. The velocity with which a charge moves in unit field is called its *mobility*. In semiconductors, the carrier concentration is often dependent on impurities present. This is particularly true where there is a large band-gap or the substance is at a low temperature. If an energy band has empty levels, it may hold electrons which may then take part in conduction. Such levels occur, for example, in the highest energy bands. Electrons entering a vacant level in the conduction band leave behind a gap or "hole" in the valence band. This permits other electrons to move up into the valence band leaving holes at a low energy level. Because of this it is convenient to consider two types of conduction. In one case the charge, $-e$, is said to be carried by an electron, and in the other the absence of an electron, due to its elevation to another band, is said to constitute a hole or a positive carrier, carrying a charge, $+e$. Thus, the free conduction electrons, moving under the action of an e.m.f., may be viewed as the movement of electric charge by negative carriers, whilst the corresponding movement of holes constitutes the motion of a charge by positive carriers.

In a pure semiconductor, conduction takes place by electron and hole pairs, since each electron that is excited leaves a hole at a lower energy level. The mobilities of these positive and negative carriers are shown in Table 1.1. Their differing mobilities are due to the fact that they are at different energy levels and travel under the action of different forces. A carrier's mobility, μ, is stated in unit field, and so is often expressed in cm sec^{-1}/V cm^{-1}, that is, in cm^{2}V^{-1}sec^{-1}.

Intrinsic Conduction

For the purposes of transistor manufacture two important materials are germanium and silicon. These elements are tetravalent, that is, they appear in group IV of the periodic table. They have a tetrahedral crystal structure similar to that of diamond, in which adjacent atoms are bound by sharing the outer valence electrons forming covalent bonds. Figure 1.2 illustrates this in one plane.

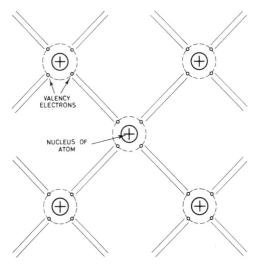

FIG. 1.2

Industrial preparation of germanium can reduce impurities to the order of one part in 10^{10}. This is largely due to the technique of zone refining, in which a liquid zone is formed in a solid ingot, and this zone is made to move along the bar of material sweeping the impurities with it. The purification of silicon is more difficult, but in the last few years much progress has been made.

Conduction in this intrinsic material is small and is made possible by the thermal energies of the electrons. Under the action of a field E, a resultant drift velocity is produced against the direction of the applied field. We can express this as:

$$v = \mu E \qquad (1.1)$$

where μ, the mobility of the carriers, is the drift velocity in unit field.

Since, as shown previously, electron mobility, μ_n, and hole mobility, μ_p, are not identical, the total current, I, flowing in an intrinsic semiconductor is given by:

$$I = I_p + I_n \qquad (1.2)$$

where I_p is the hole current and I_n is the electron current. Therefore from equations (1.1) and (1.2)

$$J = eE(n\mu_n + p\mu_p)$$

where en and ep are the respective charge densities and J is the current density. Thus the conductivity, $\sigma = J/E$ and we put $\rho = 1/\sigma$

Therefore $$\sigma = e(n\mu_n + p\mu_p) \qquad (1.3)$$

But Fowler (1936) has shown that for the thermal formation of electron–hole pairs in an intrinsic semiconductor

$$n = p = 2\frac{(2\pi mkT)^{3/2}}{h^3} \exp\left(\frac{W}{2kT}\right) \qquad (1.4)$$

(where m is the electron mass, k is Boltzmann's constant, T is the absolute temperature, h is Planck's constant and W is the energy for the formation of electron–hole pairs).

This shows the resistivity, ρ, of the material is a function of temperature. This temperature dependence of the current which flows in the semiconductor is of great practical importance. Some typical resistivities are given in Table 1.2.

Table 1.2

substance	resistivity at 300°K (ohm cm)
Germanium	65
Silicon–typical refined	250
Silicon–high purity	100,000

Extrinsic Conduction*

The electrical properties of intrinsic semiconductors can be considerably modified by the intentional addition of trace impurities in concentrations of the order of one part in 10^8. Important cases arise when the valency of the impurity is 3 or 5, causing the electrical properties of the semiconductor to be modified. *Extrinsic conduction* due to the impurity is then said to take place. This does not mean that intrinsic conduction does not also occur, but, unless the temperature is high, its effect is small compared with that due to the conduction which is due to the presence of the impurities.

A trace of impurity of group V, say arsenic, may be incorporated into the germanium lattice, each atom replacing an atom of germanium. Each arsenic atom may be considered as being completely surrounded by germanium atoms. The covalent bonds are completed with this isolated atom, an extra electron becoming available

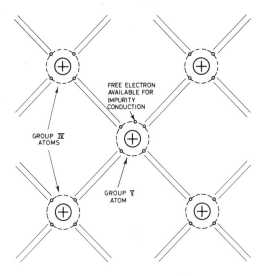

FREE ELECTRON
AVAILABLE FOR
IMPURITY
CONDUCTION

GROUP IV
ATOMS

GROUP V
ATOM

FIG. 1.3

for each atom of impurity. Impurities of this kind also include phosphorus and antimony and are called "donor" types, providing additional electrons or *n*-carriers. This technique of adding impurities to molten semiconductors in carefully controlled amounts

* Also known as "impurity conduction".

is known as "doping". Due to extrinsic conduction, doped semiconductors have reduced resistivities compared with the intrinsic materials.

At temperatures near the absolute zero, the free electrons illustrated in Fig. 1.3 remain closely bound to their own nuclei. They have a fixed energy level associated with them. It is above the valence band and below the bottom of the first conduction band of the intrinsic material. However, above temperatures of the order of $40°K$, the excess donor electrons' orbits cover several atomic distances and all these isolated donor atoms may be considered to be ionized. Under the action of an applied e.m.f. they drift in a direction imposed by the applied field. The positive nuclei left behind are static and do not drift as holes drift in intrinsic conduction. Since intrinsic conduction is taking place as well, a few holes, formed in this process, will move. Thus electrons are the majority carriers and holes are the minority carriers.

Let n be the density of free carriers and the impurity density be n_0. Then, as the temperature is raised the number of free carriers due to intrinsic conduction increases, and that due to extrinsic conduction remains substantially constant. In the case of germanium raised to $150°C$, the number of free intrinsic carriers has risen to equal the number of extrinsic carriers with normal impurity concentration. This is illustrated in Fig. 1.4.

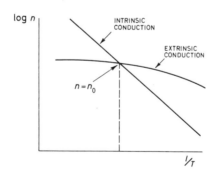

FIG. 1.4

At this temperature the semiconductor is said to become intrinsic (this may be seen from equation (1.4)), and it is nearly always necessary to operate below these temperatures. Silicon becomes intrinsic at 300°C. When the temperature of the semiconductor is lowered through this point, the material is said to become extrinsic.

Boron, aluminium and indium are examples of group III, and when these exist as impurities the lattice has one bond incomplete. This bond is filled by an electron from a neighbouring atom. This process, often repeated, may be regarded as the movement of a hole. This hole moves through several atomic distances, and, under the action of an e.m.f., becomes the majority carrier in this acceptor- or p-type material. In this case the holes or p-carriers move and the negatively charged sites are left behind.

The impurity level in the case of a group III impurity in germanium is of the order of 0.01 eV above the valence band, and for group V it is 0.01 eV below the lowest conduction level. This should be contrasted with the band-gap of about 0.65 eV.

The presence of a trace impurity of group V and its associated impurity level has the effect of raising the Fermi level above the position it normally occupies in the band-gap. Similarly, the presence of a group III impurity results in the Fermi level being lowered. Since the impurity concentration is relatively small the extent by which the Fermi level is shifted is also small. It still lies within the band-gap but displaced from its original position.

Lifetime

Minority carriers are always present in a doped semiconductor, and their concentration may be increased above their equilibrium density by incident heat or light energy. When the source of energy is removed, recombination takes place at a rate which is proportional to the excess density. This may be expressed as in equation (1.5):

$$dN/dt \propto -N \tag{1.5}$$

or $$dN/dt = -N/\tau \tag{1.6}$$

where τ is a constant depending on the semiconductor material.
One solution of this is:

$$N = N_0 \exp(-t/\tau) \tag{1.7}$$

where N_0 is the initial density when the energy source is removed. τ is the minority carrier lifetime of the material and may be regarded as the "average" time for which an excess carrier lives. For mono-crystalline germanium, τ is from 10^{-2} to 10^{-3} sec. If the semi-conductor material has dislocations of the atomic structure the life-time is very much less than this. If two slabs of material have a common surface, perhaps worked to optical limits, the dislocations are too great to produce a lifetime that would be acceptable.

Diffusion

When a concentration gradient of minority carriers exists between two boundaries in a slab of semiconductor, the carriers will diffuse in a direction such as to eliminate this gradient. The resulting dif-fusion current is in addition to any current due to the application of a field. In many types of transistor, diffusion of this kind is impor-tant, since a concentration gradient can be used to decrease the transit time of carriers across a slab of semiconductor.

For diffusion of holes, the diffusion current density, J_p, is given by:

$$J_p = -eD_p \, dp/dx$$

where D_p is the diffusion coefficient for holes and similarly D_n is the diffusion coefficient for electrons. Typical values for germanium are $D_p = 44$ cm^2 sec^{-1} and $D_n = 90$ cm^2 sec^{-1}.

Now, the characteristic length, L, is the length over which diffusion is likely to take place and $L = (\tau D)^{1/2}$ where τ and D are the appro-priate lifetimes and diffusion coefficients respectively. Thus a typical value for L is $8 . 10^{-2}$ cm. This is equivalent to the statement that the minority carrier density falls by a factor of e^{-1} in the distance L.

The *pn* Junction

There are a number of ways in which it is possible to produce a single crystal of semiconductor material with one end doped with a *p*-type impurity and the other end with an *n*-type material. The change in doping can be made to take place in a relatively short dis-tance compared with the characteristic length. We are not primarily concerned here with the techniques of manufacturing such a device, but rather with the properties of a crystal of this kind. It is essential that the impurity changes be made to take place within a single crystal structure, and without the gross discontinuities in lattice, which would inevitably take place if an attempt were made to produce a junction between two different crystals of the same substance. Figure 1.5 shows schematically a *pn* junction of this kind.

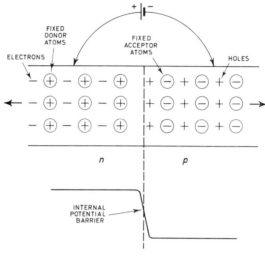

FIG. 1.5

Reverse Bias

Intrinsic conduction takes place in a semiconductor irrespective of the presence of impurities, that is, any abrupt change in the doping of a semiconductor crystal will not affect the current which flows due to this intrinsic conduction. However, providing the crystal is at a temperature well below that at which it becomes intrinsic, this current will be much smaller than the current which may flow as a result of the impurities present.

When an e.m.f. is applied as shown in Fig. 1.5, the free electrons which are present in the *n*-type germanium, due to the donor impurities, move towards the positive terminal of the supply, leaving the ionized donor atoms as fixed positive charges. In the same way the holes which are present in the *p*-type germanium, due to the acceptor atoms which are there as an impurity, are attracted towards the negative terminal leaving the ionized acceptor atoms as fixed negative charges.

Thus the application of a potential difference across the junction, with polarity as shown in the figure, results in these mobile carriers being swept from the region close to the junction. The internal potential barrier is increased with fixed sites carrying opposite charges separated by a small distance. Since the carriers which were present due to the impurity in the crystal have now been swept away, the only current which flows under these *reverse bias* conditions is the intrinsic current. Therefore the junction can be said to possess some small conductance. Also, due to the charges which are present at the ionized impurity sites, the junction possesses some small capacitance.

If the reverse bias provided by the external potential is sufficiently great, the internal potential barrier is able to give high velocities to the intrinsic carriers so that they have sufficient energy to cause ionizing collisions with the fixed atoms of the intrinsic material. This, in turn, releases more carriers so that the total current flowing increases sharply at high reverse potentials. This avalanche effect is said to result in a reverse voltage breakdown. The effect is brought about even if the breakdown region is entered for only a very short time. Its results may be permanently damaging to the *pn* junction.

Figure 1.6 shows the current–potential relationship across the reverse biased junction.

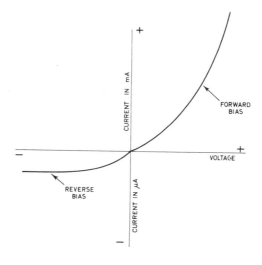

FIG. 1.6

The internal potential barrier in the vicinity of the junction is, as we have seen, due to a depletion of mobile carriers. It is known as the *depletion layer*. The width of this layer depends upon the potential difference across it, and has important bearings on the operation of the device.

Forward Bias

Figure 1.7 shows a junction forward biased with the *n*-type material connected to the negative terminal of the battery. The free electrons move towards the junction leaving the fixed donor atoms behind. A similar motion of holes takes place in the *p*-type material resulting in recombination at the junction. The internal potential

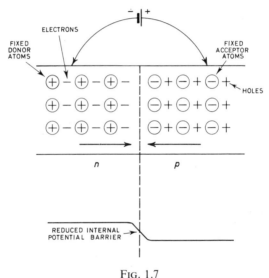

FIG. 1.7

barrier is reduced and once its effect has been overcome (as the voltage increases) a large current flows. This is shown in the forward junction characteristic in Fig. 1.6.

Since the current that flows across a *pn* junction depends on the polarity of the supply potential, its action is that of rectification and its behaviour analogous to that of a thermionic diode, the *n*-type region corresponding to the cathode and the *p*-type to the anode. Further discussion of semiconductor diodes will be postponed until Chapter 4 and again in Chapter 7.

Junction Transistors

In its early form, developed by Bardeen and Brattain in 1948, the junction transistor was made from a grown germanium crystal. That is, as the crystal was withdrawn from the melt the impurity concentration was altered. One way in which this can be done is to use the technique of overdoping. If donor impurities are added to the melt an *n*-type semiconductor results. If now just sufficient acceptor impurities are added to swamp the effect of the donor impurities, the overdoping of the material causes the semiconductor to have *p*-type properties. Successive overdoping of the melt as the crystal is withdrawn results in adjacent regions of *p*- and *n*-type material. The rate at which it is withdrawn can be altered to give sharply defined *pn* junctions and enables the width of the *p*- and *n*-type regions to be controlled. In one form of junction transistor, the crystal is then suitably cut so that a thin *n*-type region is sandwiched between two *p*-type regions. Connections are then made to all three layers. The resultant device is called a *pnp* junction transistor. Using this method *npn* junction transistors are also available. Modern circuit design may well call for the use of both of these in the one equipment. This often results in considerable simplification of circuitry, and will be frequently employed in the circuits shown in later chapters. No such facility is available with thermonic valves.

A *pnp* transistor will now be considered in some detail.

In Fig. 1.8, the emitter–base junction is forward biased since a

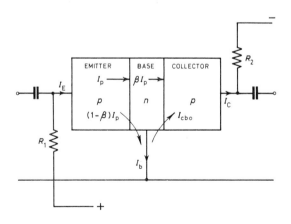

FIG. 1.8

positive potential is applied to the emitter, with respect to the base, through the resistor R_1. Now the p-type material of the emitter is relatively impure, so that its extrinsic current is much greater than its intrinsic current. Hence it contributes very many more holes than electrons to the emitter current, so that holes are the majority carriers. The ratio of these majority carriers to the total emitter current is the emitter efficiency, γ. This current must also flow into the base region. Now the base region is relatively pure. This results in high resistivity and in few donor electrons being contributed to the emitter current. This base region is made purposely thin so that there is very little recombination of carriers there. Thus a large fraction of the available majority carriers reach the collector. This fraction is the transport factor, β. The base–collector junction is reverse biased and so its current in the absence of injected carriers is small. Hence the ratio of collector current to emitter current is approximately $\gamma \times \beta$. This current gain ratio is known as α_o. Its value is commonly from 0·9 to just less than one. The techniques of manufacture are often aimed at making it as near unity as possible. In this way the current which emerges at the collector depends on the emitter current and is nearly equal to it.

The input junction being forward biased offers a low impedance whilst the output junction, reverse biased, is at high impedance. A fractional current amplification which is less than unity can thus lead to a voltage gain of much more than unity.

Figure 1.8 also shows one method by which the transistor may be used. This is the *common base* connection. The more important currents are indicated in the figure. The collector current, I_c, is seen to consist of a useful component, αI_E, which develops the output voltage $\alpha I_E R_2$ across the resistor R_2, and an undesired component, I_{cbo}, which is the leakage current due to intrinsic conduction in the reverse biased diode. It is often impossible to ignore this component of current in design as it may limit the power dissipation of the device.

Some typical values of I_{cbo} will be mentioned in detail in later chapters. At about 20°C, I_{cbo} for germanium is of the order of 10 microamps and for silicon it is very much less. Recent techniques have made the construction of transistors possible with a leakage current of the order of 1 nanoamp. These values are for typical small transistors.

I_B, in Fig. 1.8, is seen to be very small, a feature which will be of importance later. A more conventional representation of Fig. 1.8 is given by Fig. 1.9(a).

The direction of the arrow on the emitter indicates the use of a *pnp* transistor. It can be remembered as showing the direction of conventional current flow. Figure 1.9(b) shows a similar common

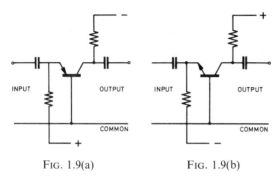

FIG. 1.9(a)   FIG. 1.9(b)

base arrangement for an *npn* transistor. Here the majority carriers* injected from the emitter into the collector are electrons. The emitter–base junction is still forward biased and the base–collector junction is reverse biased. In order to achieve these conditions, where electrons are available from the emitter, the device must be operated with the opposite potentials from those of the *pnp* transistor.

PROBLEMS

1.1   Define the term *semiconductor* in terms of the band theory. Briefly outline the properties of a semiconductor and say how these may be modified at very low temperatures.

1.2   What do you understand by a *depleted band*? Describe briefly what is meant by an empty level in a depleted band. What name is usually given to such a level? Explain whereabouts in the energy bands of a solid a depleted band may occur (a) when the solid is in a state of equilibrium, and (b) during some transition.

1.3   Explain the phenomenon of intrinsic conductivity in semi-conductors in terms of thermal excitation and recombination. In what way is the number of carriers in intrinsic conduction dependent upon temperature?

---

* The *majority* carriers of the input junction become the *minority* carriers of the output junction.

1.4   Outline the theory of conduction in a *pn* junction. Explain the reasons for any differences likely to be experienced, between conduction in a monocrystalline junction and in a junction containing gross lattice defects.

1.5   Discuss transistor action in a junction transistor from the point of view of the impurity concentration in the three transistor regions. Hence point out any differences in the resistivity of these regions. Give typical values for these resistivities.

1.6   Explain carefully how zone refining of a bar of germanium may be carried out. Why was it found difficult to extend the technique to the refining of silicon? In what way is the resistivity of a semiconductor related to its purity? Illustrate your answer with typical values.

1.7   Explain how it is that the mobilities of electrons and holes differ in the same semiconductor material at a constant temperature. How do these mobilities alter when (a) the temperature is raised, and (b) the resistivity of the semiconductor is increased?

1.8   Draw a diagram (similar to that of Fig. 1.8) to illustrate the flow of current in an *npn* transistor and employ it to explain the significance of the terms *emitter efficiency* and *transport factor*.

1.9   Explain, with reference to a suitable diagram, how extrinsic conduction takes place in a *p*-type doped semiconductor, as its temperature is raised from near the absolute zero to a high temperature above that at which it becomes intrinsic.

1.10   Describe the action of a germanium *pn* junction and sketch a typical characteristic. In what way can you explain the reduced reverse current that flows when silicon is used instead of germanium.

1.11   Discuss what connections there are between the minority carrier lifetime, the diffusion length and the base width in a junction transistor. Hence, explain what limits the lifetime of carriers, and why it is that the transistor must be made from material possessing a continuous crystal structure.

The reader who wishes to extend his knowledge of semiconductor physics should use the questions raised in these problems to direct his further reading of this subject.

BIBLIOGRAPHY

Dunlap: "An Introduction to Semiconductors", Wiley, 1957.
Goudet and Meulot: "Semiconductors, Their Theory and Practice", McDonald and Evans, 1957.

Jonscher, A. K.: "Principles of Semiconductor Device Operation", Bell, 1960.

Shockley, W.: "Electrons and Holes in Semiconductors", Wiley, 1951.

Smith, R. A.: "Semiconductors", C.U.P., 1959.

Valdes, L. B.: "The Physical Theory of Transistors", McGraw-Hill, 1961.

CHAPTER 2

Types of Transistor and Transistor Characteristics

Static Characteristics

The performance of a transistor amplifier can be investigated by first examining the static characteristics of the transistor employed. Figure 2.1 shows a typical practical arrangement for examining the characteristics of a transistor. Care should be taken in measuring currents to use a meter having a low resistance.

There are three potentials and three currents associated with the transistor. Assuming that the directions of the currents are as shown

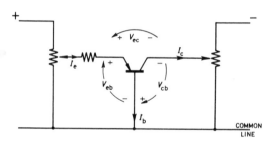

FIG. 2.1

in the figure, we may then apply Kirchhoff's laws to obtain a solution of the circuit conditions.

Therefore $$I_e - I_c - I_b = 0 \qquad (2.1)$$

and $$V_{ec} - V_{cb} - V_{eb} = 0 \qquad (2.2)$$

This technique, which does not take into account the modified behaviour of the transistor at high frequencies, really assumes that the transistor is a four-terminal network whose input and output voltages and currents can be measured. It is not an attempt to set out the physical reasons for the behaviour of the transistor.

We are then left with four independent variables, and we may choose which of the six we shall take as independent provided always that we take two currents and two voltages, the possible choices leading to six useful sets of parameters. In this chapter, we shall consider, first, just one of these sets to avoid confusion. After this others can be considered.

One such group consists of I_e, I_c, V_{eb}, V_{cb}. This is a group in which potentials are measured with respect to the base, and so represent the input and output voltages and currents in the common base connection. Hence these variables are important in this common base arrangement which was briefly described in the last chapter. By way of contrast, it may be remembered that the variables, in considering a triode valve, are I_a, I_g, V_a, V_g and of these the direct current input, I_g, is often zero. Here, no such simplification exists, and for this reason, among others, the basic function of a transistor is often said to be that of a current amplifier, whereas that of a thermionic valve is a voltage amplifier. The junction transistor is controlled by varying the current flow through the base region, whilst the thermionic valve is controlled by changes in grid voltage.

Figure 2.2 shows a set of characteristic curves obtained as a result of a practical experiment such as that shown in Fig. 2.1 and based on the four chosen variables. These curves are labelled A, B, C and D. Our four variables may be expressed mathematically thus:

$$V_{eb} = f_1(I_e, V_{cb}) \tag{2.3}$$

$$I_c = f_2(I_e, V_{cb}) \tag{2.4}$$

These may be put into partial differential form:

$$dV_{eb} = \left(\frac{\partial V_{eb}}{\partial I_e}\right)_{V_{cb}} \delta I_e + \left(\frac{\partial V_{eb}}{\partial V_{cb}}\right)_{I_e} \delta V_{cb} \tag{2.5*}$$

$$dI_c = \left(\frac{\partial I_c}{\partial I_e}\right)_{V_{cb}} \delta I_e + \left(\frac{\partial I_c}{\partial V_{cb}}\right)_{I_e} \delta V_{cb} \tag{2.6*}$$

The partial differential coefficients of equations (2.5) and (2.6) relate changes in one current or voltage with changes in another current or voltage, similarly to the way in which the mutual

---

* The suffixes used with the differential coefficients in the equations (2.5), (2.6) and elsewhere in this book are used to show which of the variables are maintained constant in each partial differential coefficient.

characteristic slope of a triode valve may be expressed as a partial differential coefficient and used to define the mutual conductance of the valve.

Since one of these has the dimensions of potential, another has the dimensions of conductance, and two are ratios, these coefficients

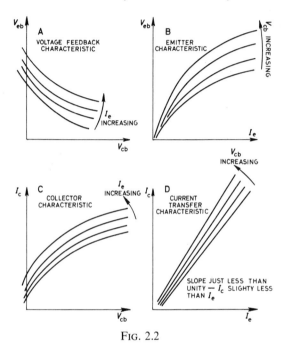

Fig. 2.2

are often called hybrid or h coefficients. They are related to the slopes of the four families of graphs in Fig. 2.2.

For example, in graph A the slope may be written as $\left(\dfrac{\partial V_{eb}}{\partial V_{cb}}\right)_{I_e}$

and in graph B the slope is $\left(\dfrac{\partial V_{eb}}{\partial I_e}\right)_{V_{cb}}$

For this reason, equations (2.5) and (2.6) may be rewritten:

$$dV_{eb} = h_i \delta I_e + h_r \delta V_{cb} \tag{2.5a}$$

$$dI_c = h_f \delta I_e + h_o \delta V_{cb} \tag{2.6a}$$

where h_f and h_o are similarly derived from C and D.

An alternative terminology is to write h_{11} for h_i, h_{12} for h_r, h_{21} for h_f and h_{22} for h_o. Both systems are in common use; the use of letters as suffixes will be adopted here.* Referring back to equation (2.5a), $h_r \, \delta V_{cb}$ in practice is very much less than $h_i \, \delta I_e$, hence:

$$dV_{eb} \fallingdotseq h_i \, dI_e \qquad (2.7)$$

Also, since $h_o \, \delta V_{cb}$ is much smaller than $h_f \, \delta_e$, from equation (2.6a) we have:

$$dI_c \fallingdotseq h_f \, dI_e \qquad (2.8)$$

Therefore, to a first order of approximation, h_i is the input resistance to a.c. It is only strictly true when δV_{cb} is zero, that is, when the output is short-circuited. Also h_f is very nearly equal to dI_c/dI_e. $dI_c/dI_e = \alpha$, where α is the small signal current amplification factor. The same limitations are true here as in the case of the input resistance.

Also, h_r relates to changes in input and output voltages under the specific condition of constant emitter current. It is the voltage feedback factor. Similarly, h_o is the output conductance, since it relates changes in output current and voltage. Some typical values are given in Table 2.1. The table may also be used to assess the validity

Table 2.1

semiconductor	transistor	type	h_i (ohms)	h_r ($\times 10^{-4}$)	h_f	h_o (μmhos)	I_c (mA)
Germanium	OC 71	pnp	35	7	0·98	1·0	1
Germanium	NKT 226	pnp	65	6	0·99	1·0	1
Silicon	2S004	npn	42	4	0·98	0·4	1
Silicon	2N336	npn	55	4	0·99	0·4	1
Silicon planar	2N699B	npn	27	0·5	0·985	0·12	1
			6·4	0·6	0·988	0·14	5
Silicon planar	2N996	pnp	27	10	0·985	0·65	1
			7	14	0·990	5·5	5

of the approximations in equations (2.7) and (2.8). It should be noted, also, that these approximations depend on small signal operation and for small values of load impedance making δV_{cb} small.

* See Appendix A for a general treatment of h parameters.

3

Common Emitter Arrangement

Equation (2.7) shows that, using practical figures, the input impedance of a common base amplifier is very low, and the output impedance which may be taken as the reciprocal of h_o is very high. Therefore, useful interconnection between two of these stages becomes difficult, except with the use of matching transformers. One solution is to replace the common base circuit, which has been considered so far, by the common emitter connection where the impedance ratio between input and output is much less. This circuit has other features which also tend to make it attractive in circuit design. Figure 2.3 shows a possible method of connection for the

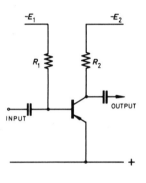

Fig. 2.3

common emitter amplifier. This basic circuit is of great importance, but certain essential modifications will be introduced later.

It will be seen that the supplies for both collector and base are of the same polarity. Providing R_1 is correctly chosen, then both collector and base may be fed from the same supply line.

Common Emitter Characteristics

Here four suitable variables for analysis are I_c, I_b, V_{ec}, V_{eb}. Proceeding as in equations (2.3) and (2.4) we may write:

$$V_{eb} = f_3(I_b, V_{ec}) \tag{2.9}$$

$$I_c = f_4(I_b, V_{ec}) \tag{2.10}$$

Equations (2.9) and (2.10) lead to:

$$dV_{eb} = \left(\frac{\partial V_{eb}}{\partial I_b}\right)_{V_{ec}} \delta I_b + \left(\frac{\partial V_{eb}}{\partial V_{ec}}\right)_{I_b} \delta V_{ec} \qquad (2.11)$$

$$dI_c = \left(\frac{\partial I_c}{\partial I_b}\right)_{V_{ec}} \delta I_b + \left(\frac{\partial I_c}{\partial V_{ec}}\right)_{I_b} \delta V_{ec} \qquad (2.12)$$

Putting these into parametric form:

$$dV_{eb} = h_{ie}\,\delta I_b + h_{re}\,\delta V_{ec} \qquad (2.11a)$$

$$dI_c = h_{fe}\,\delta I_b + h_{oe}\,\delta V_{ec} \qquad (2.12a)$$

Here the additional suffix e has been used with the parameters for common emitter operation, and the suffix b will in future be employed to imply common base operation. The extra suffix is sometimes omitted, where no confusion can arise regarding which circuit is implied, or where its use is equally applicable to them all.

A set of characteristics for common emitter connection is shown in Fig. 2.4.

Here again, the hybrid parameters are related to the slopes of the four graphs of Fig. 2.4. Some typical values for these parameters are given in Table 2.2.

Table 2.2

transistor	h_{ie} (kilohms)	h_{re} ($\times 10^{-4}$)	h_{fe}	h_{oe} (μmhos)	I_c (mA)
2N699B	2·8	3·5	70	11	1
OC 202	2·1	6·0	70	42	1
OC 71	1·5	8·0	41	42	1
ZT 23	1·6	1·1	50	2·5	1
2N105	2·9	5·5	55	16	1
2N344	1·6	6·0	22	80	0·5
2S102	0·45	0·9	18	25	5
2N996	$\begin{cases}2\cdot0\\0\cdot8\end{cases}$	1·4 \\ 2·6	70 \\ 105	40 \\ 200	1 \\ 5

Figure 2.4(D) shows a typical output family of characteristics, with equal increments of I_b between each member. For operation as

a linear amplifier, the transistor should be biased away from the saturation region where the characteristics are coincident, and away from the region of low current gain where the characteristics,

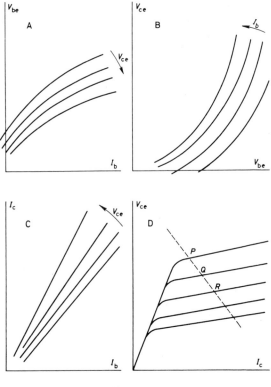

Fig. 2.4

although parallel, are close together. This is approaching the cut-off region where the input junction is no longer forward biased. A typical output voltage swing might be between the points P and R in the figure, the static bias point being that marked Q. It is also true, that for linear amplification, the input *current*, rather than the input voltage, must be proportional to the signal. Therefore, a high impedance source is often used.

The figures quoted in Table 2.2 are design centres. The manufacturer grades transistors, and guarantees a particular type of transistor to have a value of h_{fe} within a stated production spread. For example, a value of h_{fe} of 60 might be representative of transistors which, when measured, might have h_{fe} between 45 and 100. This spread is usually stated by the manufacturer.

It can be seen from the table, that h_{re} is small, and since $h_{re} \, \delta V_{ec}$ is much less than $h_{ie} \, \delta I_b$, equation (2.11a) becomes

$$dV_{eb} \doteqdot h_{ie} \, dI_b \qquad (2.13)^*$$

Thus h_{ie} is often a good approximation to the input impedance.* It is seen to be higher than h_{ib}.

Again, from the figures in Table 2.2 and equation (2.12a)

$$dI_c = h_{fe} \, dI_b \qquad h_{fe} \approx \beta \approx \alpha' \qquad (2.14)^*$$

dI_c/dI_b is the small signal current gain for the common emitter connection and is seen to be much greater than unity. It is written α' or β. The use of α' will be followed here. It should be noted that changes in I_b and in I_c have opposite sign. Therefore, α' is defined as $-\partial I_c/\partial I_b$. Now $\alpha = dI_c/dI_e$, and from equation (2.1) $I_b = I_e - I_c$.

Thus

$$\alpha' = \frac{dI_c}{dI_e - dI_c} = \frac{\alpha}{1 - \alpha} \qquad (2.15)$$

Equivalent Circuits

There are many equivalent circuits which are used to give a picture of the physical behaviour of transistors. Fundamentally these are derived from a uniform transmission line, but it is often convenient to lump the constants of such a line, and to draw the equivalent circuit in terms of a set of parameters such as the hybrid parameters. A circuit of this kind is arranged to satisfy a set of parametric equations such as (2.11a) and (2.12a). While illustrating the behaviour of the transistor, it gives no basic reason for that behaviour. One such circuit is shown in Fig. 2.5. The validity of this circuit can be checked by comparison with these equations.

The equivalent circuit can be used to deduce the input and output impedance of a practical amplifier and the dynamic voltage and current gains. The circuit (like its thermionic counterparts) is representative of a.c. conditions only, and is not used to measure

* The same limitations apply to the validity of these expressions as applied to the comparable expressions for the common base amplifier— see page 21.

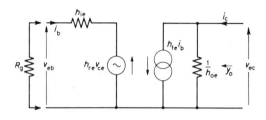

FIG. 2.5

direct potentials. In Fig. 2.5, and in the following analysis, the small changes which were assumed to occur are made sinusoidal. Therefore, v_{eb}, i_b, etc. may be used to indicate small signal alternating quantities and replace the differentials of the foregoing equations.

Input Impedance, z_{in}

From Fig. 2.5, $v_{eb} = i_b\,h_{ie} + v_{ce}h_{re}$ and $z_{in} = v_{eb}/i_b$

Therefore
$$z_{in} = h_{ie} + h_{re}\,v_{ce}/i_b \qquad (2.16)$$

But, from equation (2.12a)

$$i_b = (i_c - h_{oe}v_{ce})/h_{fe} \qquad (2.17)$$

and, if Y_L is written for $-i_c/v_{ce}$, where Y_L is the admittance of the load, equations (2.16) and (2.17) become

$$z_{in} = h_{ie} - \frac{h_{re}h_{fe}}{Y_L + h_{oe}} \qquad (2.18)$$

Equation (2.18) gives the input impedance under any specified conditions, and, in particular, when the output is short-circuited, that is, when Y_L has become infinite. Under this condition, $z_{in} = h_{ie}$. Hence, the approximation of equation (2.13) is in fact the input impedance with a short circuit load. z_{in} in fact increases as Y_L increases for all positive values of Y_L, since the second term in equation (2.18) is always negative.

Current Gain, a_i

The dynamic current gain is due to that fraction of $h_{fe}i_b$ which flows through the load.

Therefore
$$a_i = \frac{h_{fe}i_b}{i_b}\frac{Y_L}{Y_L + h_{oe}} = \frac{h_{fe}Y_L}{Y_L + h_{oe}} \qquad (2.19)$$

It is quite common for the load to be of the order of 1–5 kilohms. Therefore, Y_L is often much greater than h_{oe} and the current gain is approximately equal to h_{fe}. However, this is only strictly true when Y_L tends to infinity. Therefore, h_{fe} is the small signal current gain with a short-circuited load.

Output Admittance, y_o

The output admittance, y_o, when the input is supplied from a generator of impedance R_g can now be found.

From the right-hand mesh, $y_o = h_{oe} - h_{fe}i_b/v_{ce}$. But from the left-hand mesh, $i_b = h_{re}v_{ce}/(h_{ie} + R_g)$.

Hence
$$y_o = h_{oe} - \frac{h_{fe}h_{re}}{h_{ie} + R_g} \qquad (2.20)$$

In particular, when the transistor is driven from a high impedance source and R_g tends to infinity,

$$y_o = h_{oe} \qquad (2.21)$$

Voltage Gain, a_v, and Power Gain, a_w

By a similar method the voltage gain may be found. The power gain is an important quantity. It is the product of voltage and current gains. Whereas a thermionic valve has an extremely large (almost infinite) power gain, the power gain of a transistor is often in the range 20–40 dB.

Common Collector Arrangement

Figure 2.6 shows the common collector arrangement. This type of circuit is also known as an emitter follower due to its similarity to the cathode-follower thermionic circuit.

Again, the differential equations may be written down and the parameters deduced from them.

Here $V_{bc} = f_5(I_b, V_{ec})$ (2.22)

and $I_e = f_6(I_b, V_{ec})$ (2.23)

or, $dV_{bc} = \left(\dfrac{\partial V_{bc}}{\partial I_b}\right)_{V_{ec}} \delta I_b + \left(\dfrac{\partial V_{bc}}{\partial V_{ec}}\right)_{I_b} \delta V_{ec}$ (2.24)

and $dI_e = \left(\dfrac{\partial I_e}{\partial I_b}\right)_{V_{ec}} \delta I_b + \left(\dfrac{\partial I_e}{\partial V_{ec}}\right)_{I_b} \delta V_{ec}$ (2.25)

Equations (2.24) and (2.25) may be expressed:

$$dV_{bc} = h_{ic}\,\delta I_b + \delta h_{rc} V_{ec} \tag{2.24a}$$

$$dI_e = h_{fc}\,\delta I_b + h_{oc}\,\delta V_{ec} \tag{2.25a}$$

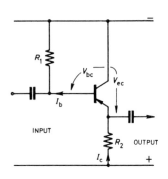

FIG. 2.6

Current Gain

The current gain, α'', is defined as dI_e/dI_b.

From equation (2.1) $I_b = I_e - I_c$

Therefore $dI_e/dI_b = \alpha'' = \dfrac{dI_e}{dI_e - dI_c} = \dfrac{1}{1-\alpha}$ (2.26)

since $\alpha = dI_c/dI_e$.

But from Table 2.3, we see that h_{oc} is small and in equation (2.25a), $h_{oc}\,\delta V_{ec}$ is much less than $h_{fe}\,\delta I_b$ for small signal operation.

Hence $dI_e/dI_b \fallingdotseq h_{fc} = \alpha''$

Similarly, the other parameters may be deduced. Some typical values are shown in Table 2.3.

Comparison between the figures in Table 2.3 and equation (2.24a), shows that the input impedance is not equal to h_{ic}, since h_{rc} is not negligible. In fact, the input impedance varies considerably

Table 2.3

transistor	h_{ic} (kilohms)	h_{rc}	h_{fc}*	h_{oc} (μmhos)
OC 71	1·5	1†	42	42
GT 33	2·5	1†	61	25

* Measured at a collector current of 1 mA
† Very nearly

with the load impedance (R_2 in Fig. 2.6), and over a wide range is approximately equal to the product of α'' and the load impedance.

Summary

If parameters are given for some transistor for one circuit configuration, it is clearly possible to deduce their values for either of the other important modes of operation. The relationships between these and other parameters are listed in Appendix A.

Table 2.4 summarizes the performance at low frequencies of the three major circuit arrangements. To obtain it we have considered one analytical approach, that of hybrid parameters, to assess the performance of a transistor in these simple circuits. It is not

Table 2.4

Transistor Amplifiers—Summary

	input impedance	current gain	voltage gain	output impedance
Common Base	low	α (just less than unity)	high	high
Common Emitter	medium	$\alpha' = \dfrac{\alpha}{1-\alpha}$ high	high	medium
Common Collector	high (approx. $\alpha'' \times$ load)	$\alpha'' = \dfrac{1}{1-\alpha}$ high	just less than unity	low (approx. source impedance $\div \alpha''$)

intended now to go through a procedure of this kind again in full, but other similar sets of parameters exist. These are used because no one set of parameters will yield simple solutions to all possible transistor circuit problems and, also, the appropriate equivalent circuits are applicable to the solution of the design of particular circuits. Also transistor data are not specified by all manufacturers in terms of the same parameters.

z Parameters

Two of the hybrid parameters were pure numbers, one a resistance and one a conductance. It might have been more convenient if they had all been dimensionally similar. It should not be assumed from this that the hybrid parameters are so awkward that they are never used, but the reader should be advised of their limitations in this respect.

One alternative approach is to choose the variables so that all four parameters are impedances. It will be shown that this leads to the T equivalent circuit of Fig. 2.7.

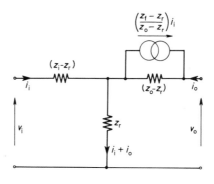

FIG. 2.7

Let V_i and I_i be generalized symbols for the input voltage and current. They will be replaced by V_{be} and I_b in the common emitter case, or V_{be} and I_e in the common base arrangement. Similarly, V_o and I_o are the output voltage and current. The method is similar to that used with the h parameters, the variables being related as follows:

$$V_i = f_7(I_i, I_o) \tag{2.27}$$

$$V_o = f_8(I_i, I_o) \tag{2.28}$$

By a process similar to that we have already employed these lead to:

$$v_i = z_i i_i + z_r i_o \qquad (2.29)$$

$$v_o = z_f i_i + z_o i_o \qquad (2.30)$$

where z_i, z_r, z_f and z_o are the parameters. Consideration of the full differential equations will show that all these parameters have the dimensions of impedance.

It is convenient to rewrite equation (2.29) in the form

$$v_i = (z_i - z_r)i_i + z_r(i_i + i_o) \qquad (2.31)*$$

and equation (2.30) may be rewritten as

$$v_o = z_r(i_i + i_o) + (z_f - z_r)i_i + (z_o - z_r)i_o$$

or $$v_o = z_r(i_i + i_o) + \frac{(z_f - z_r)(z_o - z_r)i_i}{(z_o - z_r)} + (z_o - z_r)i_o \qquad (2.32)$$

These equations are put into this form since they then easily lead to the equivalent circuit of Fig. 2.7 and equations (2.31) and (2.32) are seen to be the input and output mesh equations.

If Fig. 2.7 is taken to be representative of a transistor used as a common base amplifier, the somewhat cumbersome parameter formulae may be replaced as in Fig. 2.8, where r_e, r_b and r_c are used instead of the z parameters. These new parameters which replace them are the T parameters.

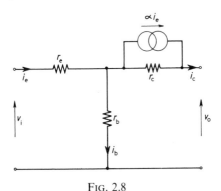

FIG. 2.8

* It should be noted that the directions chosen for the currents i_i and i_o follow the usual convention for the analysis of a general case.

The current generator simplifies to αi_e on the assumption that z_r is much smaller than z_f or z_o. This is seen to be justified from Table 2.5 since $z_i - z_r$ is equal to r_e and z_r equals r_b, and both r_e and r_b are much less than r_c which is often about 1 megohm.

Table 2.5

transistor	r_e (ohms)	r_b (ohms)	α'	I_c (mA)
OC 71	18	700	41	1
2N105	34	976	51	2
GT 47	25	500	100	1
OC 202	25	800	70	1

Figure 2.8 could have been drawn for the common emitter circuit, but it is usual to define these T parameters for common base operation, and then to derive equivalent circuits for common emitter and common collector circuits, in terms of the same T parameters that have been adopted for the common base amplifier. Some conversion tables between the h parameters and the T parameters are to be found in Appendix A.

Derivation of the T Circuit for Common Emitter Operation

To use the T equivalent circuit to represent the operation of the transistor in the common emitter mode it is first redrawn as in Fig. 2.9(a).

It is more useful to put the current generator αi_e into the form $\alpha' i_b$ so that it is a function of the input current, i_b. This is done in Fig. 2.9(b). The impedance r_c has been replaced by r_m, for it is clear

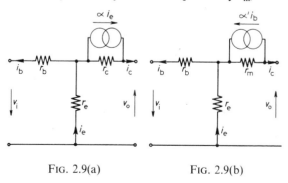

FIG. 2.9(a)   FIG. 2.9(b)

from Table 2.4 that the output impedance is different from that of the common base amplifier. It is necessary to prove the equivalence of the two figures, for they represent the same circuit under the same conditions and will, for example, have the same input impedance and current gain. In so doing, the connection between r_c and r_m will become apparent, and the validity of the use of $\alpha' i_b$ demonstrated.

If these circuits are equivalent to each other their input and output conditions may be equated.

In Fig. 2.9(a)

$$v_i = i_e r_e + i_b r_b \tag{2.33}$$

$$v_o = \alpha i_e r_c - i_c r_c - i_b r_b \tag{2.34}$$

In Fig. 2.9(b)

$$v_i = i_e r_e + i_b r_b \tag{2.33a}$$

$$v_o = -(i_e r_e + i_c r_m + \alpha' i_b r_m) \tag{2.35}$$

Comparing equations (2.33) and (2.33a) the input conditions are seen to be identical.

Equating equations (2.34) and (2.35), so that the output conditions shall be the same:

$$\alpha i_e r_c - i_c r_c - i_b r_b = -(i_e r_e + i_c r_m + \alpha' i_b r_m)$$

Now, $i_b r_b$ is approximately equal to $i_e r_e$, and both are much smaller than $i_c r_c$ and so can be neglected.

Then, putting $i_e = i_c + i_b$

$$r_c i_c - \alpha r_c (i_c + i_b) = i_c r_m + \alpha' i_b r_m$$

or $\qquad r_c(1-\alpha)i_c - \alpha r_c i_b = i_c r_m + \alpha' i_b r_m$

This expression is seen to be an identity if $r_m = r_c(1-\alpha)$. Also, it demonstrates that it is permissible to use a current generator, $\alpha' i_b$, having the sign shown in the figure.

This T-junction of resistors (or impedances) has the advantage that there is only one active element, the current generator $\alpha' I_b$. Some typical values for the T parameters are given in Table 2.5. As might have been expected from equation (1.4), all the parameters that have been deduced are, to a greater or less extent, dependent on temperature. Some parameters also depend on the collector current that flows at the time of measurement. For this reason the figures given in the tables are to be used to give a guide to the range of typical values that are to be encountered. It is not always possible to obtain from manufacturers, data which is referred to a given collector current. For example, r_e can be shown theoretically to be inversely proportional to the collector current when the collector current is small. This topic is pursued further in Chapter 3.

Input and output impedances and voltage and current gains can be calculated using the T parameters, in the same way as that using the h parameters. The reader is referred to Appendix B for further information on this topic.

Hybrid π Parameters

At high frequencies, the equivalent circuits so far discussed become increasingly inaccurate. The use of hybrid π parameters is an attempt to overcome this, since it attempts to take into account the reactances present at the junctions. However, none of these circuits may be closely relied upon when the upper frequency limit of the transistor is approached. The hybrid π equivalent circuit is shown in Fig. 2.10 as it is applied to the common emitter circuit. In

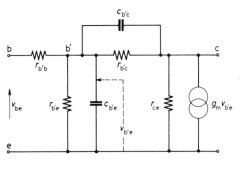

FIG. 2.10

this circuit the point b is the point at which connection is made to the base. However, the base material is relatively pure and so has a high resistivity. This is necessary in order to obtain a high emitter efficiency. There is a significant resistance between the point b and the active base region, since it is not possible to make the base contact extremely close to the active base region. This is the resistance $r_{b'b}$ and the point b' represents this active base region.

$c_{b'e}$ is the base-emitter capacitance. It is due to two capacitances, the relative importance of which depends on the nature of the junction bias.

(i) *The barrier layer capacitance.* This is proportional to the area of the emitter junction. For an abrupt junction it is proportional to $V^{-1/2}$ and for a linear gradient junction it is proportional to $V^{-1/3}$, where V is the applied bias. A fused alloy junction is typical of an abrupt junction and a grown junction is typical of a linear gradient junction.

(ii) *The diffusion capacitance.* This is proportional to $\omega^{-1/2}$ and is a function of the base width, increasing with the base width. When the junction is reverse biased the barrier layer capacitance is more important, but when it is forward biased the diffusion capacitance is so large that the barrier layer capacitance can be neglected, particularly since the input capacitance of a forward biased junction is shunted by a low resistance.

$c_{b'c}$ is the collector capacitance and is, in part, due to the capacitance of the collector depletion layer. It is therefore related to the area of the collector junction.

The mutual conductance, $g_m = -\alpha'/r_{b'e}$. Some typical values are given in Table 2.6.

Table 2.6

transistor	$r_{b'b}$ (ohms)	$r_{b'e}$ (ohms)	$c_{b'e}$ (pF)	$r_{b'c}$ (megohms)	$c_{b'c}$ (pF)	r_{ce} (kilohms)	g_m (mA V^{-1})	f_α (Mc/s)
OC 45	75	1,315	1,000	3·33	10·5	62·5	38	6
NKT 142	200	2,000	400	3·0	20	20	39	12
2N105	250	2,700	4,500	5·0	17	200	21	1
GT 41	100	790	1,560	2·6	15	122	38	4
GET 874	100	1,800	500	2·6	8·5	40	38	15
OC 202	250	1,800	2,000	2·1	29·5	35	39·5	3·2*

* f_1

The effect of the inherent capacitances of the transistor is to limit the frequency response, since the transistor is shunted by $c_{b'e}$ and there is feedback from the output to the input through $c_{b'c}$. The manufacturers indicate these limitations in one of three ways. The frequency at which the short circuit current gain when used in the common base configuration has fallen 3 dB of its low frequency value is called f_α. This was frequently used in the early stage of transistor development since the highest frequency operation is obtained in the common base arrangement. Table 2.6 includes values of f_α. Secondly, the frequency at which the common emitter current gain has fallen to unity is f_1. This is of importance since the common emitter mode is the one that is most often used. Finally, f_T is the frequency at which the common emitter current gain is calculated to fall to unity if its rate of fall at the upper frequency end of its pass band is maintained constant at 6 dB per octave (see Fig. 4.5). Thus f_1 is found by experiment, and f_T is theoretically deduced since it gives a more realistic value for the performance of a transistor whose gain might at first fall rapidly, but more gradually at higher frequencies, thus giving a high figure for f_1.

Types of Transistor

The early junction transistors were grown types, as has been mentioned. These were followed by alloy junctions. The impurities were applied to both sides of the base wafer, and by heat treatment were made to alloy with the semiconductor material, so forming the emitter and collector by overdoping. Figure 2.11 shows a section (not to scale) through an alloy transistor. The figure shows some of the more important features of the transistor. The base width should

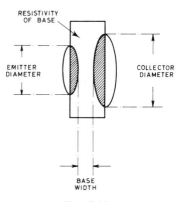

FIG. 2.11

be kept small compared with the diffusion length since at high frequencies the transit time of carriers across the base is important. Also the majority of the carriers should be able to cross the base without recombination. The doping of the emitter should be heavier than that of the base. For this reason, the resistivity of the emitter should be much lower than that of the base, in order to obtain a high emitter efficiency. However, the resistivity of the base and the dimensions and resistivity of the collector have important bearings on the power dissipation of the transistor. Thus high frequency transistors tend to become very small, and so their power handling capabilities are reduced at the same time.

One attempt to overcome the limitations, particularly of base width, of this type of transistor, is the alloy diffused transistor.

The Alloy Diffused Transistor

The upper frequency limit of alloy transistors is about 10–15 Mc/s. This is due in part to the width of the base region. Their upper frequency performance can be increased by a factor of about 3 by the incorporation of a drift accelerating field into the base region. In this technique the base has an impurity gradient introduced during manufacture. However, the alloy diffused technique can extend the upper frequency limit much beyond this. In this process the base width can now be reduced to a few microns.

In many alloy diffused transistors, the doping process is applied from one side only of the crystal slab, and the diffusion of the impurities into the semiconductor which is allowed to take place at a carefully controlled temperature, produces a drift field which also contributes to the improved characteristics of the device. The starting point in the manufacture of this transistor is the collector. This is formed from a wafer of p-type germanium on which are placed two metal pellets, one of which contains n-type impurities while the other contains both n- and p-type impurities. This is shown in Fig. 2.12.

When suitably heated in an inert atmosphere diffusion of the

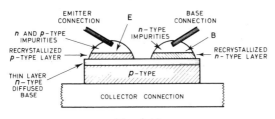

FIG. 2.12

4

impurities takes place into the germanium; that due to the p-type having a much slower rate than that due to the n-type impurities. The diffused n-type layer connected to the pellet B in the figure forms the base, and can be controlled to about 5 microns in thickness. That due to the p-type is connected to the pellet E. This contains both p- and n-type impurities but is predominantly p-type. It forms the emitter. The graded impurity density which is produced in the base region causes an accelerating field to act on the carriers in transit across the base. The resulting pnp transistor contains impurities distributed as shown in the figure.

y Parameters

The y parameters often used with this type of transistor may be defined from the differential equations (2.36) and (2.37):

$$dI_i = \left(\frac{\partial I_i}{\partial V_i}\right)_{V_o} \delta V_i + \left(\frac{\partial I_i}{\partial V_o}\right)_{V_i} \delta V_o \qquad (2.36)$$

$$dI_o = \left(\frac{\partial I_o}{\partial V_i}\right)_{V_o} \delta V_i + \left(\frac{\partial I_o}{\partial V_o}\right)_{V_i} \delta V_o \qquad (2.37)$$

These may be expressed as:

$$i_i = y_i v_i + y_r v_o \qquad (2.38)$$

$$i_o = y_f v_i + y_o v_o \qquad (2.39)$$

For the common emitter configuration, these lead to the equivalent circuit of Fig. 2.13. Some conversion tables using y parameters are to be found in Appendix A.

The parameters y_i and y_o may be expressed as $g_i + j\omega c_i$ and $g_o + j\omega c_o$ (presuming that sinusoidal voltages and currents are used in the analysis, whereas equations (2.36) and (2.37) relate to *incre-*

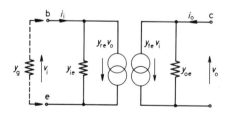

FIG. 2.13

mental voltages and currents). Some typical values for these parameters are given in Table 2.7 based on the common base configuration, a method of connection of use at high frequencies. They can be converted to common emitter parameters using Table A.4. Formulae for the voltage and current gains of the amplifier are shown in Table A.5 in terms of the y parameters.

Table 2.7

transistor	g_i (mmhos)	c_i (pF)	y_r (mmhos)	y_f (mAV^{-1})	g_o (μmhos)	c_o (pF)	f_1 (Mc/s)
OC 170	2·5	65	0·1	32	60	4·5	70
OC 171	23	6	0·6	9	350	2·6	70
AF 102	50	36	0·1	45	30	2·0	180
AF 114	15	5	0·45	16	300	2·5	75
AF 117	0·25	70	neg.	37	0·2	4·0	75

Epitaxial Transistors

In the type of alloy diffused transistor already considered, the base and emitter layers are formed by diffusion of impurities into a germanium or silicon layer. The remainder of the original, which must have a reasonably high resistivity to obtain a satisfactory breakdown voltage, forms the collector. However, the collector region should ideally have a low resistivity in order to obtain a low collector saturation resistance. Hence a compromise must be made between this and the breakdown voltage. Such transistors do not commonly make good switches.

With epitaxial construction both ideals can be achieved in the same transistor. The original silicon wafer is of very low resistivity and a thin epitaxial (table) layer of high resistivity is deposited on it. Base and emitter regions are then formed in this epitaxial layer as in the conventional alloy diffusion process. The high resistivity collector region is then very thin and the original wafer forms a low resistivity contact path. The epitaxial silicon transistor has a high cut-off frequency, a low bottoming voltage and its current gain is linear over a wide range of collector current. Some examples of this technique are illustrated in Table 2.8.

A further modification is the planar epitaxial transistor. This has a silicon oxide layer above the epitaxial layer, keeping leakage currents yet lower and yielding a higher current gain at very low collector currents. Because of the importance of this type of transistor, examples of its use will be found in subsequent chapters.

Table 2.8

transistor	type	h_{fe}	f_1*	V_{be} for $I_c = 10$ mA	V_{ce} sat. for $I_c = 10$ mA
			(Mc/s)	(volts)	(volts)
BCY 34	Germanium alloy	45	0·6	0·3	0·4
2G401	Ge alloy diffused	100	80	0·28	0·4
MDS 33	Ge alloy diffused	40	300	0·3	0·5
2S131	Silicon epitaxial	25	300	0·8	0·27
2N697	Si planar epitaxial	100	†	1·0	1·2
2N753	Si planar epitaxial	100	†	0·9	0·6

* This is a function of V_{ce} and leads to f_1 contours plotted on axes of I_c and V_{ce}. f_1 is also the gain-bandwidth product since it is the frequency at which h_{fe} has fallen to unity.

† Switching transistor.

Micro-Alloy Transistors

Another type of alloy diffused base transistor is built up from both sides of the base wafer. This is etched electrolytically as shown in Fig. 2.14. The final precision etch is controlled by the infra-red

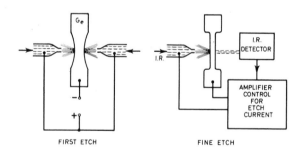

FIRST ETCH   FINE ETCH

Fig. 2.14

transmission through the thin wafer. Accurate control of base thickness is thus possible.

The etch potential is then reversed in order to plate on regions which later act as emitter and collector. This forms an alloy-type transistor, the micro-alloy type of Fig. 2.15.

The same technique can also be employed to give diffusion into the base region. The resulting micro-alloy diffused transistors, which are intended for use as switches, have no intrinsic base region, whilst those intended as oscillators and amplifiers do have an

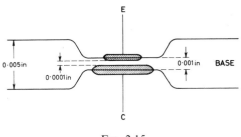

FIG. 2.15

intrinsic high resistivity layer, and, therefore, for optimum performance require a certain minimum collector-emitter voltage. Frequently, V_{ce} must exceed about 5 volts and I_c exceed, say, 2 mA.

Transistors at High Frequencies

The hybrid π equivalent circuit was a model which sought to explain the high frequency performance of a junction transistor. Alternatively, we may assume that the current gain of a transistor operating under steady state conditions is a complex quantity, and use this premise to deduce its high frequency gain.

The common base, short circuit current gain α is highest at low frequencies. Let this be α_0 and at any frequency, f, let the gain be α. Then α is a complex quantity and may be expressed in real and imaginary components or as a polar plot. Such plots show that if α_0 is real, the phase angle at which α has fallen to 0·707 of its low frequency value may vary from about 50° to over 100°, depending on the techniques used to form the junctions. This angle is greatest when a graded base is used.

It is of considerable interest to compare the performance of transistors in the three major circuit configurations. One method of approach to this problem is to express the complex nature of the current gain, as in equation (2.40), from which the relationship between f_α (common base) and $f_{\alpha'}$ (common emitter) can be deduced:

$$\alpha = \frac{\alpha_o}{1+\mathrm{j}f/f_\alpha} \tag{2.40}$$

also

$$\alpha' = \frac{\alpha}{1-\alpha}$$

and

$$\alpha'_o = \frac{\alpha_o}{1-\alpha_o}$$

Therefore

$$\alpha' = \frac{\alpha_o}{(1+\mathrm{j}f/f_\alpha)(1-\alpha_o/(1+\mathrm{j}f/f_\alpha))}$$

$$= \frac{\alpha_o}{1+\mathrm{j}f/f_\alpha-\alpha_o}$$

$$= \frac{\alpha_o/(1-\alpha_o)}{1+\mathrm{j}f/(1-\alpha_o)f_\alpha} \tag{2.41}$$

The problem may also be investigated by letting $f_{\alpha'}$ be the cut-off frequency in a common emitter circuit and then rewriting equation (2.40) for the common emitter case:

$$\alpha' = \frac{\alpha'_o}{1+\mathrm{j}f/f_{\alpha'}} \tag{2.42}$$

Then, comparing equations (2.41) and (2.42)

$$f_{\alpha'} = (1-\alpha_o)f_\alpha \tag{2.43}$$

f_1 and f_α are related by $f_\alpha = f_1/K$ where K is a constant for a particular class of transistor ($K=0.8$ for transistors with a uniform base). Further, f_α is only used to describe the performance of germanium alloy transistors at relatively low frequencies, due to the transistors' practical departure from the simple concept of the equivalent circuit near its upper frequency limit and the consequent uncertainty of the phase angle, whereas f_1 is inversely proportional to the transit time of the majority carriers. Thus f_α is not quoted for transistors operating at very high frequencies.

Temperature Effects

In the first chapter the existence of intrinsic conduction and hence of leakage currents was pointed out. These currents may be quite small in the case of common base operation, but in the same transistor they are much larger in the common emitter arrangement. Figure 2.16 shows the results obtained with a typical germanium transistor operated from a 9-volt supply.

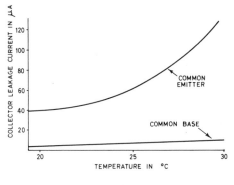

FIG. 2.16

A similar experiment with a silicon transistor shows correspondingly smaller leakage currents of only a few millimicroamps, and epitaxial transistors, particularly those with passivated surfaces have the lowest leakage currents of all.

Now, if the collector leakage current at some given temperature in a common base circuit is I_{cbo} and that occurring at the same temperature in a common emitter circuit is I_{ceo}, then, since the leakage current still flows, even in the absence of base current as shown in Fig. 2.17

$$I_{ceo} = (1+\alpha')I_{cbo} \qquad (2.44)$$

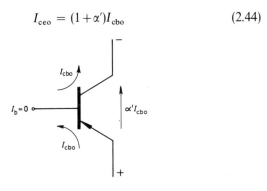

FIG. 2.17

Referring back to Fig. 2.16, therefore, it would appear that α' is of the order of 20 at 25°C for the germanium transistor used.

In the common emitter circuit the collector current, I_c, is given by

$$I_c = \alpha' I_b + I_{cbo}(1 + \alpha')$$

If the transistor is operated at high current, the resulting temperature rise can cause I_{ceo} to increase, causing the temperature to rise yet further, until, if this current is not limited by the circuit resistance, these cumulative changes result in thermal runaway and destroy the semiconductor junctions. Thermal stability is required, particularly in common emitter circuits (a common base circuit possesses good thermal stability) and a good design will achieve a low thermal stability factor.

Thermal Stability Factor, k

The reader should be careful to distinguish between the terms "stability" and "thermal stability". The former is used in the terminology of electronics to describe the measure of freedom of an amplifier from spurious oscillation.

The thermal stability is a measure of the change in collector current produced by a small change in temperature when the circuit is thermally stabilized, as compared to the change when no attempt at stabilization has been made. However, changes in I_c are due to changes in leakage current, that is in I_{cbo} or I_{ceo} as appropriate.

The thermal stability of a transistor can be defined in one of two ways:

(i) *The thermal stability*, $s = dI_{cs}/dI_{cbo}$
(ii) *The thermal stability factor*, $k = dI_{cs}/dI_{ceo}$

where I_{cs} is the stabilized collector current, and from equation (2.44)

$$\frac{1}{1 + \alpha'} \frac{dI_{cs}}{dI_{cbo}} = k$$

or
$$s = \alpha'' k \qquad (2.45)$$

A graph similar to that of Fig. 2.16 can be constructed from measurements on the stabilized and unstabilized currents or the thermal stability factor can be deduced from theoretical considerations. This subject will be pursued further in the next chapter.

Figure 2.18 shows some typical stabilizing circuits.

Circuit (a) stabilizes since an increase in I_c decreases the p.d.

across R_1. However, negative feedback is introduced at the signal frequency. This is not always desirable; it decreases gain whilst sometimes improving frequency response. In this chapter, however, the effect of this feedback on the amplifier's characteristics will not be considered. This is discussed in Chapter 4. In circuit (b) the

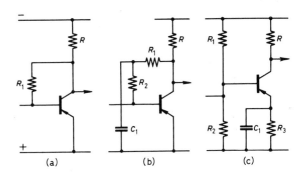

Fig. 2.18

negative feedback is eliminated via R_2 and R_1, with C_1 acting as the decoupling capacitor. It must be noticed, however, that the base current flows through R_1 and R_2.

Circuit (c) is a further improvement, although using more components than the other two. The relative merits of these circuits, from the point of view of thermal stability, depend, of course, on the values of the components used and on the current gain of the transistor. It is frequently the case that circuits (a) and (b) have a thermal stability factor, k, of the order of one half and circuit (c) in the range from one fifth to one tenth with components of the order of values commonly encountered.

PROBLEMS

2.1   Show that the current gain, a_i, of a common emitter transistor amplifier is equal to h_{fe} when it is operated with zero load.

2.2   Derive the equation for the voltage gain of a common emitter amplifier:

$$a_v = \frac{-h_{fe}}{\Delta + h_{ie}Y_L}$$

where $\Delta = h_{ie}h_{oe} + h_{re}h_{fe}$

2.3   Show from first principles that $\alpha' = \alpha\alpha''$

2.4   Deduce an expression for the input impedance of an emitter follower. By making reasonable approximations show that the input impedance is approximately $\alpha''R$ where R is the output load. Under what practical conditions might these approximations not be true?

2.5   It is often stated that $h_{ie} = (1 + \alpha')h_{ib}$, $h_{oe} = (1 + \alpha')h_{ob}$ and $h_{re} = h_{rb}$. Verify these statements, pointing out which of them are only approximate, and, using typical values, estimate the likely inaccuracy.

2.6   Write down expressions for α and α'' as measured at some frequency, f, stating that these are complex quantities. Hence find a relationship between $f_{\alpha'}$ and $f_{\alpha''}$.

2.7   Deduce from the common emitter T equivalent circuit, making reasonable approximations:
   (a) The input impedance of a common emitter amplifier with short-circuit load.
   (b) The input impedance with open-circuit load.
   (c) The voltage gain of the amplifier with a load R.
   (d) The input impedance of a common collector amplifier with a load R.
   Hence calculate values for (a), (b), (c) and (d) if $r_e = 25$ ohms, $r_b = 500$ ohms, $\alpha = 0.98$, $R = 5$ kilohms. [Ans. (a) 1,750 ohms, (b) 525 ohms, (c) 140, (d) 252 kilohms.]

2.8   Investigate carefully the justification for the statement that $(z_f - z_r)/(z_o - z_r) = \alpha$ (Fig. 2.8).

2.9   Show that the equivalent circuit of Fig. 2.13 follows from the definition of the y parameters in the common emitter mode.

2.10   Explain how the input impedance of a transistor may be regarded as a complex quantity, and comment on the mechanism responsible for its change of reactance when it is biased into conduction from a reverse biased state.

The reader is advised that assistance with some of these problems may be found in Appendix B.

BIBLIOGRAPHY

Amos: "Principles of Transistor Circuits", Iliffe, 1962.

Pritchard: Transistor Equivalent Circuits, *Proc.I.E.E.*, **106**, 1012, 1959.

Shea: "Principles of Transistor Circuits", Wiley, 1953.

CHAPTER 3

Small Signal Amplifiers at Audio Frequencies

It is helpful in analysis to consider two special types of impedance matching in small signal amplifiers at audio frequencies. These will be examined briefly before considering an amplifier of a general nature. This will make it easier to understand the operation of any practical amplifier, which does not fit precisely into one of these two categories:

1. *A voltage amplifier* is driven from a source of low, and theoretically zero, impedance, and feeds a high, and theoretically infinite, impedance load.

2. *A current amplifier* is driven from a source of high, and theoretically infinite, impedance, and feeds a low, assumed short-circuited, load.

In designing an amplifier we could consider whether either of these types could be the starting point in the design. Exact or approximate formulae could then be deduced in terms of any stated set of parameters for these special cases. These equations are usually easier to handle than the exact equations for the general case. They may be derived from consideration of the appropriate equivalent circuits.

However, they are not to be considered solely from this point of view. They are also of value since they represent the extremes of the possible range of operating conditions. If, for example, the input impedance of a voltage amplifier and of a current amplifier are known for some given transistor, the range of input impedance is consequently known for any finite load. A table of approximate formulae, Table 3.1, is given for the three useful circuit configurations in terms of the T parameters. Their derivation is a useful exercise on the material of the previous chapter, but should the reader prefer it, the derivation of the contents of Table 3.1 will be found in Appendix B.

Table 3.1

Amplifier Gain

	type of amplifier		
	voltage	*current*	*general**
Common Base Amplifier			
Load impedance, R_L	∞	0	—
Generator impedance, R_G	0	∞	—
Current gain, a_i	0	α	α
Voltage gain, a_v	$\alpha r_c/r_{eb}$	0	$\alpha R_L/r_{ee}$
Input impedance, z_{in}	r_{eb}	r_{ee}	r_{ee}
Output impedance, z_o	$r_c r_{ee}/r_{eb}$	r_c	r_c
Common Emitter Amplifier			
Load impedance	∞	0	—
Generator impedance	0	∞	—
Current gain	0	$-\alpha'$	$-\alpha'$
Voltage gain	$-\alpha r_c/r_{eb}$	0	$-\alpha R_L/r_{ee}$
Input impedance	r_{eb}	$\alpha'' r_{ee}$	$\alpha'' r_{ee}$
Output impedance	$r_c r_{ee}/r_{eb}$	r_c/α''	r_c/α''
Common Collector Amplifier			
Load impedance	∞	0	—
Generator impedance	0	∞	—
Current gain	0	α''	α''
Voltage gain	1	0	1
Input impedance	r_c	$\alpha'' r_{ee}$	$\alpha''(r_{ee}+R_L)$
Output impedance	r_{ee}	r_c/α''	$r_{ee}+R_G/\alpha''$

* The data given in the column headed "general" are only valid on the assumption that the load, R_L, is small. The reader may investigate the degree of approximation in the expressions, and in the corresponding expressions in Tables 3.2, 3.3 and 3.4 by comparing them with the more accurate expressions derived in Appendix B. For example, the current gain of a common base amplifier can be found from equation (B.10).

In Table 3.1 the following abbreviations are used

$$\alpha' = \frac{\alpha}{1-\alpha}, \qquad r_{ee} = r_e + r_b(1-\alpha)$$

$$\alpha'' = \frac{1}{1-\alpha}, \qquad r_{eb} = r_e + r_b$$

The formulae in the column labelled *general* in this table are of use in assessing an amplifier which does not approximate very well to either a voltage or a current amplifier, since they show the effect of the external collector resistance, or other effective load, R_L, and the generator impedance, R_G. The derivation of these formulae is also shown in Appendix B.

Other formulae can be derived from the equivalent circuits which are representative of the behaviour of iterative* and image† amplifiers, but since their application is somewhat more specialized they are not included here.

Amplifier Bias

The choice of the operating point of an amplifier and the means by which it is biased are decided by the compromise between a number of considerations, some of which are frequently conflicting. The collector current must be sufficiently large so that any change in the intrinsic leakage current, due to reasonable changes in the ambient temperature, does not seriously affect the collector voltage. If the collector current is too small, an increase in intrinsic current may result in the collector–emitter voltage falling to nearly zero. If the collector current is too large, it may not be possible to dissipate the energy which appears as heat at the collector-base junction. This energy would therefore cause an increase in the junction temperature and a consequent increase in the intrinsic current. This current adds to the collector dissipation so that, as explained in Chapter 2, the overall effect may be cumulative. Therefore, it may be a worthwhile practice to use the bias network to limit these changes, as shown in Fig. 2.18.

To summarize, the collector current must be sufficiently high so that the intrinsic current is only a small fraction of the whole, but not so high that the collector dissipation is exceeded. The bias net-

---

* An iterative amplifier is one whose effective load is equal to its own input impedance and which is driven from a source impedance equal to its own output impedance. For example, if three identical amplifying stages are connected in tandem, the centre one will be driven under approximately iterative conditions.

† An image amplifier is one which is matched for maximum power transfer at both its input and its output. Many tuned high frequency amplifiers are image matched.

work must provide an adequate degree of thermal stability without shunting the input excessively. These conditions must fall within reasonable tolerances for all the transistors of any given type, whose characteristics lie within a specified range.

Thermal Stability of Bias Circuits

The thermal stability factor has been defined as

$$k = dI_{cs}/dI_{ceo}$$

Figure 3.1 shows a typical bias circuit which can be examined from the point of view of thermal stability. As stated in Chapter 2, the question of negative feedback introduced by this circuit will be deferred until Chapter 4.

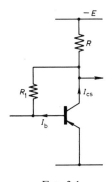

FIG. 3.1

Now, assume that V_{be} is very small compared with the other voltages. Then

$$I_b = (E - I_{cs}R)/R_1$$

where
$$I_{cs} = \alpha' I_b + I_{ceo} \qquad (3.1)$$

Therefore
$$I_{cs} = \frac{\alpha'(E - I_{cs}R)}{R_1} + I_{ceo}$$

or
$$I_{cs}\frac{(R_1 + \alpha'R)}{R_1} = I_{ceo} + \frac{\alpha'E}{R_1}$$

Therefore
$$\frac{dI_{cs}}{dI_{ceo}} = k = \frac{R_1}{R_1 + \alpha'R} \qquad (3.2)$$

Thus
$$\frac{dI_{cs}}{dI_{ceo}} = k = \frac{1}{1 + \alpha' R/R_1} \tag{3.2a}$$

which is of the form
$$k = \frac{1}{1 + \beta m} \tag{3.3}$$

Here $m = \alpha'$ and $\beta = R/R_1$

Example. If $R = 4,000$ ohms, $R_1 = 100$ kilohms and $\alpha' = 25$

$$k = \frac{100}{100 + 25 \times 4} = \tfrac{1}{2}$$

These figures are typical of this type of circuit. It should be noted that the corresponding value of s is $\alpha''k \doteqdot 25/2$, i.e. the circuit amplifies the leakage current 12·5 times.

Considering Fig. 3.2, first assume that $I_e \doteqdot I_{cs}$. Then

$$I_e R_3 \doteqdot I_{cs} R_3 = IR_1 \tag{3.4}$$

also
$$E = I(R_1 + R_2) + I_b R_2 \tag{3.5}$$

Hence
$$I = \frac{E - I_b R_2}{R_1 + R_2}$$

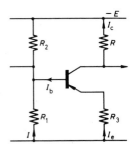

FIG. 3.2

Therefore, from equation (3.4)

$$I_{cs} R_3 = \frac{(E - I_b R_2)R_1}{R_1 + R_2}$$

Hence
$$I_b = \frac{E}{R_2} - \frac{I_{cs} R_3 (R_1 + R_2)}{R_1 R_2}$$

Now equation (3.1) applies

Therefore $\quad I_{cs} = -\dfrac{\alpha' I_{cs} R_3 (R_1 + R_2)}{R_1 R_2} + \dfrac{\alpha' E}{R_2} + I_{ceo}$

Hence $\quad dI_{cs} \dfrac{R_1 R_2 + \alpha' R_3 (R_1 + R_2)}{R_1 R_2} = dI_{ceo}$

That is

$$k = \frac{R_1 R_2}{R_1 R_2 + \alpha' R_3 (R_1 + R_2)} = \frac{1}{1 + \alpha' R_3 (R_1 + R_2)/R_1 R_2} \quad (3.6)$$

Again, this is in the form $1/(1 + \beta m)$, where β is R_3/R_{eff} and $1/R_{eff} = 1/R_1 + 1/R_2$

Example. $R_1 = 40$ kilohms, $R_2 = 10$ kilohms, $R_3 = 1$ kilohm, $R = 4$ kilohms and $\alpha' = 50$.

$$k = \frac{1}{1 + 50 \times 1 \times 50/400} \fallingdotseq \tfrac{1}{7}$$

The remainder of this chapter will be taken up with the detailed consideration of some of the amplifier circuits possible with typical transistors, so that the design procedure may be followed step by step for any other given transistor. Usually, the design may be immediately narrowed by the choice of a particular type of amplifier, but here the range of amplifiers already mentioned will be covered.

We start first, in this example, with the h parameters which it is assumed have been supplied by the manufacturer or measured in the laboratory:

$$\alpha = 0 \cdot 983$$

so that $\qquad \alpha' = 60 \quad$ (typical of the range 45–100)

$$h_{ie} = 2,500 \text{ ohms}$$

$$h_{oe} = 25 \times 10^{-6} \text{ mhos}$$

$$h_{re} = 5 \times 10^{-4}$$

These are then converted to T parameters by using relationships derived from the data given in Appendix A.

$$r_c \fallingdotseq \alpha''/h_{oe}$$

$$r_e = h_{re}/h_{oe}$$

$$r_b \fallingdotseq h_{ie} - \alpha'' h_{re}/h_{oe}$$

5

(These formulae, where approximate, are based on the reasonable assumption that $r_c(1-\alpha)$ is much greater than r_e or r_b.)

Hence we obtain $r_c = 2\cdot4$ megohms, $r_e = 20$ ohms, $r_b = 1,280$ ohms giving also $r_{ee} = 41$ ohms and $r_{eb} = 1,300$ ohms.

It should be noted that r_e is proportional to T/I_e where T is the absolute temperature of the semiconductor, and, at room temperature, r_e is approximately $25/I_e$ ohms, where I_e is in milliamps. In giving a value for r_e in the tables of data and in these figures quoted here, an operating temperature and current is therefore implied.

The mutual conductance, g_m, in common emitter configuration may be defined as follows:

$$g_m = \left(\frac{\partial I_c}{\partial V_{be}}\right)_{V_{ce}} \tag{3.7}$$

$$= -\left(\frac{\partial I_c}{\partial I_b}\right)_{V_{ce}} \left(\frac{\partial I_b}{\partial V_{be}}\right)_{V_{ce}}$$

$$= \alpha'/h_{ie} = \frac{\alpha}{r_e + r_b/\alpha''}$$

$$= \frac{\alpha}{25/I_e + r_b/\alpha''} \text{ AV}^{-1} \ (I_e \text{ in milliamps}) \tag{3.8}$$

$$= \frac{40\alpha I_e}{1 + (1-\alpha)r_b I_e/25} \text{ mAV}^{-1}$$

which tends to

$$40\alpha I_e = 40 I_c \text{ mAV}^{-1} \ (I_c \text{ in milliamps}) \tag{3.9}$$

when I_e and r_b are small and α' is large.

Thus, approximately, g_m is the same for all transistors operating at the same low collector current. This value for g_m is modified by the external circuit to give a lower dynamic value, g'_m, as in valve circuits. Also, at high values of collector current, g_m is less than the expected value. This can be seen from equation (3.8) since, as I_e becomes larger, the approximation of equation (3.9) becomes more inaccurate.

The Common Base Amplifier

This transistor, whose characteristics were quoted, will now be used as a common base amplifier, and the equations of Table 3.1

may therefore be solved and are shown in Table 3.2. From this table the performance of the transistor can be assessed under special conditions. The gain achieved by a voltage stage makes this seem the most promising for the common base amplifier, but the difficulty with the voltage amplifier is to make the load impedance high compared with the output impedance of 80 kilohms. A load of about

Table 3.2

	type of amplifier		
	voltage	current	general*
Common Base Amplifier			
Load impedance	∞	0	—
Generator impedance	0	∞	—
Current gain	0	0·98	0·98
Voltage gain	1,900	0	$R_L/42$
Input impedance	1,300 ohms	41 ohms	41 ohms
Output impedance	80 kilohms	2·4 megohms	440 kilohms
Power gain, a_w	0	0	$R_L/42$

* See footnote to Table 3.1

4,200 ohms will result in a useful gain of about 100. Another solution is to use an inductive load, which is not difficult since the inductance carries a relatively small current. However, the transient e.m.fs associated with any reactive load may cause the voltage ratings of the transistor to be exceeded, with consequent damage.

If the transistor is used in an image matched amplifier, matched for maximum power, consideration of the equivalent circuit will

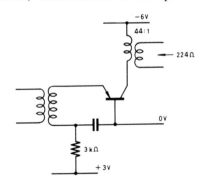

FIG. 3.3

show that a voltage gain of 37 and a current gain of 37 are possible, measured as a voltage or current ratio of that at the second base to that at the first base with a 44:1 step-down transformer. This yields a power gain of 31 dB. Stages of this sort are used at very high frequencies where other, more usual, circuit techniques are handicapped by the reduced performance of the transistors at such frequencies. A common base image stage is shown in Fig. 3.3.

Where, however, gain is not the first consideration, the common base amplifier used as a current amplifier is effectively a transformer from an input impedance of 41 ohms to an output impedance of some higher value. In Fig. 3.4 this value is 5,000 ohms, which, compared with the output impedance, R_o, of 2·4 megohms, is virtually a short circuit. Note that the generator impedance here is not high, as is demanded of a current amplifier. The voltage gain of this arrangement using the general formula for gain is about 120.

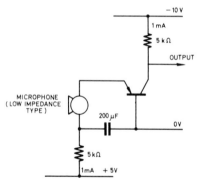

FIG. 3.4

The Common Emitter Amplifier

The same example will be followed and Table 3.1 rewritten as Table 3.3.

The common emitter amplifier is simplified by the fact that its potentials can easily be obtained from one supply, but the results of Table 3.3 are complicated by the fact that the resistors of the bias network often form a shunt on the input and any external collector resistance forms a shunt on the output. This is particularly important where the effective load is the input impedance of a subsequent stage. Some special types of common emitter amplifier will now be considered.

Table 3.3

| | type of amplifier | | |
	voltage	current	general*
Common Emitter Amplifier			
Load impedance	∞	0	—
Generator impedance	0	∞	—
Current gain	0	− 60	− 60
Voltage gain	− 1,900	0	− 1·5R_L
Input impedance	1,300 ohms	2,460 ohms	2,460 ohms
Output impedance	80 kilohms	40 kilohms	40 kilohms
Power gain	0	0	90 R_L

* See footnote to Table 3.1

Voltage Amplifier

In Fig. 3.5, the bias circuit is of the kind already referred to, but due to the transformer input, it forms no input shunt. Just as for the common base stage, gain depends on the value of L. Again, the same problems will be met due to the inductive nature of the load.

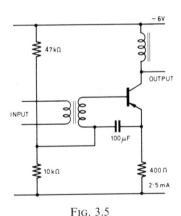

FIG. 3.5

Current Amplifier

In Fig. 3.6, the collector resistance of one kilohm is not the short-circuit load associated with a current amplifier, but it is very low compared with the 40 kilohms output resistance and may also be shunted by some capacitively coupled a.c. load. Since the input resistance is 2,460 ohms it is not seriously shunted by the bias resistor. The series resistance of 15 kilohms is to assist in raising the

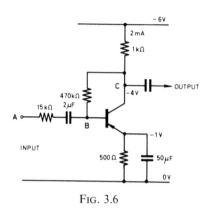

FIG. 3.6

generator input resistance, which should ideally be infinite to ensure linear current amplification. The voltage gain of this stage, with a one kilohm load, theoretically tending to zero, is

$$\frac{0.983 \times 1,000}{41} = 24$$

and hence there is a power gain of 1,440 (31·6 dB). These figures are both without taking into account the 15 kilohm resistor. The circuitry associated with a ferrite store in a computer is a typical application of a current amplifier. Here, the amplifiers are used to supply current pulses to change the state of magnetization of a number of "square loop" ferrite cores. Each ring is threaded by a number of wires and the current amplifier supplies pulses to a number of cores in series. The load of such an amplifier is often, therefore, a low impedance.

Image Matched Amplifier

The circuit of a common emitter image stage is illustrated in Fig. 3.7. This stage, which may be designed using the equivalent circuit and substituting the appropriate parameters, has a theoretical power gain of 43 dB compared with 31 dB for the common base amplifier. Careful design of the transformers is important or poor frequency response may result. However, the ratio of 5·7:1 makes it easier to achieve a good design than the 44:1 previously necessary.

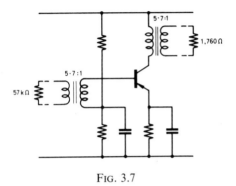

Fig. 3.7

This type of circuit is employed in tuned amplifiers where selectivity is a requirement rather than a drawback.

Iterative Matched Amplifier

A typical iterative stage is one which operates into an impedance equal to its own input impedance, and is driven from an impedance equal to its own output impedance. The reader should compare this with the current amplifier of Fig. 3.6. An iterative stage is shown connected between two other stages in Fig. 3.8. The equivalent circuit of one stage is shown in Fig. 3.9. At mid-frequencies the coupling and by-pass capacitances will be assumed to be short-circuited.

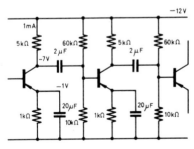

Fig. 3.8

Under these conditions Fig. 3.9 may be simplified to Fig. 3.10. This example may usefully illustrate the technique of design using the equivalent circuit.

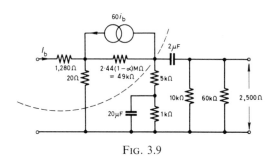

FIG. 3.9

The voltage gain can now be calculated from Fig. 3.10:

$$V_{in} \fallingdotseq 1{,}280\, I_b + (61 \times 20\, I_b) \fallingdotseq 2{,}500\, I_b$$

$$V_{out} \fallingdotseq 1{,}400 \times 60\, I_b \quad \text{ignoring the shunt} \\ \text{of the 49 kilohms}$$

$$= 84{,}000\, I_b$$

Hence   gain $= 84{,}000 \div 2{,}500 \fallingdotseq 34$

Alternatively, if it had been assumed that this was a general amplifier with a 5 kilohm load, the voltage gain calculated from the

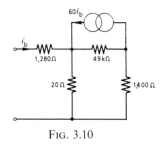

FIG. 3.10

appropriate formula is 122, a result which is much in error. This example, therefore, shows the importance of the shunting effect produced by the bias network and the following stage. It would have been better to take the effective load as 1,400 ohms, and then the calculated gain, given by $-\alpha R_L/r_{ee}$, is the same as that obtained by using the equivalent circuit of Figs. 3.9 and 3.10.

Common Collector Amplifiers

Continuing with the same example as previously, Table 3.1 may be rewritten as Table 3.4.

Table 3.4

	voltage	*type of amplifier* *current*	*general***
Common Collector Amplifier			
Load impedance	∞	0	—
Generator impedance	0	∞	—
Current gain	0	60	60
Voltage gain	1	0	1
Input impedance	2·4 megohms	2,460 ohms	$60(41+R_L)$ ohms
Output impedance	41 ohms	40 kilohms	$41+R_G/60$ ohms
Power gain	0	0	60

* See footnote to Table 3.1

The common collector arrangement is important as a current amplifier, and as an impedance transformer. As an example of its use as a matching transformer, consider a common collector stage feeding a common emitter stage with input impedance of 1,000 ohms. The equivalent circuit is as in Fig. 3.11.

$$V_{in} = 1,280\, I_b + 1,020 \times 61\, I_b$$

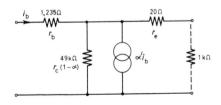

FIG. 3.11

Hence the input impedance

$$z_{in} = 1,280 + 62,220 = 63,500 \text{ ohms}$$

This should be compared with the result of using the general formula, $\alpha''R_L$, which gives $z_{in} = 60$ kilohms, and with that of equation (A. 52).

Now, consider this supplied by a second common collector stage, where the bias shunt of the stage just considered, reduces the effective load from 63 kilohms to, say, 30 kilohms. An equivalent circuit could be used here again, but the approximate formula can be seen to be sufficiently accurate. Thus the effective input impedance is $60 \times 30,000$ ohms $= 1.8$ megohms, and this figure has been matched to 1,000 ohms. A circuit of this kind is shown in Fig. 3.12 in which the input impedance has been shunted by the bias circuit.

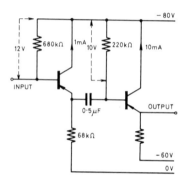

FIG. 3.12

The need for bias provides a practical limit to the high input impedance that can be obtained by this means. In Fig. 3.12 the bias resistor of 680 kilohms has become the final arbiter of the input resistance.

High Input Impedance Circuits

If it is possible to prevent the bias resistor network acting as a shunt across the input terminals of the amplifier, then its potentially high input impedance may be usefully employed. A circuit of this kind, which is shown in Fig. 3.13, has an input impedance of about 250 kilohms with unity voltage gain. Although this impedance is not as high as that of the previous circuit it illustrates a first approach to this kind of circuit. It remains to investigate its limitations and to minimize them. In Fig. 3.14 the equivalent circuit of the transistor has been drawn together with the load, R_L, and the bias resistors. It should be noted that there are two parallel paths from the point B to a supply rail. However, in this circuit, these

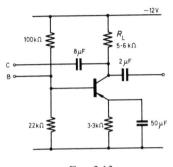

FIG. 3.13

paths only shunt r_b and r_e and not the input terminals. This circuit suffers from the drawback that neither side of the input is earthed, but the impedance from either side of the input to earth is low, thus minimizing the pick-up of unwanted noise.

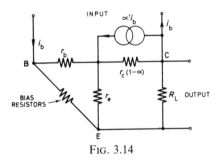

FIG. 3.14

From the equivalent circuit of Fig. 3.14 the input impedance of the amplifier may be deduced.

$$z_{in} = r_b + \frac{\alpha r_c(r_e + R_L)}{r_e + R_L + r_c(1 - \alpha)}$$

$$\doteqdot \frac{\alpha r_c R_L}{R_L + r_c(1 - \alpha)} \tag{3.10}$$

Using the data employed in the previous examples, $z_{in} = 240$ kilohms.

One way of raising the input resistance of the previous circuit is by preceding it with an emitter follower stage. A typical circuit is shown in Fig. 3.15. This circuit is essentially an example of negative

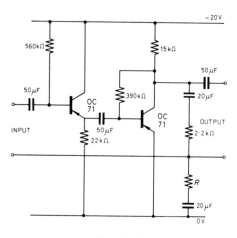

FIG. 3.15

feedback (see Chapter 4). An expression for the input impedance of this circuit and for its voltage gain, can be deduced by using the equivalent circuits of the two transistors in the same way that z_{in} was found for the circuit of Fig. 3.13. The circuit has an input resistance of about 1 megohm and a gain of 3 when R is approximately 600 ohms. When R is 5·6 kilohms the input resistance has risen to about 6 megohms whilst the input now needs to be 1 volt for 30 mV output.

Field Effect

Circuits such as those just described have been used to achieve a high input impedance. Still higher impedances can be obtained using silicon transistors but, for impedances above about 100 megohms, field effect devices must be used.

A change in the resistivity of a thin layer of a doped semiconductor crystal slab can be induced by varying the bias on another layer with which it forms a junction. In an early type of field effect transistor a current is passed, for example, through an *n*-type slab which is in the "on" state. A *pn* junction is formed with the cylindrical *p*-type modulator or gate which surrounds it. The junction is reverse biased by an external potential difference. The gate potential is used to alter the width of the depletion layer. More recently diffusion and epitaxial techniques have been used. The semiconductor material is usually silicon and a very high input impedance can be obtained, since only a very small leakage current flows, a typical figure being 25 picoamps. This effect was first noticed by Shockley in 1952. The tecnetron and the unipolar transistor are examples of this class of semiconductor valve analogue. Figure 3.16 illustrates a typical circuit arrangement.

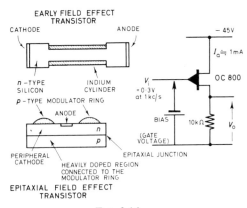

FIG. 3.16

The gate leakage current is of the order of 5 nanoamps for this transistor and the output characteristics are similar to those of a pentode. The anode potential which is just sufficient to cause saturation of anode current is called the pinch-off voltage. This saturation current is called the pinch-off current. The transistor is said to be in the triode region when below the pinch-off voltage and in the pentode region when above it. The gate electrode carries a steady bias between zero and -10 volts for example. A typical mutual conductance for a field effect transistor is of the order of 0.8 mAV^{-1} and is almost independent of frequency up to at least 1,000 Mc/s. The mutual conductance is, however, a function of temperature, rising with increasing temperature, whereas α' for a normal transistor falls at about the same rate. The input impedance falls as frequency rises, due to the gate-cathode capacitance of about 2 pF and the "Miller" anode-gate capacitance of about 1 pF. An anode slope resistance of 10 megohms is typical. This is because an increase in voltage biases off the transistor further.

Field effect transistors are able to operate at lower noise levels than conventional transistors. This is because majority carriers are used, there is no recombination, and no potential barriers to be crossed. These effects are some of the causes of noise in a normal "bipolar" transistor. This, together with their high input impedance are their chief advantages.

Transistor Noise

The noise generated in a transistor is assessed in terms of a noise factor. This is defined as the total noise power output of the transistor divided by the noise power output, measured at the same point, due solely to the noise present at the input of the transistor.

The noise factor, measured in decibels, is least for some source impedance to which the transistor is connected. This impedance is often of the order of 1 kilohm.

When a noise factor is quoted for any transistor, not only is the optimum value assumed, but it is also important to state the conditions under which it is measured. The noise factor passes through a minimum, being inversely proportional to frequency at low frequencies, then becomes independent of frequency and finally increases, due to the loss of gain and effects of transit time at high frequencies. At frequencies of the order of 250 c/s a noise factor of about 20 dB is quite common, although this may fall to about 5 dB at 10 kc/s. Transistor noise is mainly due to shot effect and thermal noise which may be considered as generated in $r_{b'b}$ (see Fig. 2.10).

Table 3.5

transistor type	noise factor (dB)	V_{ce} (volts)	I_e (mA)	source resistance (ohms)	frequency (Mc/s)
AF 117	1·5	−6	1	500	1
AF 114	8	−6	1	60	100
AF 102	6	−12	1	30	200

It increases with increase in temperature and in V_{ce} and with increasing collector current. Also, it may increase slightly from a minimum value at very low collector currents.

Typical examples of noise factors are shown in Table 3.5 together with the conditions of measurement.

PROBLEMS

3.1   Show that the T equivalent circuit for a common collector stage has three impedances, r_e, r_b and r_c/α'' and a current generator $\alpha' i_b$ by deriving its conditions from the common base equivalent circuit with elements r_e, r_b, r_c and αi_e.

3.2   By considering the appropriate equivalent circuit, show that the voltage gain of a common base voltage amplifier is $\alpha r_c/r_{eb}$. Derive an expression for its input impedance and modify it to cover the case of an amplifier with finite load, R_L.

3.3   Show that the input impedance, z_{in}, of a common base amplifier coupled for maximum power gain at input and output is given by $z_{in}^2 = r_{ee} \cdot r_{eb}$.

3.4   A transformer has impedance ratios of 2,000 ohms:50 kilohms and is to be replaced electrically by a common emitter transistor amplifier. Show that its load, R_L, must be chosen so that $\alpha R_L r_c = 10^8$.

3.5   By considering the definition of an iterative common emitter amplifier, show that its voltage and current gains are approximately equal, and obtain a value for them in terms of the parameters of the T equivalent circuit.

3.6   Show that the circuit of Fig. 3.14 has approximately unity voltage gain. What assumptions have to be made to obtain this result? Show, by quoting from typical circuit and transistor data, that these assumptions are justified.

3.7   Using the technique associated with Fig. 3.14, analyse the circuit of Fig. 3.15 to obtain approximate expressions for input impedance and gain. Hence, find a value for R so that the circuit shall have unity gain, and calculate the input impedance under these conditions. Discuss the circuit critically, pointing out its advantages and drawbacks as an integral part of a high input impedance transistor amplifier.

3.8   A transistor has a current gain of 40, and is to operate in the common emitter mode from a 12 volt supply with a collector current of 2 mA. Sketch the stage using a simple bias arrangement that is economical in component cost. Calculate the component values of the circuit and

(a) the input impedance,

(b) the voltage gain of the stage,

(c) the thermal stability factor, k, of the circuit.

In what way are (a), (b) and (c) altered when the stage is coupled to another similar one?

3.9   (a) Obtain expressions for the input impedance and voltage gain of an emitter follower in terms of the T parameters. It may be assumed that $r_c(1 - \alpha)$ is much larger than r_e and the load R.

(b) An emitter follower is to be designed to have a collector current of 2 mA and to operate from a 10 volt supply. Making reasonable assumptions, deduce the value of the input impedance and the voltage gain, taking into account any way in which these are modified by the bias network (take α as 0·985).

3.10   Making reasonable approximations, show that the voltage gain of a common emitter amplifier is $\alpha R_L / r_{ee}$. Design an npn transistor amplifier that is intended to operate with a collector current of 1 mA from a 6 volt supply. It is given that $\alpha = 0·983$, $r_e = 25$ ohms and $r_b = 1,050$ ohms. Estimate the voltage gain (a) of the stage alone, and (b) operating into another similar stage following it. [Ans. (a) 70, (b) 21.]

The reader is advised that assistance with some of these problems may be found in Appendix B.

BIBLIOGRAPHY

Blanks: Measurement and Testing of Transistors, *Proc.I.R.E.Aust.*,* **21**, 669, 1960.

Greiter: The Darlington Connection, *Wireless World*, 397, Aug. 1962.

Nisbet and Happ: The Calculus of Deviations Applied to Transistor Circuit and Network Analysis, *J.Brit.I.R.E.*,† **21**, 437, 1961.

Shockley: The Theory of *pn* Junctions in Semiconductors and *pn* Junction Transistors, *Bell System Tech. J.*, **28**, 435, 1949.

Sturley: The Frequency Response of Transistor A.F. Amplifiers, *Electronic Engng*, 466, July 1963.

Wilson: Transistor Noise; its Origin, Measurement and Behaviour, *J.Brit.I.R.E.*, **18**, 207, 1958.

    * The Institution of Radio and Electronic Engineers (Australia) was formerly the I.R.E. (Australia).

    † The Institution of Electronic and Radio Engineers was formerly the British Institution of Radio Engineers.

CHAPTER 4

Direct Coupling and Negative Feedback

There are three main classes of modification to the circuits which
have already been discussed in Chapter 3 and which are to some
extent overlapping. They increase the usefulness of the transistor
amplifier, and they offer the designer a greater scope than he could
ever have with amplifier design based on the use of thermionic
valves. These modifications are as follows:

Complementary Stages

Amplifiers designed to use both *pnp* and *npn* transistors may
simplify circuitry in a way that is not paralleled at all by valve
techniques.

Direct Coupling

Direct coupling between stages avoids the use of capacitive
coupling with its limitations at low frequencies, and is readily
accomplished due to the lower potentials employed than in valve
technology. Direct coupling is used not only for the amplification of
very slowly changing voltages or currents but may also have weight,
space or economic advantages.

Negative Feedback

Negative feedback can be used by the designer to modify input
and output impedances and to some extent increase the bandwidth
of amplifiers at the expense of gain. Unlike valve amplifiers, however, a straightforward trading of gain for bandwidth is not always
possible, since the upper frequency limit of a transistor is largely
dependent on the time taken for carriers to cross the base region.

6 69

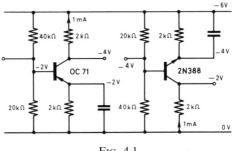

FIG. 4.1

Figure 4.1 shows two separate stages, one *pnp* (left) and one *npn* (right). Approximate potentials are shown and it will be seen that the stages could be combined profitably as in Fig. 4.2.

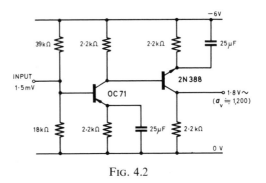

FIG. 4.2

Zener Diodes

Before the usefulness of stages of the types already described can be examined further, it is necessary to consider *zener* or *voltage reference diodes*, and the principles of their operation. In these diodes the voltage drop across a reverse-biased junction, when this is in the breakdown region, is used as a reference voltage. The effect is of particular use in silicon since a very sharp breakdown may be obtained. The breakdown voltage may be controlled by a suitable impurity content particularly for low voltages. The slope resistance for a typical zener diode, with a breakdown at 6 volts can be obtained from the voltage/current characteristics and is of the order of 10–20 ohms at the working point. The slope resistance rises approximately as the square of the breakdown voltage. It is also higher at small currents. The breakdown voltage varies with temperature, the temperature coefficient passing through a zero for a breakdown voltage of about 6 volts. Such diodes have a use wherever a fixed reference potential is required, for a wide range of current flowing, and are the semiconductor analogues of the gas-filled stabilizers. Their applications will be encountered in this and subsequent chapters. Some typical data is given in Table 4.1.

Table 4.1

Zener Diode Data

diode type (Ferranti)	voltage at 5 mA	slope in ohms at a current of:			temperature co-efficient per cent per °C
		1 mA	5 mA	20 mA	
KS 30 A	3·3	500	130	30	−0·05
KS 36 A	5·6	450	65	15	very small
KS 38 A	6·8	40	10	8	+0·05
KS 42 A	10·0	40	20	15	+0·06

Direct Coupling

The complementary stage of Fig. 4.1 could have been formed by capacitively coupling the output of the *pnp* transistor to the input of the *npn* stage. Instead, Fig. 4.2 employs direct coupling between the *pnp* and *npn* transistors. Although complementary coupling lends itself to direct coupling, it is not an essential part of a directly coupled circuit. Figure 4.3 shows some other ways in which direct coupling between two *pnp* transistors can be achieved.

In circuit (a), the first collector voltage must be small; but for amplification this stage must not be bottomed, that is, the base current must be limited so that the collector potential does not approach that of the positive line. Hence the collector current must be small. Although some drift in the output potential level is experienced with this circuit, the fairly low collector current helps to ensure low noise. This circuit is intended for the amplification of voltages of the order of a few millivolts only.

In circuit (b), the zener diode connected to the second emitter permits a larger collector–emitter voltage in the first transistor. Hence, the circuit operates for larger signal voltages than in (a). The emitter current of the second stage must be sufficiently large to bias the zener diode into its breakdown region.

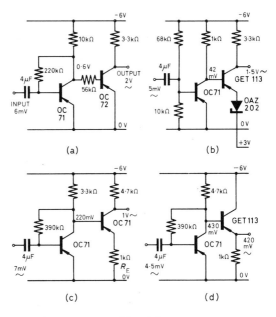

FIG. 4.3

In circuit (c), the cost of a zener diode is saved, but the resistor, R_E, causes negative feedback. For an approximate estimate of the voltage gain of the second transistor the formula of Table 3.1 becomes:

$$a_v = \frac{-\alpha R_L}{r_{ee} + R_E}$$

Thus, with an unbypassed resistance of 1,000 ohms, this second stage has its voltage gain reduced from 115 to 4·7 with certain consequent improvement in frequency response. Also, the loading of the second stage on the first is reduced by the presence of R_E.

In circuit (d), the first stage gives high voltage gain since it works into the high input impedance of an emitter follower stage. The second stage gives high current gain.

In some applications, the level of the direct voltage output may be important. In all these examples the output potential can not change its sign with respect to the positive common line. Here it is always more negative than this level. Alternatively, by making the negative line common, or perhaps by using *npn* transistors throughout, a potential of the opposite sign can be obtained. Where it is necessary for this potential to change sign, however, a double supply (e.g. ±6 volts) is frequently used. Some circuits of this kind are shown in Fig. 4.4.

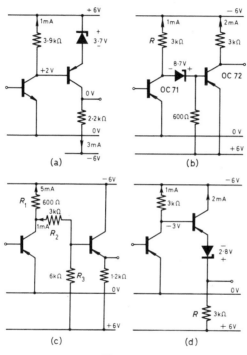

FIG. 4.4

In circuit (a), a complementary amplifier is used. Such amplifiers can be made thermally stable by suitable bias circuits. In this example a zener diode is used.

Circuit (b) is used where the second transistor has a sufficiently high base current to maintain the zener diode at the breakdown voltage; this factor must influence the choice of the previous load, R, for the zener current must pass through R also.

Circuit (c), although economical of components, introduces an attenuation into the signal path and this circuit is only useful when

R_2 is small compared with R_3. The magnitude of the positive supply potential will be an important factor in determining the size of R_3.

In circuit (d), the slope resistance of the diode is small compared with R, and hence the main output potential can be varied at will without influencing the gain of the circuit, nearly all the alternating output potential falling across R.

Negative Feedback

Negative feedback may be used to stabilize static working voltages and currents, or to make the dynamic gain of an amplifier largely independent of the characteristics of the individual transistors. This can be done to such an extent that amplifier design can be carried out with no more than the barest information about the small signal parameters, provided always that operation is within the frequency range of the devices. For example, in Fig. 4.5, if a current gain of n dB is required, satisfactory operation up to some

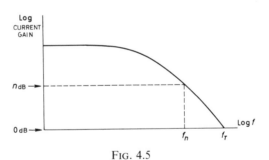

FIG. 4.5

frequency, f_n, can be expected. Provided this frequency is known, within this limit the gain-bandwidth product is substantially constant.

If negative feedback is used for dynamic purposes, it also reduces gain, alters impedances and may increase bandwidth.

Figure 4.5(a) shows a block diagram which represents an amplifier, a part of whose output is fed back to its input. The gain of the amplifier before feedback is applied is A_v, so that in the figure, $A_v = V_o/V$.

If the fraction of the output voltage, V_o, which is fed back is β, then the gain with feedback, a_v, is V_o/V_i. But $V = V_i + \beta V_o$. Therefore, $a_v = V_o/(V - \beta V_o) = A_v/(1 - \beta A_v)$.

In general, both A_v and β are complex but if $|1 - \beta A_v|$ is greater than unity, the gain is reduced. This is the case with negative feedback. The gain, a_v, is seen to depend increasingly on β as the loop gain, βA_v, is increased, so that variations in A_v become of less

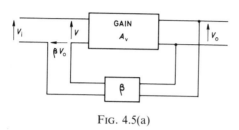

FIG. 4.5(a)

importance. Thus, the effects of variations in the transistor parameters are reduced if negative feedback is used, the extent of the reduction depending on the amount of the feedback.

In Fig. 4.5(a), it will be seen that the feedback was taken in parallel with the output and applied in series with the input.

Dynamic Negative Feedback

There are a number of ways by which amplifiers which use negative feedback can be classified. One of the most useful is that in which the point from which feedback is taken is considered. The feedback may be taken in parallel or in series with the load. Similarly, examination is made of the point to which the feedback path is returned. Here it may be in parallel or in series with the signal input. This leads to four types of feedback, being the four possible combinations of series and parallel input and output conditions. The effects of these four types of feedback are summarized in Table 4.2. A detailed analysis, of which this table is a summary, is shown in Appendix C, where the four basic circuits are treated in a simplified manner.

These four types of feedback are illustrated in the remainder of this chapter.

Table 4.2

Types of Negative Feedback

	feedback in parallel at the output		feedback in series at the output	
	feedback in parallel at the input	feedback in series at the input	feedback in parallel at the input	feedback in series at the input
Input resistance	reduced	increased	reduced	increased
Output resistance	reduced	reduced	slightly increased	slightly increased
Voltage gain with open-circuited load	reduced	reduced	unaltered	unaltered
Current gain with short-circuited load	unaltered	unaltered	reduced	reduced

Feedback in Series at Both Input and Output

The circuit shown in Fig. 4.6 has already been discussed from the aspects of operating point and the thermal stability of the bias network. It will now be considered as a feedback amplifier. The output current develops a voltage across R_E. This causes a marked fall

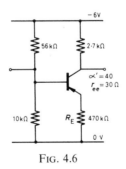

FIG. 4.6

in the voltage gain of the stage and increase in its input impedance as shown in Appendix C.

A circuit of this kind has been used in feedback amplifiers for carrier telephony where R_E may be an output transformer, the feedback being taken from a tapping on the transformer primary. The increased input and output impedances (see Table 4.2) enable the amplifier to be used in conjunction with equipment designed originally for valve circuitry.

The stage shown in Fig. 4.6 has an input impedance of the order of 20 kilohms, which is shunted by the bias network. Because its input impedance is relatively high, it should be fed from a low impedance source. This will result in maximum voltage transfer. Also, the stage has a high output impedance, and therefore to obtain a high current transfer at the output, it should be fed into a low load resistance. This method of deliberately introducing an impedance mismatch between source and load is of importance, since it leads to the design of a composite stage consisting of two transistor amplifiers, one of which has series feedback at both input and output, and the other has parallel feedback. A stage of this kind forms the basis of an amplifier which has a gain largely independent of transistor parameters.

The transconductance or mutual conductance of a single transistor series feedback stage is (if $R_E \gg r_{ee}$):

$$\left(\frac{\partial I_o}{\partial V_i}\right)_{V_o} = 1/R_E \tag{4.1}$$

This result is due to a simplification of equation (C.3a) in Appendix C.

Feedback in Parallel at Both Input and Output

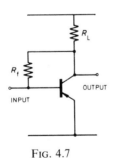

FIG. 4.7

Here the current fed back is proportional to the output voltage. This circuit has already been suggested as a simple bias arrangement of moderate thermal stability. In such cases the feedback resistor would probably have a high resistance, and if feedback is to be avoided the circuit of Fig. 2.18(b) could be employed.

When, however, feedback is intended, care must be taken to ensure that the requirements of linear operation and thermal stability are still met, whilst providing the desired feedback. In some cases, the main feedback paths will be capacitively coupled, particularly where feedback at very low frequencies is not intended. The chief effects of feedback in this circuit are the reduced current gain and reduced input impedance. Again, using the mismatch technique, a low input impedance amplifier should be fed from a high source impedance generator. Similarly, the reduced output impedance of this stage makes it suitable for feeding a high impedance load. In both these cases, fractional changes in the load conditions have only a small effect on the linearity of the system.

It can also be shown that the input impedance with feedback, z_{in}, is given by

$$z_{in} = \alpha'' r_{ee}\left(1 - \frac{R_L}{R_L + R_f/\alpha''}\right) \qquad (4.2)$$

This result is due to a simplification of equation (C.10a).

For a single stage of this kind, the transresistance of the stage is

$$\left(\frac{\partial V_o}{\partial I_i}\right)_{V_i} = \frac{dV_o}{dI_i} \eqsim R_f \qquad (4.3)$$

This result is due to a simplification of equation (C.14).

On the assumptions previously outlined, alternate stages having feedback in series at both input and output, and stages having feedback in parallel at both input and output can be operated satisfactorily, the two transistors making one design unit (see Fig. 4.3(c)). A number of these units can then be connected together to make an amplifier of sufficient gain for some particular application. The overall gain of two of these stages can be estimated as the product of the transconductances and transresistances of the units of which it is made. But for the gain of these stages to be predicted and to be reproducible in production with any certainty, they must be as nearly independent as possible of the transistor parameters and isolated from each other by the mismatch between the stages. The circuit of Fig. 4.8 illustrates this. Its voltage gain can be calculated on the basis of equations (4.1) and (4.3) and also more accurately using equations (C.3a) and (C.14) which are reproduced here for convenience.

The gain estimated approximately from equations (4.1) and (4.3)
is

$$\frac{R_{f_2}}{R_{E_1}} = \frac{22 \times 10^3}{470} = 47$$

A more accurate estimate is obtained as follows:
The transconductance of the first stage

$$g_{m_1} = \frac{\alpha}{r_{ee} + R_E} \qquad (C.3a)$$

and the transresistance of the second stage

$$R_{T_2} = \frac{R_f}{1 + (R_f + R_L)/\alpha' R_L} \qquad (C.14)$$

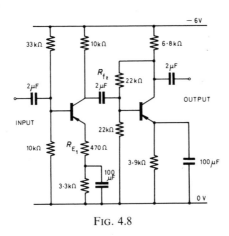

FIG. 4.8

If $\alpha = 0.98$ and $r_{ee} = 40$ ohms and taking α' as 50, these equations
give:

$$g_{m_1} = 0.98/510 = 1.9 \text{ mAV}^{-1}$$

and $$R_{T_2} = 19 \text{ kilohms}$$

Hence the overall gain $= 1.9 \times 19 = 36.1$
This lower figure is the more accurate of the two and may be taken
as typical of the gain of stages of this kind. Uniform gain can be
expected (to within about 10 per cent) for a wide range of germanium

alloy transistors for which the data given are only of the correct order.

The complete amplifier of Fig. 4.8 will have a high input impedance given by equation (C.1):

$$z_{in} = \alpha''(r_{ee} + R_E) \qquad (C.1)$$

Using the figures already quoted, it can be seen that the input impedance is, in fact, determined here by the bias network resistors which shunt the input limiting it to about 8,000 ohms. This, taken into consideration with the reduced output impedance of the second transistor amplifier, means that the mismatch technique is still followed in coupling together circuits such as that of Fig. 4.8.

Feedback in Parallel at the Input and in Series at the Output

In Fig. 4.9, it can be seen that the output current develops a voltage which feeds back a current, via R_f, to the input. This kind of circuit particularly reduces the input impedance and the current gain. If the input to the stage be shorted to a common supply line then feedback cannot be applied, so that the extent of any feedback will, in practice, depend on the impedance of the source

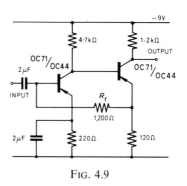

FIG. 4.9

driving the stage. However, it must also be remembered that this stage has a low input impedance, so that this will only be of importance for values of source impedance less than this.

Figure 4.9 shows a typical feedback pair circuit. Assuming the values quoted previously to apply to this transistor, we evaluate the input impedance from equation (C.15):

$$z_{in} = r_{ee}\left(\frac{R_E + R_f}{r_{ee} + R_E + R_f/\alpha''}\right)$$ (C.15)

$$= 300 \text{ ohms}$$

The stage also has a current gain of R_f/R_E—from equation (C.18a)— which is here equal to 10, so that the voltage gain of about 40 is obtained for each feedback pair. An amplifier made up from such stages, using OC 44 transistors intended for somewhat higher frequency operation, has been used as a wideband amplifier with a bandwidth of 2 Mc/s, input impedance of 50 ohms and an output impedance of 800 ohms.

Figures 4.9 and 4.9(a) are of the same general type, but in Fig. 4.9(a) the current gain is seen to be $10,000 \div 100 = 100$. A flat

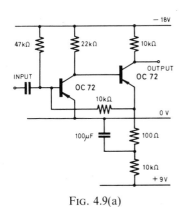

FIG. 4.9(a)

response up to 60 kc/s is obtained with this circuit with medium gain alloy transistors. The input impedance is approximately 100 ohms and the output impedance is about 10 kilohms. These figures should be noted in conjunction with Table 4.2.

Feedback in Series at the Input and in Parallel at the Output

In Fig. 4.10 the current through R_f is proportional to the output voltage. Hence the voltage across R_E is proportional to the output voltage. One of the main advantages of this type of circuit is its high input impedance. The effect on the current gain will depend on the

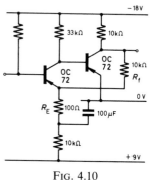

FIG. 4.10

impedance of the load, being unaltered if the load is shorted, whilst, as shown in equation (C.22), the voltage gain is reduced to approximately R_f/R_E. In the example illustrated here, the input impedance is about 100 kilohms and the output impedance about 300 ohms. A high current gain is maintained to about 100 kc/s.

Compound Feedback

Since one of the purposes of negative feedback is to produce any desired input and output impedance with adequate gain and good frequency response, circuits have been devised with more than one

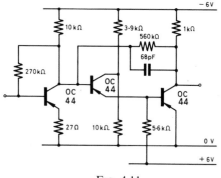

FIG. 4.11

feedback path. When different modes of feedback are used in these paths, this is described as compound feedback. Compound feedback is a useful tool to modify circuit impedances.

Figure 4.11 shows one part of an industrial amplifier utilizing parallel feedback at both input and output with two feedback paths. Here the d.c. conditions have been satisfied by the signal feedback components permitting a directly coupled amplifier to be used. With this circuit and these transistors, it would be expected that a good frequency response would be maintained up to about 50 kc/s.

In Fig. 4.12 the 100 ohms in the emitter circuit of the first transistor increases the input impedance to about 18 kilohms (series feedback at input and output). The 100 kilohm resistor only stabilizes

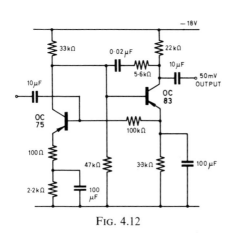

FIG. 4.12

the d.c. levels (since the 3,300 ohm resistor is bypassed). The 5,600 ohms and the 0·02 μF are an example of frequency sensitive feedback, and provide negative feedback at high frequencies (parallel feedback at input and output) over the second stage. The circuit values have been adjusted for use as a preamplifier for playback in a tape recorder. Figure 4.12 shows an example of compound feedback, since the type of feedback is not the same in each path, whereas in Fig. 4.11 the type of feedback is the same by each path. Therefore Fig. 4.11 does not illustrate a true example of compound feedback.

Negative Feedback at High Frequencies

Design of untuned amplifiers using negative feedback, is similar to that of comparable amplifiers at lower frequencies but using instead, either alloy-diffused or epitaxial transistors. Figure 4.13 shows a feedback amplifier designed on the mismatch principle with a 40 dB voltage gain and a bandwidth from 10 c/s to 20 Mc/s.

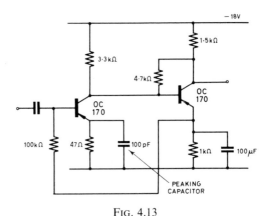

FIG. 4.13

The low frequency response could be improved by using a compensating capacitor in series with the 4,700 ohms feedback resistor as in Fig 4.12. The peaking capacitor reduces the amount of negative feedback at high frequencies. As the gain falls the feedback is made to fall also, maintaining the gain of the amplifier constant.

Figure 4.14 shows a video amplifier with a gain of about 20 dB, consisting of two common emitter stages with frequency-dependent

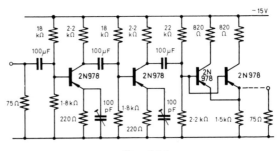

FIG. 4.14

feedback, and a parallel emitter follower output capable of supplying a peak output current of about 20 mA. The 1,500 ohm resistor prevents accidental damage should the 75 ohm termination be removed. Since the emitter resistors are high compared with r_e for the 2N978, the gain is virtually independent of the value of α'.

Equalization of Response

The gain at low frequencies is always greater than that at high frequencies, and it is often necessary for equalization of gain to be carried out. In practice a single stage may be equalized, and a number of such stages used to obtain the requisite gain. A circuit resonant just above the maximum video frequency is employed as shown in Fig. 4.15(a). The capacity may in fact be the self-capacity of the

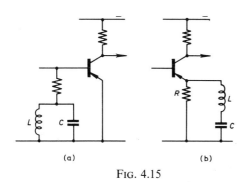

(a) (b)

FIG. 4.15

inductance when the circuit may be regarded as that of a shunt peaking coil.

A second method is illustrated in Fig. 4.15(b). Again the LC circuit is resonant at slightly above the maximum video frequency. R produces negative feedback, modified by the tuned circuit. If R is shunted by C alone the amplifier may be compared with that of Fig. 4.13. The performance with the inductance is slightly favourable compared with that of the capacitor alone.

Operational Amplifiers

One important application of directly coupled amplifiers is that of the operational amplifier. An operational amplifier is a directly

7

coupled amplifier of high gain and carefully prescribed frequency response. Its overall gain is reduced by heavy negative feedback, so ensuring a high degree of electrical stability. By symmetrical design and thermal coupling with common heat sinks, a high degree of thermal stability is also achieved. This is important since direct coupling is used giving amplification at zero frequency. The final thermal drift of an operational amplifier is often the limiting factor on its sensitivity.

The amplifier of Fig. 4.16 is assumed to have high input impedance, low output impedance and high gain before feedback is

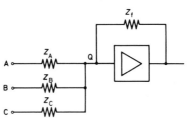

FIG. 4.16

applied. The feedback is assumed to be by an impedance Z_f, and the series impedances are $Z_A, Z_B, Z_C, \ldots, Z_N$. In the following treatment of the circuit, the point Q is assumed to be at the potential of the common line.

The output voltage, v_o, is given by:

$$v_o \doteq -Z_f \sum_{J=A}^{N} \frac{v_J}{Z_J} = -Z_f \left(\frac{v_A}{Z_A} + \frac{v_B}{Z_B} + \cdots + \frac{v_N}{Z_N} \right) \qquad (4.4)$$

Equation (4.4) implies a phase inversion in the amplifier; this is necessary in order that Q shall be at the potential of the common line. If the various impedances are specified as resistors or pure capacitances then equation (4.4) can be simplified further.

(a) $Z_A, Z_B, \ldots$ and Z_f are all resistive.

$$v_o = -R_f \left(\frac{v_A}{R_A} + \frac{v_B}{R_B} + \cdots \right) \qquad (4.4a)$$

The output voltage is proportional to the sum of the input voltages.

(b) $Z_A = Z_B = Z_C = R_K$; $Z_f = R_f$.

$$v_o = -\frac{R_f K v}{R_K} \tag{4.4b}$$

The output voltage is proportional to K times the input voltage.
(c) Z_A capacitive; $Z_f = R_f$.

$$v_o = -R_f C_A \frac{dv_A}{dt} \tag{4.4c}$$

The output voltage·is proportional to the first differential of the input voltage.
(d) $Z_A = R_A$; Z_f capacitive.

$$v_o = -\frac{1}{R_A C_f} \int_0^t v_A \, dt \tag{4.4d}$$

The output voltage is proportional to the integral of the input voltage.

The operational amplifier can thus be used to simulate analogue addition (and subtraction), multiplication, differentiation and integration. Analogue computers use high quality potentiometers to set up the coefficients and operational amplifiers with suitable external networks for feedback and input, to produce solutions of differential equations.

Figure 4.17 shows a typical directly coupled amplifier in which

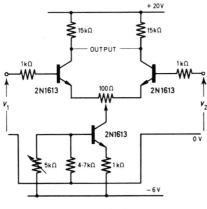

FIG. 4.17

the inputs are applied symmetrically. It is suitable for use as the input stage of a high gain computing amplifier. Planar silicon transistors are almost mandatory for this application, and great care is taken to use a common heat sink, since, to minimize thermal drift, the transistors should be matched for their leakage current/temperature characteristic. The transistor in the emitter circuits of the matched amplifier provides a constant current source, so that the input impedance of the amplifier shall be very high (several megohms). The potentiometer is used to adjust the base–emitter voltages of the input transistors to be equal.

Since the gain of this circuit is still a function of temperature even when leakage currents, base–emitter voltages and operating temperatures have been matched, it is now common practice to replace each input transistor by a complementary feedback pair. The overall drift can now be reduced to an extent corresponding to a voltage of less than 10 μV at the input per centigrade degree.

Voltage Drift of Operational Amplifiers

The gain of the circuit of Fig. 4.17 is dependent on temperature. Its gain will be lower than that of many circuits intended for use as operational amplifiers. In these amplifiers voltage drift is an important problem. The voltage drift which can be expected may be estimated if a drift generator, V_d, is postulated. This is illustrated in Fig. 4.18.

From Fig. 4.18, if the input is assumed to be short-circuited between the points A and A':

$$I_f + I_{in} = I_i \tag{4.5}$$

i.e.
$$\frac{V_o - V_i}{Z_f} - \frac{V_i}{Z_A} = \frac{V_i + V_d}{R_{in}} \tag{4.6}$$

But
$$\frac{V_o}{V_i + V_d} = a_v$$

or
$$V_o/a_v - V_d = V_i \tag{4.7}$$

From equation (4.6):

$$V_i\left(\frac{1}{R_{in}} + \frac{1}{Z_A} + \frac{1}{Z_f}\right) = \frac{V_o}{Z_f} - \frac{V_d}{R_{in}}$$

And from equation (4.7):

$$\left(\frac{V_o}{a_v} - V_d\right)\left(\frac{1}{R_{in}} + \frac{1}{Z_A} + \frac{1}{Z_f}\right) = \frac{V_o}{Z_f} - \frac{V_d}{R_{in}} \qquad (4.8)$$

Equation (4.8) gives the drift voltage, V_d, which produces a corresponding output voltage for an operational amplifier with known voltage gain, and hence gives the effective drift voltage, V_o.

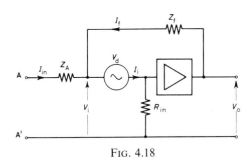

FIG. 4.18

If Z_A, $Z_f \gg R_{in}$ and a_v is large, equation (4.8) reduces to

$$V_o = \frac{V_d Z_f}{R_{in}} \qquad (4.8a)$$

Now $V_d = dI_b R_{in}$. Hence the output drift voltage, V_o, is given approximately by $V_o = dI_b Z_f$.

The changes in base current are chiefly due to changes in current gain and in leakage current. If these are known for some temperature range, then the drift voltage which can be expected can be estimated.

For example, if a base current of 40 μA is present and the current gain changes by 0·6 per cent. per centigrade degree, a change of 50 centigrade degrees (from 25 to 75°C) produces a change in base current of

$$\frac{0·6}{100} \times 50 \times 40 \ \mu A = 12 \ \mu A$$

For silicon transistors operating over this temperature range, the change in leakage current, $dI_{cbo} = 2 \ \mu A$ approximately.

Hence the total change in base current is 14 μA, and for $Z_f = 100$ kilohms the drift output voltage is 1·4 volts. This example is included to show the importance of temperature compensation and control.

There is still another factor to be taken into account in assessing the drift of a directly coupled amplifier. If, for example, the extrinsic base current is to be maintained constant, it is found that the voltage, V_{be}, necessary to do this, is a function of temperature, falling as temperature rises. Since most simple bias supplies tend to produce a constant forward bias voltage, there is a further increase in collector current due to this cause. This also tends to increase the collector dissipation and hence the leakage current also. One method which has been used to control the junction temperature is to employ balanced amplifiers. In this way, any change in V_{be} in one transistor is mirrored by a similar change in the other transistor of the balanced pair. As a further precaution the transistors may be held in holes drilled in a large copper block or heat sink. There is a further discussion of heat sinks, and of changes in V_{be} due to changes in temperature in Chapter 6.

High Voltage Stages

When a large output stage is required, such as in a video amplifier coupled to a cathode-ray tube grid, when a 50–80 volt swing is required from the output transistor, the first approach is to use transistors able to operate at high peak inverse voltages and therefore capable of large collector swings. Figure 4.19 shows a circuit

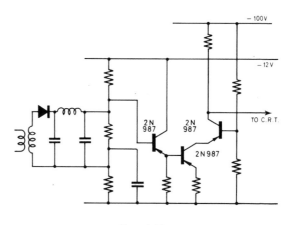

FIG. 4.19

capable of producing a 60 volt swing. In order to minimize the Miller effect, an emitter follower is used between the video detector and video output transistor. Also, since the output stage is driven from a low impedance circuit, it has high thermal stability, whilst the high impedance load on the detector enables high efficiency and good linearity to be obtained. The two output transistors are connected to form a cascode circuit, the upper transistor of which must take the greater part of the voltage drop, since the base of the lower transistor will never be positive with respect to its emitter. This problem always makes it difficult to use two transistors in series, making a large swing possible without entering the breakdown region.

Transistors are available with maximum ratings up to 500 volts but these are at present expensive. One method of sharing the voltage swing, using the mass-produced low voltage types, is the beanstalk amplifier illustrated in Figs. 4.20 and 4.20(a).

In Fig. 4.20, the swing of the potential at collector 1 depends on the value of R and on the current swing. If R_1 and R_2 are made equal,

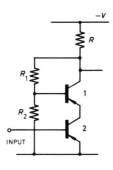

Fig. 4.20

so that the junction of these resistors is at the potential of collector 2 (except for the small V_{be} of the upper transistor), then the potential at collector 2 is half that at collector 1. Thus the transistors share the total voltage swing. Construction of an equivalent circuit for the two transistors shows that each of them provides gain, so that the output may swing between approximately V and $2V_{be}$.

This concept is illustrated further in Fig. 4.20(a), which is a practical beanstalk amplifier. It is again fed from an emitter follower, to provide a low source impedance for the output stage and matched to the high impedance of the video load. Two potential dividing chains are needed to stabilize the voltage swing of each transistor, and the small capacitors help to maintain the gain at high frequencies.

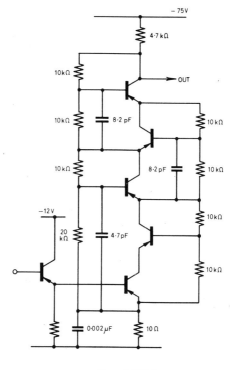

FIG. 4.20(a)

PROBLEMS

4.1   Draw an equivalent circuit and estimate the voltage gain of the amplifier illustrated in Fig. 4.2, making reasonable assumptions about typical transistor parameters. [Ans. If $r_{ee} = 40$ ohms and $z_{in} = 2$ kilohms for 2N388, $a_v = 1,200.$]

4.2   Deduce a general expression for the input impedance of an amplifier with feedback in parallel at both input and output (equation (4.2)).

4.3   Use the T parameters to draw an equivalent circuit of Fig. 4.6, and hence show that the current and voltage gains are reduced and the input impedance is increased by the inclusion of R_E.

4.4   An alloy transistor has $r_{ee} = 50$ ohms and $\alpha = 0.980$. It uses an external 1,000 ohms emitter resistor and has an effective collector load of 1·5 kilohms. Plot a graph showing the variation in voltage gain with the variation in that part of the emitter resistance which is unbypassed. Why is it that this graph is only valid for a transistor driven from a very low impedance source?

4.5   A transistor has $\alpha = 0.990$, $r_e = 25$ ohms, $r_b = 1,500$ ohms. It has a 3 kilohm load and bias is provided by a 60 kilohm resistor between collector and base. Calculate its current gain and input impedance, (a) ignoring the negative feedback, and (b) taking into account the feedback produced by the 60 kilohm resistor. [Ans. (a) 100, 4 kilohms; (b) 17, 670 ohms.]

4.6   Construct a simple T equivalent circuit for Fig. 4.17, choose typical values for R, R_1 and R_2, and hence determine approximately its voltage gain and input impedance.

4.7   Explain carefully what is understood by the mismatch technique in amplifier design, illustrating your answer with (a) alternating stages having overall series, and overall parallel feedback, and (b) a number of similar stages each of which consists of a feedback pair. Contrast these methods from the point of view of voltage gain.

4.8   (a) A transistor feedback pair uses an emitter resistor, R_E, in the second stage and two feedback resistors, $\frac{1}{2}R_f$, in series from this emitter to the base of the first stage. Explain how it is that when this circuit is examined, there is no increase in the output voltage when the a.c. feedback path is shorted by a capacitor to the common rail from the junction of the two feedback resistors. What can you deduce about the drive conditions in this case?

(b) Design a feedback pair of this kind, matched at its input to 75 ohms, and having a current gain of 10, into a 1,000 ohm load.

4.9   A transistor has $r_{ee} = 50$ ohms, $\alpha = 0.987$ and must use a load of 5,000 ohms. Show how the mismatch technique may be used to produce a two-stage amplifier module. If an overall voltage gain of 50 is required from the module, find the relationship between the emitter resistor, R_E, of one stage, and the feedback resistor, R_f, of the other. Hence assign practical values to R_E and R_f to obtain the desired gain. Also calculate the input impedance of the module. [Ans. Approx. 7,500 $R_f = (50 + R_E)(375 + R_f)$ where R_f is in kilohms and R_E is in ohms.]

4.10   A transistor with $r_{ee} = 35$ ohms, $\alpha = 0.980$ is used as an amplifier with an effective load of 1,000 ohms. A 100 ohm emitter resistor is bypassed by a 0·1 μF capacitor. Sketch a graph of the voltage gain and input impedance against frequency for the stage over the audio range. Assume that the transistor parameters are entirely real over this range.

The reader may, if he so desires, obtain help to some of these problems from the material of Appendix C.

BIBLIOGRAPHY

Bertoya: High Resistance Transistor Circuits, *J.Brit.I.R.E.*, **26**, 13, 1963.

Cherry: An Engineering Approach to the Design of Transistor Feedback Amplifiers, *Proc. I.R.E.* (*Aust.*), **22**, 303, 1961.

Cox and Harrison: Transistors in Reactor Control Instruments, *J.Brit.Nucl.Energy Soc.*, **2**, 49, 1963.

Griffin: Some Design Techniques for Low Drift D.C. Amplifiers, *Electronic Components*, 612, June 1963.

Helsdon: Transistors in Video Equipment, *J.Brit.I.R.E.*, **19**, 753, 1959.

Yarker: A Simplified Assessment of Transistor Amplifier Performance, *Electronic Engineering*, 554, Aug. 1962, and letters to the editor, 843, Dec. 1962.

Zener: Theory of Electrical Breakdown of Solid Dielectrics, *Proc. Roy. Soc.*, **185**, 523, 1934.

CHAPTER 5

Tuned Amplifiers

This chapter will be devoted to the principles of operation of tuned transistor amplifiers. These are frequently image matched stages. An example will first be taken of an amplifier operating at a frequency of 500 kc/s. For alloy transistors operating at frequencies of this order and above, the equivalent circuits of Figs. 2.5 and 2.9 do not adequately describe the operation of the transistor. The hybrid π equivalent circuit of Fig. 2.10 is a better approach.

The hybrid π parameters enable the behaviour of the transistor at high frequencies to be analysed on sound physical principles. Provided only one frequency or a narrow band of frequencies is to be considered, the analysis of the transistor and the consequent synthesis of an amplifier can be greatly simplified by adopting this circuit or the π equivalent circuit of Fig. 5.1, which has been developed from it. One reason, in particular, for redrawing the equivalent

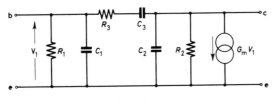

Fig. 5.1

circuit, is that in the early part of the design we need to have the internal signal feedback shown as due to R_3 and C_3 in series. If, as with alloy transistors, this feedback is appreciable, an alternative feedback path must be provided. When the transistor is used in the common base mode the internal feedback is in phase with the input, reinforcing it and, if sufficiently large, leads to instability and oscillation. When the common emitter mode is used, the internal feedback is approximately in antiphase with the input. This leads to reduced gain and thus, unless precautions are taken to counteract

95

this feedback, poor amplification results. With the alloy diffused family of transistors, C_3 may be so small that even at quite high frequencies such precautions are unnecessary, with a consequent simplification in the following work.

By Kirchhoff's laws it can be shown that the circuits of Figs. 2.10 and 5.1 are electrically equivalent, and that

$$C_3 = \frac{c_{b'c}}{1 + \dfrac{r_{b'b}}{r_{b'e}} - \dfrac{r_{b'b}c_{b'e}}{r_{b'c}c_{b'c}}}$$

or, since the last term in the denominator is small

$$C_3 \doteqdot \frac{c_{b'c}r_{b'e}}{r_{b'e} + r_{b'b}}$$

and

$$R_3 = r_{b'b}\left[1 + \frac{c_{b'e}}{c_{b'c}}\right] + \frac{1 + r_{b'b}/r_{b'e}}{r_{b'c}\omega^2 c_{b'c}^2}$$

Again, the last term is small at high frequencies and can often be ignored.

Also

$$G_m = \frac{g_m}{1 + r_{b'b}/r_{b'e}}$$

These, and formulae derived from them, can be obtained from the hybrid π circuit, but for the circuit designer it may be more important to be able to find such formulae quoted, than to go to the trouble of deriving them. For this reason their derivation is not given here.

Some typical values of the simplified parameters at 500 kc/s for germanium alloy transistors are listed here to illustrate the validity of the approximations that have been made.

$r_{b'c}$	2–5 megohms	R_3	5–10 kilohms
$c_{b'c}$	5–15 pF	C_3	5–15 pF
g_m	38 mAV^{-1}	G_m	35 mAV^{-1}

The values of R_1, R_2, C_1 and C_2 will be considered later. Here it is important to note that $c_{b'c}$ and $r_{b'c}$ of Fig. 2.10, or C_3R_3 of Fig. 5.1, represent a phase shifting network which is inherent in the transistor and which is responsible for feedback from collector to base, analogous to the interelectrode capacities and resulting Miller effect in triode valves. Where it is necessary to use triodes at high frequencies, it is common practice to feed back an antiphase voltage to neutralize the effect of the feedback which exists due to the internal capacitances. The same technique is employed here. If the reactive component only of the feedback current is cancelled by using a purely capacitive external feedback path from some suitably phased point, the method is called *neutralization*; if both real and imaginary components are cancelled by a *CR* feedback network, it is called *unilateralization*. This is only strictly possible at one given frequency. However, if unilateral behaviour is achieved over the frequency range of the amplifier, the possibility of dynamic instability from this cause is eliminated and, in tuned amplifiers, response curves are no longer grossly asymmetrical.

If a tuned amplifier stage is designed to have an adequately low thermal stability factor, and if C_3 is sufficiently small, it can be both thermally and dynamically stable without unilateralization. Some examples of such circuits are given later in this chapter.

In Fig. 5.2 a parallel feedback path is used, the unilateralizing feedback components being marked R and C. Once a stage has been

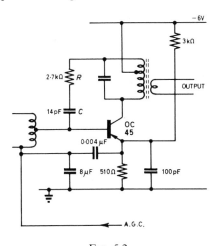

Fig. 5.2

unilateralized, it can, from the point of view of the feedback, at the frequency for which the components are valid, be considered as though there were no connection between its input and output circuits, as shown in Fig. 5.3. Table 5.1 shows some typical values relating to Fig. 5.3 at about 500 kc/s. In the table the input and output impedances are given. The individual component values can often be deduced from low frequency values or, in some cases, they are quoted by the manufacturer.

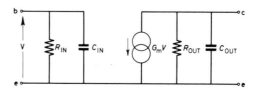

FIG. 5.3

Table 5.1

transistor	Z_{in} (ohms)	Z_o (kilohms)	typical power gain (dB)
2N641	3,000	1,000	40
2N370	2,000	200	35
GET 873	750	35	33
GT 42	1,600	40	35

A typical image matched stage will now be designed using the following transistor data. The same process could profitably be repeated as an exercise by the reader using some known manufacturer's product. From the given data the equivalent circuit of Fig. 5.4 can then be constructed.

z_{in}	1,600 ohms	z_o	40 kilohms
C_3	14·3 pF	R_3	5·6 kilohms
G_m	36 mAV^{-1}		

For image matching, $n^2 = z_o/z_{in} = 40,000/1,600 = 25$. Hence $n = 5$. (Note that the calculation uses n^2 since this is a case of impedance matching.)

Also, due to the use of the transformer, the voltage available to drive the feedback current has been reduced in the ratio $n:1$. Hence C_f must be equal to nC_3 (not n^2C_3) and R_f must be equal to R_3/n for the feedback to be correct in magnitude and phase.

Thus here $C_f = 5 \times 14·3 = 71·5$ pF

and $R_f = 5,600 \div 5 = 1,120$ ohms.

The shunting effect of the feedback components on the input circuit and via the transformer on the output circuit, must be taken into consideration.

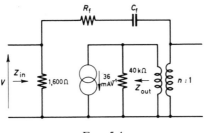

FIG. 5.4

From low frequency measurements or by using the following approximate relationship:

$$c_{in} \doteqdot \frac{c_{b'e}}{1 + (\omega c_{b'e} r_{b'b})^2}$$

it can be found that in this case

$$c_{in} \doteqdot 1{,}020 \text{ pF}$$

Similarly, using

$$R_{in} \doteqdot \frac{r_{b'e}}{1 + \omega^2 c_{b'e}^2 r_{b'e} r_{b'b}}$$

we obtain $R_{in} \doteqdot 690$ ohms

In the same way, c_{out} can be shown to be approximately 22 pF, and R_{out} approximately 59 kilohms. These values are quite typical of germanium alloy transistors.

Also, the series combination of C_f and R_f may at this stage be changed for ease of calculation later into the parallel equivalent case, C_p and R_p.

From elementary a.c. theory it is known that $R_p = (R_f^2 + X_f^2)/R_f$. So that here $R_p \doteqdot 20$ kilohms.

Similarly, using $X_p = (R_f^2 + X_f^2)/X_f$, where X is the reactance of C at the given frequency, we obtain $X_p \doteqdot 66$ pF.

As stated previously, C_p and R_p shunt the input and C_p/n^2 and $n^2 R_p$ shunt the output. (Again n^2 is used with impedance matching.)

$$C_p/n^2 = 2 \cdot 6 \text{ pF}; \qquad n^2 R_p = 500 \text{ kilohms}$$

The foregoing calculations result in the equivalent circuits of Fig. 5.5. The parallel components in Fig. 5.5(a) are combined in Fig. 5.5(b) to show the resistive and reactive elements of input and output.

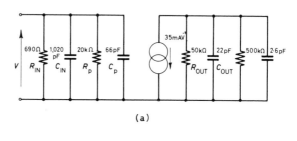

(a)

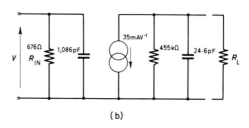

(b)

FIG. 5.5

Amplifier Gain

The gain can now be calculated on the basis that no component shows any imperfection other than those already considered. The transformer, for example, falls short of this. The gain so calculated, is therefore a maximum. However, due to circuit losses, the figure in practice will be about 5–10 dB less than this.

In Fig. 5.5, the input power $= V_{in}^2/R'_{in}$ and the output power $= V_{out}^2/R_L$, or, if the load is correctly matched, $R_L = R'_{out}$.

Hence, the output power $= (\frac{1}{2}G_m V_{in})^2 R_L = \frac{1}{4}G_m^2 R'_{out} R'_{in}$.

Here the power gain $= 35^2 \times 49.5 \times 10^3 \times 676/(4 \times 10^{-6}) = 10,240 = 40.1$ dB.

In order to tune to 500 kc/s the tuning capacitance available is 24·6 pF, plus the reflected input capacitance of the following stage. Here, that would be for a similar following stage, $1,086 \div 25 = 43.4$ pF, i.e. a total of 68 pF.

It should be noted, however, that if instead of a similar stage, the amplifier should be followed by the highly capacitive load of a diode detector the following calculations must be amended. This is due to the reflected capacitance of the load on the tuned circuit.

This gives an inductance, $L(=1/c\omega^2)$ of 1/680 henries, and hence $\sqrt{L/C}=10^5/22$. The selectivity factor, $Q(=(1/r)(\sqrt{L/C}))$, can now be found. Here r is the resistance at 500 kc/s of the winding (allowing for skin effect) and for practical values of r, the practical selectivity, Q', which this equation implies is very high. Should the amplifier have a signal applied to it which consists of an audio amplitude-modulated wave, cutting of the sidebands would result.

Q' is also given by $\omega/\delta\omega$ or $f/\delta f$ and if a passband of 9 kc/s is assumed, i.e. resolving up to the 4·5 kc/s sideband, then $Q'=500/9=56$.

An unloaded selectivity factor, Q, of perhaps twice this, say 110, is quite usual. To achieve a selectivity factor of 110 the L/C ratio must be decreased, whilst the product LC remains constant since the frequency must be unchanged. To avoid an extremely high value of additional capacitance, the primary is frequently tapped as shown in Fig. 5.6.

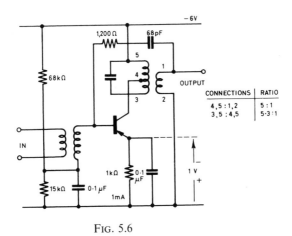

FIG. 5.6

To obtain Q equal to 110 with an effective resistance of, say, one ohm, $\sqrt{L/C}=110$, i.e. $L/C=12,100$.

Also $$LC = 1/\omega^2 = 1/(\pi^2 \times 10^{-12}) \doteqdot 10^{-13} \qquad (5.1)$$

8

Substitution gives

$$L^2 = 12,100 \times 10^{-13}$$

or $$L = 110 \times 10^{-6}/\sqrt{10} \fallingdotseq 35 \ \mu\text{H} \qquad (5.2)$$

Then, from equations (5.1) and (5.2)

$$C = \sqrt{10} \times 10^6/(110 \times 10^{13}) \fallingdotseq 2,900 \ \text{pF}$$

Now the output capacitance of the transistor is about 25 pF, and so an external capacitance is needed of $2,900 - 25$, i.e. 2,875 pF. If this is to be achieved with, say, a mean capacitance of 100 pF and a turns ratio, T, so that the circuit tunes to the same frequency, $T^2 = 2,875/100$, or $T = 5\cdot3:1$ approximately.

This value has been written into Fig. 5·6, where the transformer primary is the tuning inductance of the resonant circuit. Finally, if loading, as supposed, reduces the selectivity factor from 110 to 56, the power loss which results is $10 \log_{10} (Q/Q')^2$ dB.

Hence power loss $= 20 \log 110/56 = 6$ dB.

Hence the effective power gain of the stage is $40\cdot1 - 6 = 34\cdot1$ dB.

Piezo-Electricity

Certain crystalline materials, including quartz, rochelle salt and a number of ceramics, suffer a deformation of shape when a potential difference is applied between certain faces of the crystal. Also, when they are subjected to strain, a potential difference is developed across the crystal in certain selected directions. These two phenomena lead to a resonance effect, the electrical performance of the crystal being similar to that of a highly selective tuned circuit. The crystal physically flexes at its resonant frequency, and to a lesser extent at a number of other frequencies, known as overtones, which are integral multiples of the fundamental resonant frequency.

Ceramic Filters

The operation of ceramic filters depends on the piezo-electric effect in lead zirconate titanate. Filters have been produced with this material, whose impedance matching characteristics have made it possible to use them to replace tuned interstage transformers in some applications. One form consists of a disc having a fully silvered face on one side and the other face carrying two electrodes, as shown in Fig. 5.7.

Discs of this kind can be operated at their resonant frequency, or at an overtone, by applying the signal between the central dot and the silvered rear face. The piezo-electric effect causes a voltage to be

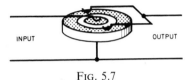

INPUT   OUTPUT

FIG. 5.7

produced at the same frequency as the signal, but at a lower impedance between the ring and the rear face.

Such discs often operate at their first overtone, and possess a transformation ratio of the order of 10:1, depending on the relative capacitive reactances of the dot and ring electrodes to the other face. They thus possess a suitable transformation ratio to act as a coupling element between amplifier stages. However, if a signal at the fundamental frequency or some other overtone of the disc is applied to the amplifier, the amplifier would be likely to have some gain at this frequency. This is avoided by using another type of ceramic element consisting of two plane electrodes only, on opposite sides of a disc. This can be used as a filter where no transformation ratio problems exist. A circuit is shown in Fig. 5.8 where these

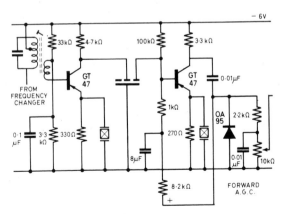

FIG. 5.8

filters are used in conjunction with germanium alloy transistors in the I.F. and detector circuit of a broadcast receiver. It will be seen that the filter in the emitter circuit of the second transistor, which operates in its fundamental mode, provides negative feedback at all frequencies except that for which it is resonant. It thus helps to reduce gain at those other frequencies to which the other ceramic filters might respond.

Unilateralization is often unnecessary even with alloy transistors. The negative feedback assists stability, and their small size and the economic price for which they can be marketed are their chief advantages.

Selectivity is good and the gain is of the same order as that of a comparable conventional amplifier. However, the chief drawback of these filters is the need to provide a direct current path for the collector currents of each stage. The resistance used, while essential, inevitably acts as a shunt on the resonant disc.

Automatic Gain Control

In a radio receiver or television tuner, the signal strength which is received varies from one station to another. Thus, if the audio volume or the video contrast were adjusted correctly for one station, it might be grossly incorrect for another. To minimize the problems associated with this effect, it has been the practice for many years to employ circuits for automatic gain control. Then, once the manual controls have been set for one station, they will be approximately correct for other stations whose signal strength at the receiver may be considerably different. These circuits operate efficiently for all but the extremes of signal strength.

Automatic gain control in radio receivers has in the past been arranged by obtaining a direct voltage level from the last I.F. amplifier whose amplitude was proportional to the mean carrier level of the modulated signal received, and using this to reduce the gain of preceding stages. This method may be termed "reverse A.G.C.". Transistor circuits frequently employ a "forward A.G.C.", in which the rectified A.G.C. voltage is supplied to the base circuit of an R.F. amplifier, in a way which will increase the collector current as the signal carrier increases. A series resistor (see Fig. 5.9) in the collector circuit has a greater voltage drop across it when a large collector current is flowing, thus lowering the collector–emitter voltage of the stage and so reducing its gain.

In the circuit shown here, the R.F. amplifier has a fixed bias provided by the potential divider across the H.T. supply, so that the A.G.C. diode is reverse biased until a predetermined level results in delayed A.G.C. Forward A.G.C. is particularly useful with transistor

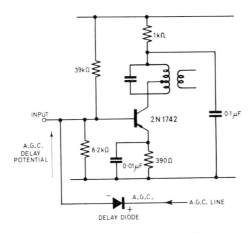

FIG. 5.9

circuits, since overloading does not occur until a very high signal level is received, and it occurs when the collector potential on the transistor is at a minimum.

Operation with Alloy-Diffused and Epitaxial Transistors

Transistors having an impurity density gradient in the base, which has the effect of greatly reducing the transit time of the charge carriers through the base region, have thus a higher cut-off frequency than alloy types with the same physical dimensions. The graded base is responsible for the high resistivity barrier between the collector and the active region of the base, resulting in a higher breakdown voltage and a lower feedback capacitance of the order of 1–2 pF. An f_T of 100 Mc/s and a power gain of 15 dB at 50 Mc/s is now quite commonplace. The smaller feedback capacitance avoids the need for unilateralization, at all but the highest frequencies, and even here the positive feedback associated with common base operation may sometimes be used to advantage.

Tuned Amplifiers at Very High Frequencies

The operation of amplifiers at very high frequencies has been difficult for two reasons. First, the transistor types which would operate at these frequencies were developed later than the more pedestrian alloy transistors. With the advent of the alloy diffused transistor, and, more recently, the silicon planar epitaxial transistor, the limitations of the earlier types have been overcome.

Also, the operation of any circuit at frequencies of the order of 100 Mc/s requires a fresh approach to the concepts of circuit elements. At lower frequencies, one meets the imperfections of circuit elements. For example, a carbon resistor has distributed capacitance, or a coil has resistance in its windings. However, at very high frequencies the inductance of straight leads, although low, may represent an appreciable inductive reactance. Similarly, the capacitance between wiring and a metal chassis, or between one circuit and another may be low, but, nevertheless, still represents an important capacitive link which must be taken into account in circuit design.

Figure 5.10 shows a typical 100 Mc/s R.F. stage. It should be noted that, in this case, the common base configuration is used, since at this frequency the gain of the transistor is beginning to fall.

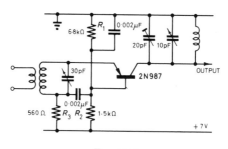

FIG. 5.10

The negative line is earthed, bias being provided by R_1, R_2 and R_3. When common base is used in an unneutralized stage, the feedback is positive and increases the gain, but the circuit gain and phase shift are in this case such that instability is avoided. The main problem in this type of circuit is usually that of avoiding oscillation. Neutralization is, in any case, often extremely difficult, since the feedback components inherent in the transistor vary with frequency.

The usual approach, therefore, is to mismatch either the source or the load, the loading being adjusted to ensure that the gain is not sufficient to cause oscillation.

A small preset capacitor is included between base and emitter, so that the feedback is adjusted to be in phase with the input signal. Its capacitance is increased until the circuit oscillates and then decreased sufficiently so that the circuit remains stable. This technique can be employed at any high frequency to extend the range of a given transistor. The alternative is, of course, to use a transistor with a higher f_T, when these adjustments would be unnecessary.

Often at high frequencies the collector is taken to the earthed line directly. This will reduce stray capacitance and may improve the inherently poor power-dissipating capability of the transistor. It should be noted that at V.H.F., the volume of semiconductor present is of the order of 10^{-6} cu. in. Transistors of this size, when used at 300 Mc/s, are capable of dissipating 250 mW in free air at 25°C when case and collector are in direct contact. This is illustrated in Fig. 5.11 which shows two common collector stages at the lower frequency of 45 Mc/s.

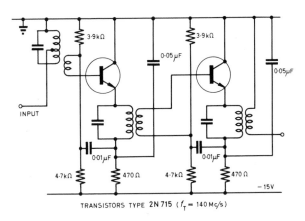

TRANSISTORS TYPE 2N 715 ($f_T = 140$ Mc/s)

FIG. 5.11

No neutralization is needed, because the internal feedback in this type of transistor is very low and, with the gain required, the circuit is stable. Such circuits usually have a gain of less than about 20 dB in order to ensure stability.

Common base circuits are used where essential, but the higher gain and small impedance transformation ratio of common emitter circuits, make them attractive at frequencies well below f_T when control of gain is more easily achieved with the negative feedback associated with these circuits.

At frequencies well below f_T, impedance levels are at least ten times lower than for valves, and Q values fifty times lower. Thus, a valve power-matched tuned amplifier operating at 45 Mc/s will have a "natural" bandwidth of about 1·8 Mc/s compared with the transistor counterpart of over 20 Mc/s. This natural bandwidth is that obtained when the inductances are tuned, not only by their stray capacitances, but also by the input capacitance of the transistors. To reduce this natural bandwidth, capacitance must be added in series with the input capacitance of each stage to prevent it tuning the previous collector load. Therefore, the power loss, W_L, will increase. $W_L = Q_o^2/(Q_o - Q_w)^2$, where Q_o is the Q of the coil and Q_w is the working Q of the circuit.

To obtain a bandwidth greater than the natural bandwidth, conductance is added in parallel with the coil, and the gain falls according to the relationship

$$(\text{power gain})^2 \times \text{bandwidth} = \text{constant.}$$

This relationship is only valid well below f_T.

Figure 5.11 represents a circuit of this latter type whilst Fig. 5.12 shows a typical narrow band amplifier.

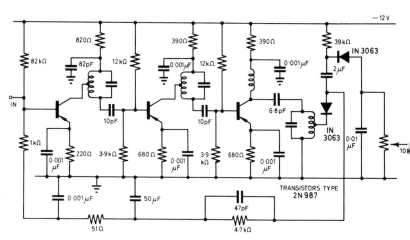

FIG. 5.12

Figure 5.12 is the circuit of a sound I.F. amplifier from a television receiver working at about 38 Mc/s. The Q of each stage is about 40, corresponding to a 1 Mc/s bandwidth. The collector loads of the first two stages have a step-up ratio of 2:1, so that the required capacitance to produce this Q (350 pF) is reduced to 85 pF approximately. The first stage is arranged to have forward A.G.C. The right-hand diode is a noise limiter of the rate-of-rise type, which clips signals greater than 1 volt peak, at frequencies below 3 kc/s, beyond which the clipping level drops progressively.

Frequency Changers

It is generally true that amplifiers perform increasingly inefficiently as their frequency of operation is raised. It is often necessary in telecommunications to employ amplifiers which have very high gain and whose input signals are at some known high frequency. This is the case in the reception of radio or video signals. The method employed is to use only limited amplification at the signal frequency, and to mix the amplified signal with the output of a local oscillator. Under certain circumstances, the result of such mixing is to generate a number of new frequencies, one of which is the difference frequency between that of the oscillator and that of the incoming signal. By means of a suitable oscillator frequency, this difference frequency, or *intermediate frequency*, as it is often called, can be made much lower than the signal frequency and hence easier to amplify.

The amplifier circuits shown in Figs. 5.6 and 5.8, might well have been intermediate frequency amplifiers operating at about 500 kc/s. Hence, to receive a frequency of 2 Mc/s the local oscillator might, for example, have been tuned to 1·5 Mc/s so that the *frequency changer*, in whose circuit the signals are mixed, might have a component of output current at the intermediate frequency.

One of the simplest frequency changers or mixers is the single transistor converter circuit of Fig. 5.13.

The collector load, T_1, of this common base amplifier is tuned to the intermediate frequency. The transistor also acts as a Hartley oscillator* whose frequency is chiefly determined by L_1 and C_1. C_3 provides input matching, and C_2 and L_2 are tuned to the intermediate frequency. Since the oscillator circuit cannot here be easily

* See Chapter 9.

isolated from the signal circuit, oscillator pulling and signal intermodulation may result. Oscillator pulling can be reduced by A.G.C.

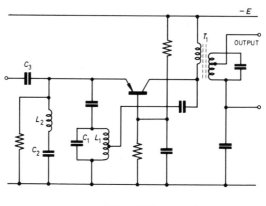

FIG. 5.13

If forward A.G.C. is used, and its use is becoming more common,
the overload level of the stage is increased. Now, it is well known
that intermodulation occurs under the non-linear input conditions

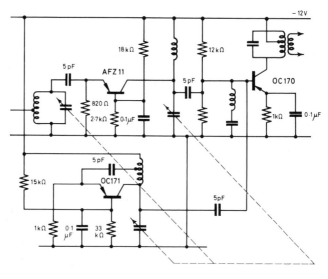

FIG. 5.14

of overloading. Therefore, forward A.G.C. reduces the intermodulation also.

Figure 5.14 shows a circuit which is suitable for use at 100 Mc/s, and where signal and oscillator circuits have been carefully isolated.

The R.F. amplifier operates in the common base mode which gives high gain at high frequencies. The local oscillator is a separate circuit, coupled only by a small capacitance to the base circuit of the frequency changer. This provides a high degree of isolation for the oscillator, so that frequency pulling is greatly reduced. In general, circuits of this complexity are unnecessary at lower frequencies, of the order of 1 Mc/s. It is only when the oscillator frequency is close to that of the signal that these measures are necessary.

Conversion Conductance

The conversion conductance of a frequency changer, g_c, can be defined as the ratio of the component of alternating short circuit collector current at intermediate frequency, i_2, to the component of alternating input voltage at signal frequency, v_1.

i.e. $$g_c = i_2/v_1 \qquad\qquad (5.3)$$

Now, in Fig. 2.10, if the reactance of the capacitance $c_{b'c}$ is high at the operating frequency, and the resistances $r_{b'c}$ and r_{ce} are high compared with other component values, and the reactance of $c_{b'e}$ is low compared with the resistance of $r_{b'e}$ (see Table 2.6), then the figure can be simplified as shown in Fig. 5.15.

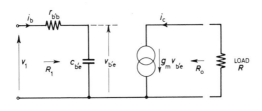

Fig. 5.15

It should be remembered that the output of the amplifier is at intermediate frequency, and that the input is effectively shorted for this frequency. The stage can then be considered as unilateralized. Except for this point, the following argument is quite general.

From Fig. 5.15, we obtain

$$v_1/i_b = R_1 = r_{b'b} - j/c_{b'e}\omega \tag{5.4}$$

and

$$i_c = g_m v_{b'e} \tag{5.5}$$

Hence

$$\frac{i_c i_b}{v_1} = \frac{g_m v_{b'e} c_{b'e}\omega}{r_{b'b} c_{b'e}\omega - j} \tag{5.6}$$

From Fig. 5.15

$$i_b = j v_{b'e} c_{b'e}\omega \tag{5.7}$$

From equations (5.6) and (5.7)

$$i_c/v_1 = \frac{g_m}{1 + j r_{b'b} c_{b'e}\omega} \tag{5.8}$$

and from equations (5.5) and (5.7)

$$i_c/i_b = \frac{g_m}{j c_{b'e}\omega} = \alpha' \tag{5.9}$$

Now, for small values of emitter current, I_e

$$g_m \doteqdot I_e/25$$

Hence, from (5.9)

$$c_{b'e} \doteqdot g_m/j\omega\alpha'$$

Hence, in equation (5.8), $c_{b'e}$ and g_m are functions of I_e, and, substituting i_2 for i_c, it can be seen that g_m is a function of I_e. Now if I_e varies at the oscillator frequency, the conversion conductance which results is due to the variation of the transconductance at this frequency also.

Hence, from equation (5.8)

$$g_c = \frac{g_m}{1 + j r_{b'b} c_{b'e}\omega} = g(t)$$

Now, the conversion power gain, a_W, is the ratio of the output power at I.F. to the input power at R.F., and, if Fig. 5.15 represents a frequency converter, a_W is given by equation (5.10).

$$a_W = \left(\frac{i_2 R_o}{R_o + R}\right)^2 RR_1/v_1^2$$

$$a_W = \left(\frac{g_c R_o}{R_o + R}\right)^2 RR_1 \qquad (5.10)$$

where R_o is the output impedance at I.F. and R_1 is the input impedance at R.F.

PROBLEMS

5.1 A tuned amplifier stage has an output impedance of 90 kilohms and an input impedance of 2·5 kilohms. The series internal feedback components are 200 ohms and 12 pF. Sketch the equivalent circuit showing feedback from the secondary of the collector transformer, labelling component values where possible.

5.2 Draw a hybrid π equivalent circuit for an alloy transistor and give a physical basis for the elements of the circuit. Explain how this circuit is of use in tuned amplifiers.

5.3 Verify the approximations for C_3 and R_3 given in this chapter. To what degree of accuracy can they be relied upon (i) at 10 kc/s, (ii) at 1 Mc/s and (iii) at 20 Mc/s? Assume that the other characteristics of the transistor are those suggested early in this chapter.

5.4 Construct an equivalent circuit based on the T parameters, but containing both resistive and reactive elements, and use it to explain how the feedback in the common emitter mode is essentially negative, and how that in the common base mode can lead to oscillation.

5.5 Explain how selective amplifiers may be designed which use ceramic filters as resonant elements.

  (i) What are their chief advantages?
  (ii) What measure of frequency stability would you expect from these filters?
  (iii) For what frequency range would you expect these filters to be available? State your reasons.

5.6 Outline the problems associated with the design of tuned amplifiers at high frequencies. Explain why it is that the design of this type of amplifier is often carried out using the Y parameters.

Sketch a Y parameter equivalent circuit labelling the elements with their real and imaginary component values.

5.7   Contrast the design of "front ends" for F.M. tuners and domestic medium wave receivers.

BIBLIOGRAPHY

Crawford: Piezoelectric Ceramic Transformers and Filters, *J.Brit.I.R.E.*, **21**, 353, 1961.

Duncan: Mismatch Design of Transistor I.F. Amplifiers, *Proc. I.R.E. (Aust.)*, **23**, 147, 1962.

Jannson: High Amplification Using Junction Transistors, *Mullard Tech. Comm.*, **26**, 174, 1957.

Jones: Transistor I.F. Amplifiers Using Double Tuned Coupling Transformers, *Mullard Tech. Comm.*, **47**, 259, 1961.

CHAPTER 6

Power Amplifiers

A transistor power amplifier may be defined as a transistor amplifier in which a high power gain, as distinct from a voltage or current gain alone, is required, converting direct power from the supplies into alternating power delivered to a load. Power stages frequently operate at high collector currents. It has already been shown that certain small signal amplifiers often have high power gains*. In the present case large signal amplifiers only will be considered. It is important to remember that small signal parameters do not usually apply with large signal operation. It will be assumed here that the appropriate large signal parameters are employed.

Power stages may work in class A or class B, or for switching service in an extreme class C which is sometimes known as class S. The use of these terms will become apparent as practical amplifiers are examined. Switching amplifiers will be considered further in Chapter 10.

Class A Stage

Figure 6.1 illustrates some of the limitations on the operation of a power amplifier. Voltage breakdown must be avoided, both between collector and emitter, and between collector and base, and also the dissipation of power within the transistor must not be excessive. The maximum power dissipation which can be permitted will depend on the resistivity of the junctions, on the type of transistor (e.g. a micro-alloy construction is likely to dissipate less power with safety, than a planar epitaxial having the same volume of semiconductor), and on the method of mounting the transistor to remove heat from it to the air around it.

At high values of collector current, the current gain becomes less. This region of low current gain should be avoided if the transistor is

* See page 27.

being used as a linear amplifier. Also, to prevent distortion, bottoming* must not be permitted. That is, the transistor must not be so hard on, that the potential across it has fallen to a very low saturation value. When a transistor has bottomed, its current gain will be extremely small. The current gain may also be small for low values of base current. The maximum power dissipation that the

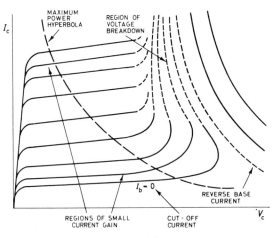

FIG. 6.1

manufacturer permits, P_{max}, can be indicated on the output characteristics, since it is given by $I_c V_c = P_{max}$. This is the maximum power hyperbola in Fig. 6.1.

Figure 6.2 shows a simple class A amplifier and its corresponding load lines. A load line is the locus of points on the output characteristic which satisfies the $I_c–V_c$ conditions for the transistor working with a known load. Here it will be assumed that V_c and I_c remain in

* Bottoming implies that the collector–emitter potential has become extremely small, of the order of 200 mV, and that the collector current is limited by the resistance of the external circuit. On the other hand, saturation strictly implies that the collector current has reached a maximum value, determined by the transistor, and which cannot be increased by any further increase in base current, whatever the value of the external resistance. In this sense, transistors do not readily saturate (whereas the emission of a tungsten filament valve does). Here, however, following common usage, the terms "bottoming" and "saturation" are treated as synonymous.

phase and that the locus is a straight line. The a.c. load line should touch the limiting parabola of Fig. 6.1 for maximum power, but the swing should be restricted to within the bounding regions which have been described, and which may be appropriate in the particular application for which the power stage is intended. Equal increments of I_b should cut off equal intercepts on the load line.

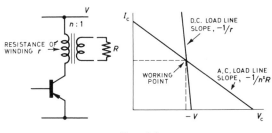

FIG. 6.2

Thus a class A stage must operate over the relatively linear part of the characteristic, whilst for switching service the conditions would not be so stringent.

Figure 6.3 shows a typical output characteristic with the maximum power hyperbola and a typical load line superimposed on it.

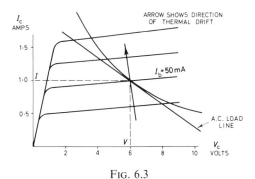

FIG. 6.3

If, in the figure, the mean current is I and the mean voltage is V, then the d.c. power supplied is $V \times I$. In order to find the maximum possible efficiency, it will be assumed that the whole length of the load line is employed. This may be approximately true, particularly with silicon epitaxial transistors, where the linearity of current gain

9

is maintained to high values of collector current and the bottoming voltage is low. Under these conditions, the maximum r.m.s. alternating current is $I/\sqrt{2}$ and the maximum r.m.s. alternating voltage is $V/\sqrt{2}$. Thus the alternating power delivered to the load is $\frac{1}{2}VI$, giving a maximum efficiency of 50 per cent. This means that the maximum power delivered to the load is equal to the mean power dissipated in the transistor. From Fig. 6.3 it can be seen that the battery supplies 6 watts for 3 watts output power.

Now, the mean collector current is 1 amp and the characteristic shows that a mean base current of 50 mA is needed to produce this. The signal base current to give the maximum swing of collector current is $50/\sqrt{2}$ mA r.m.s. Also, for a change in base current of 10 mA, the corresponding change in base–emitter voltage might be found from the input characteristics of the transistor to be 40 mV, and the input impedance is thus 4 ohms.

With an input impedance as low as this there is also the problem of the drive needed to the stage. The power gain of this amplifier can now be calculated, since 5×10^{-3} watts are needed at the input to obtain an output of 3 watts. This is a gain of about 28 dB.

Figure 6.4 shows the circuit of a typical class A amplifier. It will be seen that, in order to obtain a low value of k, the thermal stability

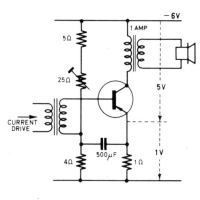

FIG. 6.4

factor, and to keep the pre-signal bias level constant on the application of a signal, a high bleed current is needed. The input transformer is connected so that the bias network does not shunt the input. With so low a value of emitter resistor, it becomes very difficult to decouple it adequately. (At the lowest frequency in use, this capacitor should have a reactance one order lower than the resistance of the resistor it bypasses.) This resistor must be a low value because of the high emitter current, and, on the other hand, it is frequently included in order that the circuit shall have reasonable gain.

The high emitter currents and dissipations in power amplifiers mean that such stages are often operated at, or near, maximum junction temperatures (75–100°C for germanium and 150–200°C for silicon). Thermal stability is of great importance, because increasing temperature, causing an increase in leakage current and a consequent further increase in temperature, may result in thermal runaway, destroying the junctions and preventing further transistor action. In the case of small signal amplifiers, even if the transistor were turned hard on, the collector load so limits the collector current, that although linear amplification would be prevented by excess leakage current, the transistor would not be destroyed, the junctions never reaching their maximum operating temperature. It can be shown mathematically, that the limiting condition for this "built-in safety valve", is that when the transistor is heavily conducting, the collector–emitter potential falls to at most one half of the supply potential. With power amplifiers this is seldom the case, since their loads usually have very low resistance to direct current. Hence care should be taken in the design of bias circuits, and in the adequate dissipation of heat (mainly from the collector junction) by the use of a heat sink.

In Fig. 6.4, the symbol used for the transistor is intended to show that the collector is in direct electrical and thermal contact with the case in which it is encapsulated. This is almost universal practice for power transistors. The following section on heat dissipation applies to all types of power amplifier.

Heat Sinks

If the junction temperature is T_j and the ambient temperature is T_{amb} then $T_j - T_{amb} = p_c\theta$, where $p_c = V_{ce}I_c + V_{be}I_b$. The second term is small and can often be neglected.

Here p_c is the collector dissipation and θ is the total thermal resistance measured in centigrade degrees per watt. This thermal equation is frequently regarded as analogous to Ohm's law,

since thermal resistances, in series and parallel, may be manipulated
in a similar manner to electrical resistances in the computation of
the total thermal resistance. Thus the total thermal resistance
between the junction and the surrounding air can be split up into
resistances, for example, between the semiconductor wafer and the

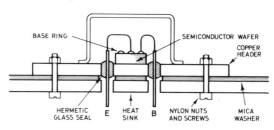

FIG. 6.5

header, through the header, and the resistance from the header to
the heat sink. Some of these resistances are under the control of the
transistor manufacturer, and some under the control of the circuit
designer. From a knowledge of the maximum ambient temperature
which can be expected, and the maximum permissible junction
temperature, the designer is able to find the thermal resistance he
must not exceed. Then he must be able to make this compatible
with circuit requirements.

It is important that the maximum permissible temperature is not
exceeded either due to accidental surges or during pulse operation.

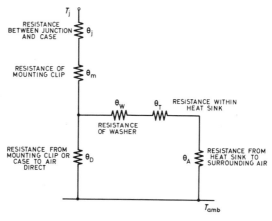

FIG. 6.6

The result of such excess dissipation may be immediately catastrophic, or may produce a gradual deterioration in the performance of the transistor. Increased leakage current caused in this way may, for example, result in eventual thermal runaway. Reduced current gain can also be due to excess junction temperature.

Figures 6.5 and 6.6 illustrate some of the thermal resistances to which reference has already been made. In Fig. 6.5, a section through a typical power transistor shows the heat paths, and these are put into an electrical analogue form in Fig. 6.6.

The effectiveness of a heat sink depends on several factors which will now be considered.

Thermal Conductivity of the Metal

This is only important for high power dissipation when copper must be used. Aluminium is a better conductor than steel and hence it is often to be preferred. If, however, large heat sinks are called for in the design of the power amplifier, it may be convenient for these to form the case of the instrument, when it may be advantageous to employ steel for its strength. The transistors can be bolted into recesses which have been pressed into the metal. Care should be taken that the metal is not made thinner in the recess by pressing.

The Thickness of the Metal

Providing the metal is not very thin, say not less than $\frac{1}{16}$ in, this is of relatively less importance than some of the other factors, but very thin metal (as can be found on printed circuit cards) does not make a very effective heat sink.

Surface Area

This is a very important factor since it is, in part, responsible for θ_A, the resistance from the heat sink to the surrounding air. This resistance is usually due to both convection and radiation from the heat sink.

Surface Conditions

The effectiveness of the heat sink is greatly increased by blackening the surface, since dull black surfaces are good radiators of heat.

Radiation is proportional to the emissivity of the surface. Some typical relative emissivities are polished aluminium (0·05–0·1), clean copper (0·15), steel (0·7), anodized aluminium (0·76), matt black paint (0·9–0·95).

Orientation and Situation

Air should be capable of passing freely over the heat sink. It should be shielded from other heat sources. Heat sinks should be so mounted as to assist in cooling by air convection. Forced convection may be necessary for dissipating high powers.

Mounting Clips

Transistors can be attached to a heat sink by mounting clips or by washers. Conducting lead washers and insulating mica ones are in use, but an insulated heat sink is preferable to the use of washers. Lead washers are used to make good thermal contact between the heat sink and the transistor, whereas mica washers are used when the transistor case (often in electrical contact with the collector) must be insulated from the heat sink whilst remaining in thermal contact. At high frequencies, the use of mica washers is particularly undesirable, since they may form an undesirable capacity between the header (and the collector) and the heat sink.

Cavities

The existence of cavities must be avoided. Burrs should be removed from the metal of the heat sink, and silicone grease may be applied to the underside of the transistor. With cavities present hot spots can occur, and, in any case, thermal resistances will be in excess of those calculated.

An example will be worked to illustrate these principles.

Example. A power transistor can dissipate 14 watts and has a maximum junction temperature, T_j, of 150°C. The analogue developed from Fig. 6.6 is tabulated here for this transistor. A comparison will now be made to find the maximum ambient temperature permissible, so that the maximum junction temperature shall not be exceeded.

Thermal resistance between junction and case, θ_j 1·8°C/watt
of mica washer, θ_w 1·7°C/watt
of a blackened aluminium heat
   sink of 9 sq. in. surface area, θ_A 5·6°C/watt
of a similar heat sink of
   polished aluminium, θ_A 8·1°C/watt
from case of transistor to
   air direct, θ_D 30·0°C/watt

(a) *Polished heat sink*
(i) With washer

Total thermal resistance, $\theta = 1·8 + \dfrac{30 \times 9·8}{39·8}$

$$= 9·1°C/watt$$

$$150 - T_{amb} = 14 \times 9·1$$

Thus $T_{amb} = 22·6°C$ maximum

(ii) Without washer

Total thermal resistance, $\theta = 1·8 + \dfrac{30 \times 8·1}{38·1}$

$$= 8·1°C/watt$$

$$150 - T_{amb} = 14 \times 8·1$$

Thus $T_{amb} = 36·6°C$ maximum

(b) *Blackened heat sink*
(i) With washer

Total thermal resistance, $\theta = 1·8 + \dfrac{30 \times 7·3}{37·3}$

$$= 7·8°C/watt$$

$$150 - T_{amb} = 14 \times 7·8$$

Thus $T_{amb} = 40·8°C$ maximum

(ii) Without washer

$$\text{Total thermal resistance, } \theta = 1\cdot8 + \frac{30 \times 5\cdot6}{35\ 6}$$

$$= 6\cdot5^\circ\text{C/watt}$$

$$150 - T_{amb} = 14 \times 6\cdot5$$

Thus $\qquad T_{amb} = 59^\circ\text{C maximum}$

Of these four calculations, in practice, in the absence of forced air-cooling, only the last of them would probably be adequate for the majority of applications. Manufacturers publish heat sink data for their products, or formulae to enable the minimum heat sink size to be related to a particular dissipation. Such a curve, applicable to the example already developed, is shown in Fig. 6.7.

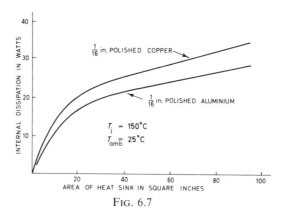

FIG. 6.7

The difficulty of dissipating the heat generated within the transistor and the 50 per cent efficiency of working, suggest that class A is a wasteful method of operation. One approach to this problem is to use heat sinks with multiple fins, and another is to use class B operation. Both of these techniques will be considered here.

Multiple Fin Heat Sinks

The resistance, θ_A, can be considered as being due to two parallel resistances, one of which is a function of the radiation from the surface of the sink and one due to convection of the surrounding air. If these are called θ_R and θ_C respectively, they may be added by the reciprocal law. θ_R is a function of the emissivity of the surface and is important, except where forced air-cooling is employed, when θ_C becomes sufficiently small to be the determining factor in θ_A. θ_C depends on the shape and the surface area of the heat sink. For forced air-cooling, θ_A is given by $A^{2/3}V^{1/2}\theta_A =$ a constant. V is the velocity of air flow, and A is the exposed surface area of the heat sink.

When multiple fins are used (without forced air-cooling) θ_R is usually greater than θ_C, since radiation is shielded by adjacent fins. θ_R may be considered to be divided by a shielding factor, F, which varies in practice between 0·1 and 1·0. For example, for a stack of square heat sinks of side 4 in, $F = 0·1$ when the fins are 0·2 in apart and $F = 0·4$ when they are 1·2 in apart. The radiation resistance of this heat sink might, if blackened, be 9°C/watt. If its convection resistance were also 9°C/watt, which is a probable figure for an aluminium fin, this yields a value for θ_A of 4·5°C/watt. From data of this kind and a knowledge of the shielding factor, multiple fin heat sinks can be designed.

Maximum Voltages

It is often the case that the maximum voltage which can be permitted across the base–collector junction is about 25 per cent greater than that between the emitter and collector when the base is open-circuited. These breakdown voltages are due to avalanche multiplication, causing α to tend towards unity at high collector voltages. The corresponding tendency of α' to rise to infinity is responsible for the lower limitation on V_{ce}*. The manufacturer's figure for $V_{ce\text{-}max}$ should be observed for class A stages although it can be increased somewhat, depending on the stability of the circuit. The value given for $V_{cb\text{-}max}$ may be used for common emitter stages, where the full voltage is only applied when the input base–emitter junction is reverse biased. This is the case for many switching circuits and for some of the class B stages which follow, provided always that the design is not complicated by a load which is predominantly inductive.

If power transistors are operated beyond these limits, in the

* See Fig. 6.1.

avalanche mode, an additional problem is that the thermal resistance of the transistor itself is higher than when used in the normal way. This is due to a concentration of the current near the emitter, so that the semiconductor material is unequally heated. This applies in the case of pulse amplifiers operated at high voltage.

Calculation of Output Power

From the output characteristics and the load line drawn on them, the peak swing, V_p, can be found. We have $V_p = V - V_{min}$, where V is the supply voltage and V_{min} is the knee voltage.

When the transistor is cut off, the collector voltage swings towards breakdown, V_{bd}. ($V_{ce\text{-}max}$ is not used here, since this treatment is quite independent of the configuration employed.)

Then, in order to avoid operation in the avalanche region

$$\tfrac{1}{2}(V_{bd} - V_{min}) \geqslant V - V_{min} \text{ (i.e. greater than } V_p)$$

Now the maximum output power

$$= \text{(r.m.s. output voltage)}^2/\text{load} = V_p^2/2R_L$$
$$= (V_{bd} - V_{min})^2/8R_L \tag{6.1}$$

Thus the maximum power can be calculated for a given transistor on an adequate heat sink using equation (6.1). These calculations apply at both high and low frequencies and so are used in the design of both audio and R.F. power amplifiers.

Class B Stages

The chief disadvantage of class A power amplifiers was the high standby dissipation. This can be overcome by class B working, but, as is well known, in audio amplifiers push–pull operation must be used also to overcome the intolerable distortion which would otherwise result.

Efficiency of Class B

Let the instantaneous current be i, and let the corresponding instantaneous internal dissipation be p, where
$$p = E_c i - i^2 R = E_c i(1 - iR/E_c) = E_c i(1 - i/I)$$

Then, putting $i = I_p \sin \omega t$, the power, P, delivered by one transistor is given by

$$P = \frac{1}{2\pi} \int_0^\pi E_c I_p \sin \omega t \left(1 - \frac{I_p}{I} \sin \omega t\right) d\omega t$$

$$= E_c I_p \left(\frac{1}{\pi} - \frac{1}{4}\frac{I_p}{I}\right) \tag{6.2}$$

But, for maximum signal, $I_p = I$ and $P = E_c I (1/\pi - \frac{1}{4})$

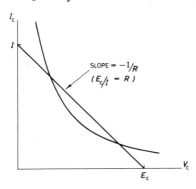

FIG. 6.8

Also, the power delivered to the load by one transistor under these conditions is

$$\tfrac{1}{2} \times E_c/\sqrt{2} \times I/\sqrt{2} = \tfrac{1}{4}E_c I \tag{6.3}$$

Therefore, efficiency ($=$ power delivered $\div$ total power)

$$= 100 \times \tfrac{1}{4} \times \pi \text{ per cent} = 78\cdot5 \text{ per cent}$$

The maximum internal dissipation is found by differentiating equation (6.2) and equating to zero:

$$\frac{\partial P}{\partial I_p} = E_c/\pi - \tfrac{1}{2}E_c I_p/I$$

$$= 0 \quad \text{when } I_p = 2I/\pi$$

Substituting this value in equation (6.2) gives the maximum dissipation:

$$P_{\text{max}} = \frac{2E_c I}{\pi}(1/\pi - 1/2\pi)$$

$$= E_c I/\pi^2 \doteqdot \tfrac{1}{10}E_c I \quad \text{(in each transistor)} \tag{6.4}$$

Hence the useful power delivered (from equations (6.3) and (6.4)) is approximately 10/4 times (or 250 per cent) the total maximum internal dissipation, or five times that of one transistor. However, because the saturation voltage of the transistor is not zero, efficiencies somewhat less than this are obtained in practice.

The advantages of high efficiency, and the consequently smaller battery drain than with class A, leads to the use of class B amplifiers. It must be remembered, however, that the regulation demands on the power supplies will be greater than for a class A stage, owing to the extreme current swings which take place.

Common Emitter Class B Stage

Referring to the circuit of Fig. 6.9, if the transistors are working over the maximum possible swing, the peak inverse voltage is equal to twice the direct supply potential. Hence, first the heat sink and transistor are chosen for a given maximum internal dissipation, and

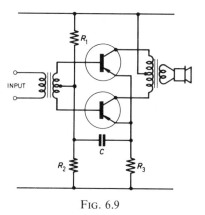

Fig. 6.9

then the supply potential is chosen to be not greater than half the breakdown voltage. Here, it is the manufacturer's figure for $V_{cb\text{-max}}$ which is used, but with a safety factor owing to the forward bias provided here. If ideal class B operation is worked, the non-linearity of the characteristics at low collector currents would produce cross-over distortion of the output signal. R_1, R_2 and R_3 in Fig. 6.9 are chosen to bias the transistor sufficiently into the conducting region to avoid this distortion, C being required as a by-pass.

If the supply potential falls, as in a partly used battery, the cross-over distortion becomes worse, and may, in battery-driven ampli-fiers, determine the useful end of the battery life, by the amount of distortion which can be tolerated. In an amplifier designed to deliver 1 watt of power, typical quiescent collector currents would be 3–10 mA.

Matched transistors are always to be preferred so that each transistor has equal drive, and there is no resultant direct current flux in the output transformer. This also keeps even harmonic dis-tortion low. Often designs of this type use negative feedback. That shown in Fig. 6.10 reduces the gain by 6 dB at 400 c/s. Phase shift

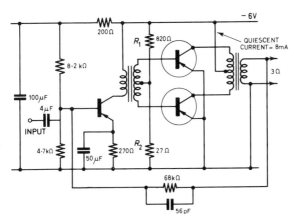

FIG. 6.10

at high audio frequencies tends to make the feedback ineffective at above about 5 kc/s. The amount of feedback is therefore increased by the 56 pF capacitor at high frequencies, so that the amplifier gain is greatly reduced, and distortion at high frequencies therefore avoided.

An alternative method of feedback is to use emitter resistors as shown in Fig. 6.11. This method is common at high powers, where the first purpose of the resistors is to limit the emitter current and so prevent destructive thermal runaway. This is important with single ended class B amplifiers such as that in Fig. 6.11. It can be seen that an output transformer is not required, with a consequent saving in cost, but the driver transformer has two secondaries and for equal drive these secondaries should be bifilar wound.

If the transistors are well matched, there will be no direct current through the load, and the drawbacks of the bifilar driver and tapped power supplies are offset by the advantages of low cost and avoiding the distortion inherent in an output transformer.

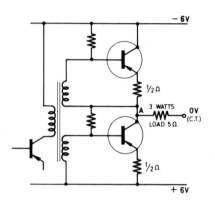

FIG. 6.11

This type of circuit suggests the use of stages in which no transformers at all are used. This idea will be developed further, later in the chapter.

The maximum output power can easily be estimated in a stage of this kind, for the output transistors can be regarded as causing the point A in the figure to swing between plus and minus 6 volts. If it is assumed that the potential at A has a sinusoidal waveform, then the r.m.s. output voltage is $6/\sqrt{2}$. The power available to a 5-ohm load is therefore 3·6 watts. In practice a somewhat lower figure may be obtained. This analysis yields a maximum power for *any* transistors connected in this way with these supplies, an ample drive and a 5-ohm load.

Common Base and Common Collector Stages

Common base stages need a high current drive ($\alpha \doteqdot 1$ gives small current gain), and common collector stages require high voltage drive, since they possess a voltage gain of only unity. Amplifiers of these types are sometimes used for special purposes.

Amplifier Design

An experimental class B amplifier will now be designed capable of delivering 2–3 watts of power to a 3-ohm loudspeaker and operating from a 14 volt supply. An arbitrary decision is to use a symmetrical design rather than a single ended one.

The transistor must stand an inverse voltage of 28 volts at peak working and hence this must influence the choice of transistor. The circuit might be similar to that of Fig. 6.9.

To avoid cross-over distortion a small quiescent current is allowed to flow. Too large a current is wasteful, too small does not avoid distortion. Three milliamps per transistor is normal for transistors dissipating internally up to about 1 watt each. Either the transistors are matched or separate bias networks are used for each transistor so that each quiescent collector current may be adjusted to a predetermined value.

Next, the common emitter output characteristics are examined. A load line is constructed on them so that one half of the area of the triangle cut off between the load line and the axes represents the output power contribution of one transistor; i.e. the power output of the two transistors is twice this, and in Fig. 6.12 is given by $\frac{1}{2}(14-1)\frac{4}{10} = 2\cdot6$ watts.

In class B operation, the maximum dissipation is exceeded for

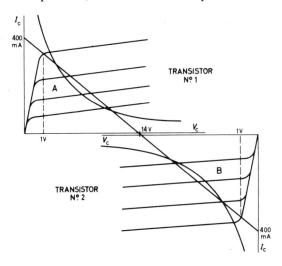

FIG. 6.12

part of each cycle, and the dissipation is less than the maximum for part also. It is essential that the average dissipation per cycle is less than the permitted maximum.

In a fuller treatment, the thermal time constant and the thermal pulse stability factor are two constants which could be introduced to explain the performance of the transistor, when it undergoes momentary excursions beyond its normal dissipation. These terms have been mentioned here, to point out to the reader that it is possible for this type of service to result in excessive junction temperatures. It will be assumed here, however, that the maximum junction temperature is not exceeded.

In Fig. 6.12 the area of triangles A and B = peak I_c × peak V_{ce} = $\sqrt{2}$(r.m.s. I_c) × $\sqrt{2}$(r.m.s. V_{ce}) = 2 × power output.

The slope of the load line is $130/4 \fallingdotseq 32$ ohms. Hence the ratio of the output transformer to match to a 3 ohm load is $\sqrt{(32/3)} = 3 \cdot 3 + 3 \cdot 3 : 1$.

The emitter resistor R_3 cannot be large or the gain will be reduced. It could be wound with copper or nickel wire to make use of the high positive temperature coefficient of these metals, and afford some measure of stability. At maximum current about $\frac{1}{10}$th of the supply voltage should be dropped across it.

Hence $R_3 = 1 \cdot 4/0 \cdot 4 \fallingdotseq 3$ ohms.

Not only does leakage current increase with temperature, due to thermal energies causing an increase in the intrinsic current, but the value of V_{be} for a given extrinsic collector current falls by about 2·4 mV per centigrade degree rise. The base–emitter voltage will be about 150 mV for a germanium transistor, and will be almost independent of the power rating of the stage. Other forms of temperature compensation will therefore be considered, which give better protection against changes in the ambient temperature.

From the input characteristic of the transistors used, it is found that the base–emitter voltage changes by 50 mV for a change in base current of 400 μA. Thus the input impedance is 125 ohms at each bifilar winding.

The maximum input power and the power gain can then be found to complete the design.

Diode Bias

An alternative method of bias stabilization is to use a forward biased junction diode in place of one of the bias resistors (R_2 in

Fig. 6.10). Ideally, a germanium diode should be used with germanium power transistors and a silicon one with silicon transistors. In practice, the cheaper germanium junction diode will often serve. The voltage drop across the diode is substantially equal to the voltage "knee" of the input characteristic. Also, the value of R_1 in Fig. 6.10 can be chosen so that the quiescent bias current is slightly greater than the peak base current. The diode should be placed on the same heat sink or under the same thermal conditions as the output transistors. It then tends to provide compensation for them. When using the diode, temperature changes causing voltage variations in the drop across the diode, and those due to the transistor are similar, thus compensating for variations in the input characteristic from this cause.

Compensation for temperature changes can also be made by using a thermistor with a high negative temperature coefficient of resistance, or combination of thermistor and resistor in the emitter circuit. Such a combination tends to be more linear in operation than a thermistor alone. Alternatively, a silicon resistor with a positive temperature coefficient can be used as part of the chain providing current in the base circuit.

Distortion in Class B Stages

(i) Even Harmonic Distortion

This arises from mismatch of current gain in the output transistors. If the values of α' are in the ratio $5:4$, over 5 per cent second harmonic distortion is produced, while 5 per cent discrepancy in the values of α' causes 1 per cent distortion.

Mismatch of f_α causes unequal phase shift in the pair at high frequencies. Both even and odd harmonics are produced. The effect can be minimized in audio amplifiers by providing heavy negative feedback at high frequencies.

Ringing of the output or driver transformer on transients also causes, chiefly, even harmonic distortion. The effect can be eliminated over a wide frequency range by a series CR circuit across the transformer winding concerned.

(ii) Odd Harmonic Distortion

This is more important in many audio amplifiers than even harmonic distortion, since the ear easily accepts a small percentage

10

of even harmonic distortion. This is not the case with odd harmonics. Its chief cause is non-linearity of the current gain. If the design specifies a maximum third harmonic, m_3, which can be tolerated, this can be estimated from the formula:

$$m_3 = \frac{(\frac{1}{2}I_c - I'_c)}{(I_c + I'_c)} \times 100 \text{ per cent}$$

where I_c is the maximum collector current (produced by a base current I_b) and I'_c is the collector current corresponding to $\frac{1}{2}I_b$.

Cross-over distortion is also important. It has already been explained that this is reduced by forward biasing the power stage. The extent of the forward bias is a compromise between reduction of harmonics and economy of operation.

Transformerless Class B Stages

The use of transformers can be avoided, although usually by circuitry which is slightly more complex than that already described. Complementary stages can be used as one practical way of keeping the circuitry as simple as possible. This is illustrated in Fig. 6.13. It has already been explained (see p. 130) that this necessarily limits the power which any transistors can supply to a given load.

The potential at A is just more negative than 12 volts in order that the OC 76 shall be conducting; that at B is more positive in

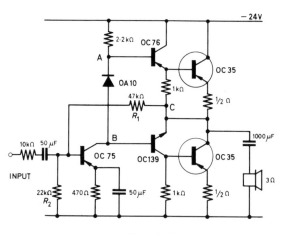

Fig. 6.13

order to bias the *npn* OC 139 into conduction. The quiescent current of about 6 mA is adjustable by R_1 and R_2. The junction diode (forward resistance about 200 ohms) is used (as previously) to give added thermal stability; a resistor may be used instead with slightly poorer stability. D.C. conditions are controlled by negative feedback so that the bias current of the first stage is set by the output potential at C. An output of about 100 mW is obtained from the OC 76/ OC 139 pair. Higher power can be delivered if the output stage is followed by a further power stage. This enables a conventional 3 ohm speaker to be used as load.

Using 24 volt supplies the possible output power has a theoretical maximum of about 24 watts into a 3 ohm load. The circuit of Fig. 6.13 can only provide an output of about 8 watts for an input of about 650 mV, with a total distortion of 3 per cent. The total battery current is about 800 mA under these conditions. Hence the d.c. power of 19·2 watts represents an overall efficiency of 40 per cent.

Improved performance can be obtained using a further stage. The circuit of Fig. 6.14 shows a 10 watt amplifier having a total distortion of 0·7 per cent at 1 kilocycle and an improved frequency response.

In Chapter 4 (see Fig. 4.18) it was suggested that a cascode circuit could be used for those amplifiers where it was important to operate at a relatively high voltage. As might, therefore, be expected,

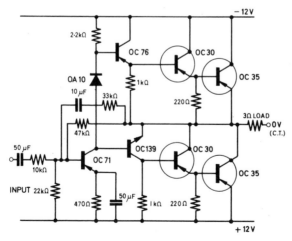

FIG. 6.14

this kind of circuit has been used to obtain high output power. Now it has been explained that in cascode operation, most of the applied voltage falls across one of the transistors in the cascode pair. This would seem to limit its usefulness as a high voltage stage, but it must be remembered that the transistor across which the high voltage falls is operating in the common base mode, and hence $V_{cb\text{-}max}$ rather than $V_{ce\text{-}max}$ is the limiting factor. Since it is frequently the case that $V_{cb\text{-}max}$ is 25 per cent higher than $V_{ce\text{-}max}$, then operating into a constant load, the output power is raised in the ratio $5^2 : 4^2$ i.e. by over 50 per cent.

Figure 6.15 is typical of a transformerless output stage of this kind. The two cascode pairs of this class B output stage are driven

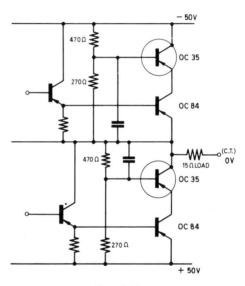

FIG. 6.15

in a similar way to that which has just been described, but the output transistors are of particular interest. In this circuit, the greater part of the supply voltage falls across the OC 35 transistors ($V_{cb\text{-}max} = 60$ volts) which are operating in the common base mode. The OC 84 transistors must supply the peak current (1 amp max.) but at a lower collector voltage. It is also of interest to note that the frequency of operation will now be limited by the smaller transistors, since each OC 84 operates as a common emitter amplifier. It is likely that $f_{\alpha'}$ for the OC 84 is about 20 kc/s ($f_1 = 1$ Mc/s and α' is at least 60 at 50 mA). This should be adequate for service as an audio amplifier.

PROBLEMS

6.1 (a) What do you understand by the concept of thermal resistance as applied to heat sink design?

(b) A power transistor has a resistance of 2°C/watt between junction and case and 30°C/watt between the case and the surrounding air. A washer is necessary and has a resistance of 1·5°C/watt. If the transistor has to work in an ambient temperature of 45°C (maximum junction temperature 75°C) when dissipating 3 watts, find the maximum thermal resistance that can be tolerated, and the resistance of the heat sink necessary. [Ans. 10°C/watt, 8·3°C/watt.]

6.2 (a) A germanium transistor can dissipate 5 watts and has a maximum junction temperature of 75°C. Find the maximum ambient temperature at which it can be operated in each of the following cases: (i) With a mica washer of resistance 2°C/watt on a heat sink of resistance 5°C/watt; (ii) On the same heat sink but without the washer. The resistance from junction to case is 1·8°C/watt and from the case of the transistor to air direct is 28°C/watt.

(b) At what ambient temperature could the transistor operate on a heat sink of infinite thermal capacity? [Ans. (a), (i) 34·8°C, (ii) 44·8°C; (b) 66°C if no washer is used.]

6.3 A *pnp* transistor power amplifier has a current gain of 25 and an emitter resistance of 0·5 ohm. Between the base and the positive rail is a resistance of 4 ohms. Between the base and the negative rail is a 5 ohm resistor and a 20 ohm potentiometer in series. How must the travel of the potentiometer be restricted if the thermal stability factor, k, must not exceed one fifth? [Ans. Not greater than $9\frac{2}{7}$ ohms making the usual approximations.]

6.4 Show that with a resistively loaded amplifier, destructive thermal runaway can only occur if, under class A conditions, less than one half of the supply voltage is dropped across the load.

6.5 (a) Discuss the factors which determine the choice of transistor for use as a class A power amplifier. In particular, explain under what conditions the maximum rated collector–emitter voltage may be employed in calculations.

(b) A transistor has a bottoming voltage of 0·5 volt. If its current gain may be assumed to be linear for all voltages greater than this, find the maximum efficiency which can be obtained for class A operation if the maximum collector voltage is (i) 6 volts and (ii) 20 volts. [Ans. (i) 41 per cent; (ii) 47·5 per cent.]

6.6   (a) The output transistors in Fig. 6.10 have a current gain of 50. If the quiescent collector current is 8 mA at 20°C, find the voltage, V_{be}, across R_2 at this temperature.

(b) If V_{be} falls by 2·4 mV per degree C rise, find the temperature at which it has fallen to one-half. If R_2 consists of a 56 ohm resistor which is not temperature sensitive and a thermistor whose resistance is 56 ohms at 20°C in parallel with the other resistor, find the resistance the thermistor need have when V_{be} has fallen to one-half its original value, in order to compensate correctly for this variation. [Ans. (a) 186 mV; (b) 58·7°C, 17·7 ohms.]

6.7   A transistor operates as a class A power amplifier with a mean current of 400 mA. It uses an emitter resistor of 1·5 ohms. What is the ideal temperature coefficient for this resistor, if it is assumed that it is the only temperature sensitive passive element in the circuit and that V_{be} falls by 2·4 mV per degree C rise? Hence discuss the suitability of a number of specific materials for the construction of this element. [Ans. −0·004/°C.]

6.8   (a) Discuss the need for thermal stability in a transistor amplifier and explain the possible effects of under-estimating this need in (i) a small signal amplifier, and (ii) a large signal (power) amplifier.

(b) A germanium transistor can dissipate a maximum of 10 watts and must operate in an ambient temperature of 40°C. If its junction temperature must not exceed 80°C find the thermal resistance of the heat sink which must be used. The thermal resistance from the junction is 1·0°C/watt and from the case to the air direct is 25°C/watt. What is the maximum power it could dissipate under these conditions without the use of an external heat sink? [Ans. $3\frac{9}{22}$°C per watt, $1\frac{7}{13}$ watts.]

BIBLIOGRAPHY

Greiter: Transistor Amplifier Output Stages, *Wireless World*, Jan.–May 1963.

Palmer: Some Aspects of the Effects of Temperature on Junction Transistors, *Electronic Components*, 749, July 1963.

Roddam: Sliding Bias Amplifiers, *Wireless World*, 241, May 1962.

Webber: Temperature Stabilisation of Transistors in Class B Amplifiers, *Proc.I.R.E.(Aust.)*, **20**, 726, 1959.

CHAPTER 7

Semiconductor Diodes

A typical diode characteristic is shown in Fig. 7.1. Reference has already been made to a particular type of diode, the zener diode, in Chapter 4. Its characteristic is similar to that shown in Fig. 7.1 except that the increase of current in the reverse voltage region is very sudden in the vicinity of the turn-over voltage. The magnitude

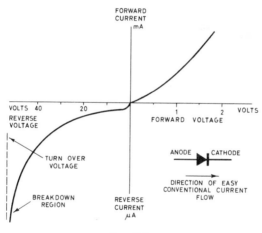

FIG. 7.1

of this voltage is controlled by the extent of the doping of the semi-conductor materials. The zener diode is an example of a silicon junction diode.

In electronics, both point-contact and junction diodes are used. The purpose of this present section is to distinguish between them, and to outline their properties and applications. However, the application of junction diodes as power rectifiers will be considered in Chapter 8.

In general, diodes pass a relatively large current when forward biased by only a small potential, have a characteristic which passes through a true zero, and, when reverse biased, pass a much smaller current until the turn-over voltage is approached. Unless the current is limited in this turn-over or breakdown region, permanent damage can occur due to overheating of the diode. A diode is therefore designed for a peak reverse voltage, and if this is exceeded for even a few microseconds its rectifying properties may be permanently destroyed.

Diode Dissipation

The maximum dissipation which may be permitted in a semiconductor diode depends on the temperature of operation. The maximum forward current must be reduced at high temperatures. Also, if high reverse voltages are applied to the diode, the reverse current which flows, even at low temperatures, although small, must be examined to find whether it causes excessive dissipation in the high impedance of the reverse-biased diode.

Point-Contact Diodes

The point-contact diode is a development of the period 1938–42 of the catswhisker of early radio receivers. Introduced as a radar detector, one form consists of a sharp sprung tungsten wire, held against a crystal of n-type germanium or silicon. Diffusion takes place at the point of contact, resulting in the formation there of a small region of p-type material. Thus a pn junction is formed with rectifying properties. It has a small junction area and is capable of only very low power dissipation. The wire is, in this example, connected to the p-type anode and the semiconductor wafer is the cathode of the diode. The maximum reverse voltage depends on the resistivity of the semiconductor crystal, heavy doping lowering the resistivity and resulting in a low reverse voltage. However, a heavily doped diode will permit a higher forward current to flow and such diodes find use as detectors up to high frequencies. The thermal dissipation of point-contact diodes is usually lower than for some other types of semiconductor diodes. The forward voltage of point-contact diodes is often about one volt for even a small current flow. This is higher than for many other types of diode.

Junction Diodes

The important properties which are particularly characteristic of *pn* junction diodes formed by alloy, diffusion or epitaxial techniques are the forward voltage drop, the peak reverse voltage and the switching behaviour. Junction diodes can be made from either germanium or silicon. A typical forward current is 100 mA with a corresponding forward voltage of 0·4 volt for a germanium diode, or 0·7 volt for a silicon diode. However, due to their much smaller reverse leakage currents, silicon diodes have much higher voltage ratings than for comparable germanium diodes. Forward voltages are lower for junction than for point-contact diodes.

Gold Bonded Diodes

These are structurally point-contact diodes where the tungsten sprung wire has been replaced by a gold or gold alloy wire. The characteristics of gold bonded diodes are a compromise between those of point-contact and junction diodes. Forward current can be higher than in the comparable tungsten wire type and the reverse-forward impedance ratio is higher.

Switching Behaviour of Diodes

The switching behaviour of a diode cannot be discovered solely by reference to characteristics similar to those of Fig. 7.1, for the junction capacitance of the diode must be examined and an explanation found for the phenomenon of carrier storage. These are of particular importance in switching circuits at high frequencies.

Reverse Recovery

When a *pn* junction diode is conducting, holes are injected from the *p*-type material into the *n*-type region, and, when it is suddenly switched from the forward to the reverse biased condition, these holes make the diode heavily conductive in the reverse direction for a short time. Thus, when the current is reversed a charge is injected into the anode, whose magnitude depends on the carrier storage in the *n*-type material in the diode. This is the phenomenon of carrier storage which is responsible for the time delay in the reverse current falling to the leakage value. The charge may be regarded as being stored in a "storage" capacitance. Such a capacitance is a function of the applied voltage. Because of this, it is usual to quote a hole storage time constant for the diode rather than to give a capacitance for some definite voltage. Figure 7.2 shows the recovery current, I_R, and the recovery time, t_{rr}. It will be seen that t_{rr} is arbitrarily defined with reference to the 10 per cent I_R level.

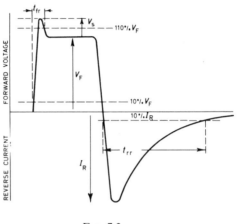

FIG. 7.2

The mechanism of hole storage should not be confused with the capacitance of the reverse biased diode, which is also a function of the diode voltage. Hole storage is a transient phenomenon, whilst a junction capacitance is always present in the reverse biased diode. Junction capacitance will be considered later in this chapter.

The reverse capacitance and hole storage of junction diodes are higher than for point-contact diodes.

Forward Recovery

When a point-contact or junction diode is biased into conduction, stored charge builds up in the n-type region and its resistance decreases, so that when the diode is switched on in series with a load, the voltage across the diode is higher at first than it is subsequently. This is shown in Fig. 7.2. In this figure, V_s is the excess forward recovery voltage and t_{fr} is the forward recovery time. Sometimes, $V_F + V_s$ is called the forward recovery voltage, but this voltage depends on the current flowing, which must be stated if $V_F + V_s$ is specified. Also, the rise time of the current pulse applied to the diode and that of the oscilloscope used in measurement may have to be taken into consideration when t_{fr} is assessed.

As an example of a fairly fast forward recovery germanium junction diode, the characteristics of the AAZ 12 show that a typical recovery time is 40 nanosec. V_F depends on the circuit resistance, but assuming that a forward current of 400 mA flows, $V_F + V_s = 0.8$ volts.

Point-contact diodes are used for video and audio detectors, and noise limiters. They can also be used for logical circuits, but the relatively high forward voltage is an important limitation to the number of circuits which can be connected in series. Where high peak currents at clock rates up to 1 Mc/s are used, gold bonded diodes are to be preferred.

Germanium junction diodes are more robust than other types. They may be used for thermal stabilizing circuits, for high current pulse drive for ferrite memories, and for power rectifiers. Silicon junction diodes have very high reverse voltages, and since they can operate at higher temperatures than germanium junctions they are of particular value as power rectifiers. Some of the more important characteristics of some semiconductor diodes are given in Table 7.1.

Table 7.1

Point-contact and Junction Diode Data

diode	type	note	forward V and I		typical capacity at 0V	peak inverse voltage
			(V)	(mA)	(pF)	(V)
OA 10	Ge junction	low carrier storage	0.3	10	6	30
OA 5	gold bonded		0.4	10	1	100
AAZ 12	Ge junction	low carrier storage	0.2	10	10	30
GD 8	point-contact	industrial	1.1	10	1	100
MS 1 H	Si junction	miniature	0.8	10	5	60
OA 211	Si junction	power rectifier	0.65	10	10	800
1 N 914	Si junction	mesa constrn.	1.0	10	4	90
FD 600	Si junction	planar epitaxial	0.7	10	5	80
M 54 CAY	Ga As	development type	<1.1	10	<1	10

Planar Epitaxial Diodes

Planar epitaxial diodes have been introduced, along with transistors made by similar techniques. Amongst the advantages of these diodes are fast recovery time ($t_{rr} = 1$–5 nanosec) and high conductivity. These features are due to the presence of the epitaxial layer, which makes it possible to reduce the effective resistance of the semiconductor crystal on which the diode is formed. A very thin n-type layer is grown on to a high conductivity n-type crystal slab, and after etching, a p-type material is diffused on this, maintaining a crystal structure free from gross lattice defects. The diffusion depth is usually much less than for conventional junction diodes. Thus, for a given dissipation, higher currents can flow in the diode, while, due to the oxide layer laid down over the diode, surface leakage current is particularly small.

When using pulse circuits (see Chapter 10), which use silicon planar transistors operating at high frequencies, it is essential also to use planar diodes, since conventional diodes would otherwise mask the good high frequency performance of the transistors.

Gallium Arsenide Diodes

A recent development of the point-contact diode is to use gallium arsenide as the semiconductor material. Such diodes can be used up to a maximum temperature of 150°C. Switching times of the order of 5 nanosec have been reported.

Diode Logic

Any device which has two states of operation can be used to perform logical functions. Thus a switch can be on or off and relays may be energized or de-energized. Mechanical methods such as these are often too slow to meet the needs of systems designers, and, since they involve mechanical movement, it is often stated that they are too unreliable.

Transistors can be operated in such a way that they are either reverse biased and practically non-conducting, like an open switch, or forward biased and heavily conducting, like a switch which is closed and passing current. Diodes too may be forward or reverse biased. These devices are faster in operation than a switch or a relay and they involve only the movement of a charge. For these reasons they are potentially of great use in the design of logical machines such as digital voltmeters, in digital computers, and in counting systems such as digital frequency meters. For a fuller treatment of this topic the reader is referred to the bibliography.

Diode Gates

Semiconductor diodes are used for the circuit modules of diode gating systems. Such modules are frequently employed for pulse routing. The speed with which they operate depends on the type of diode which is employed. Figure 7.3 shows a typical coincidence or

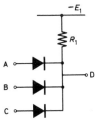

FIG. 7.3

"and" circuit in which inputs are applied to the arms labelled A, B and C. In practice, "and" circuits may have many more arms than this. It can be seen that the output at D is equal to the lowest forward voltage of any one of the diodes, so long as current can flow in one or more of the input circuits. However, when all the diodes have been reverse biased, only their leakage currents flow through R_1. Since a typical reverse current for a germanium point-contact diode is about 30–40 μA, the potential drop across the load R_1 of 10 kilohms is about 1 volt. Now the forward voltage for point-contact diodes at the small forward currents concerned is about 1 volt. Therefore, for a supply voltage, E_1, of 12 volts, D can be made to have a swing of 10 volts. The "on" current through R_1 of approximately 1 mA must be carried by one or more of the diodes.

If silicon junction diodes are used, advantage can be taken of their lower leakage current to give a greater voltage swing. If planar epitaxial diodes are used, not only is the leakage current small, but high forward currents can be obtained. This reduces false indication due to operation of the gates on transients. The fast recovery time of these diodes leads to rapid operation of the gates.

The statement that the circuit of Fig. 7.3 is that of an "and" element, implies that the more negative of the two voltage levels at D is taken as representing an output at D, whilst the less negative represents the absence or negation of an output. If these voltage levels also apply at the inputs, then it has just been shown that only when all the inputs are present is an output also present at D. This is written $A.B.C=D$. It may be remembered as "A and B and C equals D".

Instead of constantly referring to these voltage levels, it is more usual to remember them as "1" and "0". This is because the levels themselves are only important in the initial design. The function of the system is more easily understood with this shortened terminology. Here, the more negative level is "1" and the less negative is "0". For this reason, the circuit can be described as that of an "and" element, only when this "negative level" convention is employed. The operation of Fig. 7.3 could therefore be explained by saying that there is a "1" at D only when a "1" is present simultaneously on all the inputs A, B and C.

Figure 7.4 shows an "or" circuit (on the basis of a negative level convention) in which E, F and G are the inputs and H is the output.

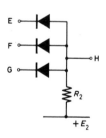

Fig. 7.4

The potential of H will differ from that of the supply, E_2, by only the voltage drop across R_2 due to the leakage current of the diodes when they are reverse biased. However, if one or more of the inputs are taken to a negative potential, then the potential at H will differ from that of the most negative of the inputs by only the forward voltage of the diode. Since only one of the inputs needs to be taken to a negative potential in order to make H negative, the circuit of Fig. 7.4 is called an "or" gate. It is common to use an "or" gate following an "and" gate like that of Fig. 7.3. For this to operate satisfactorily, the current taken by the "or" gate must not materially affect the potentials of its inputs. Hence R_2 will probably be a resistance an order higher than R_1 in the preceding "and" gate.

An example of this kind of circuit is shown in Fig. 7.5. Here, the inputs might perhaps be derived from photocells operated through

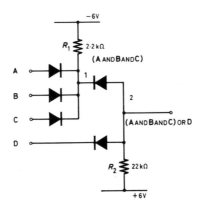

Fig. 7.5

holes in a punched card. As the circuit is arranged, only when a particular combination of inputs is received will an output be obtained from the gate.

In this example, when negative voltages are applied to the correct inputs a negative output potential is obtained. This network produces an output under the conditions shown in the diagram. However, if point-contact diodes are used in the circuit of Fig. 7.5 the potential of point 1 in the figure will be switched between approximately -5 and -1 volt when A, B and C change between 6 volts and zero. Similarly, point 2 is switched between -5 and -1 volt by switching the input D. Thus the most negative potential which can exist at point 2 is -5 volts. It can therefore be seen that the voltage swing of the output is restricted by the forward voltage drop across the diodes.

The use of gold-bonded diodes or junction diodes with their lower forward voltages make it possible to use more diode gates in cascade. Alternatively, transistor amplifying stages are used to maintain the level of the voltage changes.

Diode gates readily lend themselves to modular construction, and are the first of a number of circuits which will be encountered which are available commercially as "prefabricated building bricks" as part of a large system. Even using point-contact diodes, such elements are capable of operating at switching speeds of the order of 5 microsec, but one of their chief limitations is their low power handling capacity.

Capacitance of a Junction Diode

The capacitance of a reverse biased junction diode was discussed in connection with hybrid π parameters in Chapter 2. It was explained there that the barrier layer capacitance is a function of the voltage applied to the diode. The charge density in the barrier layer is reduced so that this layer becomes a region of high resistivity and so acts as a dielectric, the width of which becomes greater as the reverse voltage is increased. The junction capacitance for a linear gradient junction is given by:

$$C = K(V/A)^{-1/3} \tag{7.1}$$

where K and A are the effective dielectric constant and junction cross-sectional area respectively, and V is approximately equal to the applied voltage. (The applied voltage $= V - E$, where E is the contact potential.) These constants can be eliminated if the expression is put in terms of dC/dV:

$$dC/dV = -KA^{1/3}/3V^{4/3}$$

whence, substituting from equation (7.1), $dC/dV = -C/3V$.

The voltage sensitivity, S, is defined as $S = -\dfrac{1}{C} dC/dV$

Therefore $\qquad\qquad S = 1/3V$

S is seen to be independent of K and A. From this simplified theory it appears that S is not temperature sensitive, since it depends only on V. This is not quite true, however, although for diodes intended for use as variable capacitances, the use of silicon minimizes leakage current, and epitaxial or planar construction reduces this current further. The leakage current represents a resistive loss to the capacitor, and, together with the inductance and resistance of its leads, and the resistance of the material between the leads and the active region of the junction, makes it possible to construct an equivalent circuit for the diode as shown in Fig. 7.6.

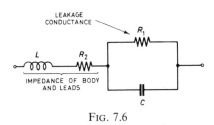

FIG. 7.6

Typical values are $L = 0.5 \times 10^{-9}$ H, $R_2 = 4$ ohms for a small junction diode. R_1 depends on the junction material and the value of the reverse voltage.

The performance of some diodes is shown in Table 7.2. The germanium diode OA 10 is included for comparison, and because some early work was carried out with this diode when silicon diodes were only just becoming available. The Q factor of diodes, intended for

Table 7.2

Diodes for use as Variable Capacitances

diode	capacitances	Q factor at 12 volts
OA 10	6 pF at -2 V, 0·5 pF at -15 V	400 at 30 Mc/s
BA 110	20 pF at -0.4 V, 5 pF at -20 V	5,000 at 2 Mc/s, 500 at 30 Mc/s
BA 111	100 pF at -0.4 V, 28 pF at -20 V	6,000 at 300 kc/s, 100 at 30 Mc/s

use as capacitances, is of importance since it is a ready indication of R_1 in Fig. 7.6. Hence Q factors are included in the table.

Although hole storage limits the usefulness of diodes in the forward direction, junction diodes, reverse biased as capacitors, have been found to perform well up to several thousand megacycles per second. Among some of their applications are automatic band sweep oscillators, remote tuning control of R.F. amplifiers, and the linearization of a sawtooth or ramp function generator, where the use of a variable capacitance diode tends to linearize the exponential CR charging curve.

A typical remote tuning circuit is shown in Fig. 7.7. The capacitor C_1 gives direct current blocking. The diodes are used in series opposition to avoid the asymmetrical clipping of the waveform, which

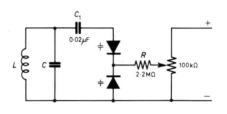

FIG. 7.7

might otherwise occur with a tuned circuit shunted by a single diode. If signal amplitudes are small compared with the minimum reverse bias, this precaution may not be necessary. The resistance R is made as high as possible since it shunts the diodes, lowering their Q.

Silicon Four-Layer Diodes

These diodes are also known commercially as *pnpn* diodes, Shockley diodes or thyristors. Their structure is shown in Figs. 7.8 and 7.9.

With the anode negative, as shown in Fig. 7.8, the unit consists of

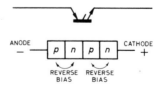

FIG. 7.8

two reversed biased diodes in series, and only the reverse leakage current flows. With the anode positive as shown in Fig. 7.9, still only the leakage current flows due to the reversed biased diode formed by the two central sections. If the total current through this junction is I, and the reverse saturation current is I_1, then the current at any potential is given by a relationship of the following form:

$$I = \frac{xI_1}{1 - xy}$$

x and y are functions of the applied voltage. At low voltages, x is approximately equal to unity, but it increases rapidly as the voltage

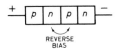

REVERSE
BIAS

Fig. 7.9

is increased. When xy is much less than unity, I is small and the diode has high impedance. As the breakdown voltage is approached, xy approaches unity although y remains small and I is large, the diode now having a low impedance. As the current increases, y tends to unity whilst x falls. This implies that dx/dV changes sign, and the diode has a large negative resistance. These effects are due to multiplication resulting from collision of carriers with un-ionized atoms. Finally, no further multiplication takes place as I increases, the centre junction being forward biased and the whole diode acting

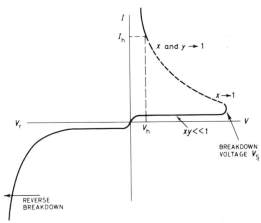

Fig. 7.10

like a simple forward biased junction. The characteristic of the diode is shown in Fig. 7.10.

The diode finds use as a sawtooth oscillator, pulse generator and counter. Some further data regarding typical diodes are shown in Table 7.3.

Table 7.3

Silicon Four-layer Diodes

diode type	V_s (V)	I_h (mA)	I_s less than (μA)	V_h (V)	maximum leakage current (μA)	V_r minimum (V)	I_{max} average (mA)
4D20–3	20	1–6	125	0·5–1·2	15	12	50*
4D200–23	200	5–45	125	–do–	15	120	50*
4AD20–5	20	1–10	125	–do–	15	12	300†
4J200–25	200	9–45	250	–do–	35	120	300†

* 2 amp pulse   † 20 amp pulse

Applications of Four-Layer Diodes

Figure 7.11 shows a sawtooth oscillator. The resistor R_1 must permit a current, less than the holding current I_h, to flow in the on-state. The holding current is the minimum current which must flow to keep the centre junction forward biased. The capacitor C charges until V_s is reached, when it is discharged through the diode. The sketches A, B and C show the waveform of the output at the point 1 in the diagram as the resistance R_2 is progressively increased. The

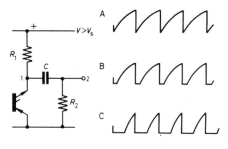

FIG. 7.11

output at the point 2 can be considered as the first output differentiated, that is, a series of negative pulses. When R_2 is much less than R_1, R_1 and C control the repetition rate. Figure 7.12 shows a variation producing an approximately square pulse. The voltage across the diode differs from that across the capacitor, due to the

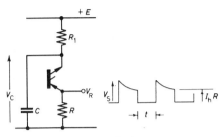

FIG. 7.12

holding current flowing through R. When $V_c - V_R < V_s$, the diode switches to the off-state, and V_R falls to zero until V_c becomes greater than V_s when the diode switches on again.

If T is the time between pulses,

$$V_s \doteqdot E(1 - e^{-T/CR_1}) \qquad (7.2)$$

If the output pulse exists for a time, t,

$$I_h R \doteqdot V_s e^{-t/CR}$$

For example, putting $T = CR_1$, $V_s = E(1 - e^{-1}) \doteqdot \frac{2}{3}E$

Hence, using a 4D20–3 diode, $E = 30$ volts and for a 10 volt output pulse, a relationship between R and R_1 can be found from equation (7.2), for a $1:1$ mark-space ratio:

$$10 = 20e^{-CR_1/CR}$$

i.e. $$2 = e^{R_1/R}$$

Therefore $$\log_e 2 = R_1/R$$

or $$R_1 = 0.69R$$

CR_1 is also defined from the pulse repetition rate and the fact that the current through R_1 must be less than I_h. Hence C, R and R_1 can be found for any specified set of conditions.

The switching action of a *pnpn* diode can be employed to operate it as a pulse generator. The point-contact diode, D_1, is used in Fig. 7.13 since it presents a high impedance to the negative pulse. The trigger square wave raises the voltage across the *pnpn* diode, D_2,

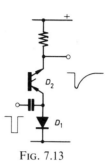

FIG. 7.13

so that it is switched into conduction. Hence a negative-going pulse with relatively small energy content can initiate a higher energy output pulse.

A two-state circuit can be constructed to be monostable, bistable or astable depending on the value of the supply potentials and the limiting resistors. Figure 7.14 is an example of a circuit of this type.

The bistable circuit in Fig. 7.14 has one diode in the on-state passing a current of 10 mA, which is greater than the holding current for the diodes which are used. The common resistor maintains the voltage to the off-state diode at 50 volts. Since the holding voltage for the 4D80–3 is 80 volts, the circuit is stable. On receiving

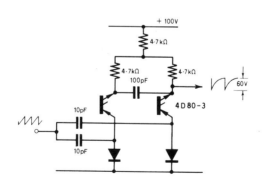

FIG. 7.14

a negative-going pulse, the on-state circuit shorts the pulse it receives, whilst the off-state circuit presents a high input impedance to it. V_h is exceeded momentarily and the diode switches on, the falling potential at its anode being passed as a negative pulse to the other diode, switching it off. The output pulse has a peak amplitude of 50 volts.

The Tunnel Diode

This diode was first produced by Esaki (1958). It is a junction diode in which the impurity doping is very heavy. In conventional transistors there are about 10^{15} impurity atoms per c.c., but here, typically there may be about 10^{20} atoms per c.c. This has the effect of eliminating forbidden energy levels between the filled donor band and the partly filled conduction band. In an n-type material, therefore, the Fermi level is in the conduction band. Similarly, in a p-type material there is no forbidden region between acceptor levels and the filled valence band. Thus the Fermi level lies in the valence band. This is shown in Fig. 7.15. The two conditions for a tunnel diode are a narrow junction and an energy band overlap.

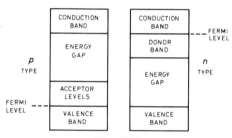

FIG. 7.15

Thus in an unbiased tunnel diode where the Fermi level is continuous the energy diagram is as shown in Fig. 7.16. Germanium was used for early tunnel diodes, but it seems that gallium arsenide and indium antimonide may offer advantages in the future.

This doping reduces the width of the depletion layer to 10^{-6} cm (100 angstroms). This is because the extreme change of doping at the junction causes a proportionally large charge to be produced when mobile carriers are cleared from the junction. Since the semiconductor material has a fixed potential barrier, characteristic of

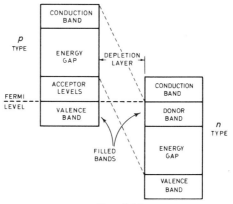

FIG. 7.16

that material, this can be produced by moving the carriers a much smaller distance. Two typical diode characteristics are shown in Fig. 7.17. One of these shows the forward characteristic when the ambient temperature is 25°C, and the other when it is 60°C.

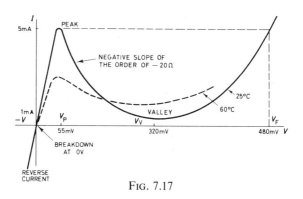

FIG. 7.17

The peak current/valley current ratio is an important characteristic of the diode. It is about five in the figure. The name "tunnel diode" arises, because when the quantum theory is used to explain the behaviour of the diode, there is shown to be a finite probability of an electron "tunnelling" a potential barrier, particularly if this barrier is very thin, as it is here. The uncertainty of the position of an electron is such that, if it is near to the barrier, the probability of it being beyond the barrier can be estimated, even though in terms of the classical theory it does not possess enough energy to surmount it. Therefore, referring back to Fig 7.16 a reverse voltage moves the n-type material down on the diagram causing electrons to move from the filled valence band into the partly filled conduction band. When the opposite potential is applied, the n-type material is moved up in the figure, and at first carriers move from the donor to the acceptor band. Further increase in potential brings the donor band opposite the energy gap of the p-type material and the current falls. Finally, as in an ordinary diode, the potential barrier is small and electrons move from the donor band to the p-type conduction band.

Tunnel diodes have been made from a number of semiconductors. Typical properties of some of these diodes are illustrated in Table 7.4.

Table 7.4

Tunnel Diodes

		semiconductor material		
	germanium	*silicon*	*gallium arsenide*	*gallium antimonide*
Peak voltage, V_p	55 mV	65 mV	150 mV	40 mV
Valley voltage, V_v	320 mV	420 mV	500 mV	220 mV
Forward voltage, V_f	480 mV	720 mV	980 mV	500 mV
Peak/valley ratio, I_p/I_v	5–8	3	10	15
Maximum temperature	100°C	200°C	175°C	100°C

The equivalent circuit of the diode in the negative resistance region is shown in Fig. 7.18. At low frequencies, the inductance of the leads, L, and the series resistance, R_s, may be disregarded.

From Fig. 7.18, the series impedance of the diode, z, is given by

$$z = R_s + j\omega L - \frac{jR}{RC\omega + j}$$

$$= R_s + j\omega L - \frac{R + jR^2 C\omega}{R^2 C^2 \omega^2 + 1} \tag{7.3}$$

The resistive cut-off frequency, f_c, is defined by the condition that z becomes imaginary. This occurs when $R_s - R/(R^2 C^2 \omega^2 + 1) = 0$.

Therefore $\omega^2 = (R - R_s)/R_s R^2 C^2$

or $$f_c = \frac{1}{2\pi RC}\sqrt{\frac{R}{R_s} - 1} \qquad (7.4)$$

Which is real only if $R > R_s$.
Usually $R \gg R_s$

then $$f_c \doteqdot \frac{1}{2\pi C\sqrt{RR_s}} \qquad (7.5)$$

This result is often stated for the maximum frequency of oscillation.

FIG. 7.18

The physical significance of the way in which a tunnel diode may operate as a circuit element may be understood with reference to Fig. 7.19.

A load line is drawn across the diode characteristics, whose slope is $-1/R_L$, where R_L is the resistance of the load. The load line may be defined as the locus of the operating point of the diode. Amplification and oscillation can be achieved when the load line only intersects the negative resistance slope of the characteristic as in line 1. If, in addition, the line intersects other parts of the characteristic,

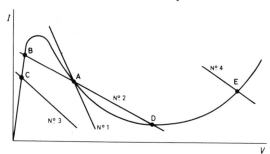

FIG. 7.19

such as at B and D (line 2), then the device has two stable states. Bistable circuits can be used for counting and for certain logical functions, where the two stable states can be used to represent the presence or absence of stored information. For this reason, such circuits are called "memory circuits". If the operating point only moves between B and A, so that there is one stable and one astable point, then the diode can be used for frequency conversion and frequency multiplication. Lines 3 and 4 are examples of load lines in which only one positive slope is intersected. Also, the slope of each of these lines is greater than $-1/R$ where $-1/R$ is the slope of the negative characteristic. Circuits which operate under these conditions have been used as threshold detectors and monostable elements.

The distinction between oscillation and amplification can be seen by investigating equation (7.3). If the series resistance of the diode, R_s, is considered as part of the external load, the real part of the diode impedance is given by equation (7.6):

$$\text{Real part of } z = \frac{-R}{1+R^2C^2\omega^2}, \text{ since } R \text{ is negative} \qquad (7.6)$$

The imaginary part of the impedance is given by:

$$\text{Imaginary part of } z = \omega L - \frac{R^2C}{1+R^2C^2\omega^2} \qquad (7.7)$$

Now for oscillation the imaginary part of the impedance must be zero and this must lead to a real value of ω.

Therefore, from equation (7.7) (putting the imaginary part of z equal to zero)

$$1+R^2C^2\omega^2 = R^2C/L$$

or $$\omega^2 = \frac{1}{LC} - \frac{1}{R^2C^2} \qquad (7.8)$$

which is positive if $\qquad L < R^2C \qquad (7.9)$

Substitution of the value of ω given by equation (7.8), into the equation for the real part of the impedance given by equation (7.6), shows that the diode acts as a negative resistance of value $-L/CR$ at this frequency. Thus, from equation (7.4), for oscillation, R must be greater than $R_s + R_L$ (switching will occur when $R_s + R_L$ is greater than R) but for amplification there is the additional requirement that L/CR is less than $R_s + R_L$.

A typical oscillator circuit is shown in Fig. 7.20. The resistance chain R_1, R_2 and R_3 is used to bias the diode to the negative resistance region. The voltage across C_1 provides this bias, and the diode oscillates at a frequency determined by the series inductance, L_1, and the diode parameters.

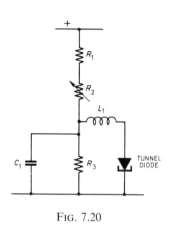

FIG. 7.20

Tunnel Diode Amplifiers

It has been shown that, for amplification,

$$L/CR < R_s + R_L < R$$

Now, in order to have a wide range of possible values for $R_s + R_L$, it is necessary to make L/CR very much less than R. To prevent any deterioration in high frequency performance, it is necessary to select the diode for low inductance, and to keep the external inductance of the leads to a minimum. It then remains to bias the diode to a point on its characteristic such as A in Fig. 7.19. Stable amplification is achieved in practice when $R_s + R_L$ is slightly less than R. As the value of R_L is further reduced, the gain increases and the bandwidth decreases until oscillation occurs as given by the inequality (7.9).

It is useful to regard the equivalent circuit of the tunnel diode (Fig. 7.18) as establishing an explanation for the physical reasons for its behaviour. The circuit of Fig. 7.21 is based on this circuit, and is useful for calculations of power gain when the diode is used as an amplifier.

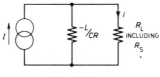

Fig. 7.21

$$\text{The power in the load} = i^2 R_L \tag{7.10}$$

where

$$i = \left(\frac{-L/CR}{R_L - L/CR}\right)I = \left(\frac{-L}{CRR_L - L}\right)I \tag{7.11}$$

The maximum input power (when I is equally shared by the load and the generator impedance) $= \frac{1}{4}I^2 R_L$ (7.12)

Hence the power gain, a_w = the power in the load $\div$ maximum input power

Therefore

$$a_w = \frac{4L^2}{(CRR_L - L)^2} \tag{7.13}$$

It can be seen that a_w becomes infinite when $R_L = L/CR$ which is the condition for the commencement of oscillation.

The Backward Diode

It was seen in Fig. 7.17 that the tunnel diode has a breakdown at zero voltage. If, in manufacture, the forward current of a heavily doped diode is made small, the reverse current may be still large, and can be compared to the forward current of a junction diode of conventional type. The small forward current of this diode, when operated at low voltages, can be compared with the reverse current of a conventional diode. Since the reverse current is used as a forward current the device is known as a backward diode, and since operation of the diode depends on tunnelling it is capable of high frequency operation. A typical characteristic is shown in Fig. 7.22 and data in Table 7.5.

If a backward diode is used between say $-200\,\text{mV}$ and $+200\,\text{mV}$, the current flowing may be in the ratio $10\,\text{mA}:10\,\mu\text{A}$, that is, $1{,}000:1$. The backward diode can, for example, be used as a logic

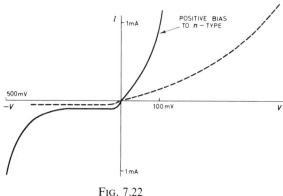

Fig. 7.22

gate at the low voltages which will be encountered using tunnel diodes, when the voltage level may be so small that point-contact or junction diodes are not very suitable. This is illustrated in Fig. 7.23 which shows a typical "and" gate.

Table 7.5

Backward Diodes

diode type	forward voltage for 1 mA (mV)	reverse voltage for 1 mA (mV)	capacity (pF)	series inductance (nH)
1 N 3353	80	510	4·0	1·0
JK 100 A	110	450	90·0	2·0

The two problems encountered with tunnel diode circuits are the low voltage swing which is available from the diode and the difficulty, common to all two terminal devices, of separating input and output. In logical circuits, like that of Fig. 7.23, the first problem is overcome by using backward diodes for coupling, and the second problem is overcome by strobing the supply potentials to successive stages so that there is a unidirectional flow of information.

Backward diodes do not exhibit valley characteristics. This may be explained by noting that, although the diode junction is very narrow, which is one requisite for tunnelling, the diode has no band overlap. The bands are virtually uncrossed at zero voltage so that negative bias raises the occupied valence band to be opposite an empty conduction band, thus allowing tunnelling to take place, whereas forward bias further uncrosses the bands to prevent tunnelling.

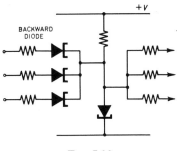

FIG. 7.23

The Tunnel Diode Relaxation Oscillator

If the capacitor is omitted in Fig. 7.20, it is possible, with suitable choice of component values, to operate the oscillator as a relaxation oscillator. The previous discussion of tunnel diode oscillators assumed that A (Fig. 7.19) was the operating point, and that the slope of the load line was slightly greater than that of the characteristic at this point. Small signal operation was implied, so that the slope of the characteristic was approximately constant over the range which was considered.

If, now, the circuit is as shown in Fig. 7.24, when the supply voltage is switched on, the voltage across the diode increases so that it follows the path ABC. This is due to the inductance which restricts the rate of change of current. At the unstable point, C, the onset of the negative slope causes the potential to switch to the stable point D. The sudden increase in voltage will cause a back-e.m.f. to be

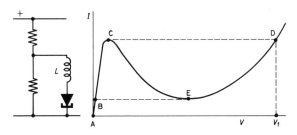

FIG. 7.24

developed across L, which will cause the diode current to drop. If this back-e.m.f. is sufficiently large (depending on an adequately large inductance), the current will fall to E, and, since any further small decrease in potential is unstable, the potential will switch to B, when the cycle BCDE will be repeated.

The oscillator will operate at low audio frequencies if a sufficiently large inductance is used. Its upper frequency limit depends on the capacitance of the diode and its circuit, which prevents a sufficiently large back-e.m.f. being available. The relaxation path is then not completed. At high frequencies, when this path is not covered, the operation is similar to that of the small signal oscillator.

PROBLEMS

7.1 (a) Contrast the performance of point-contact and junction rectifiers with that of copper oxide and thermionic rectifiers. Point out where, in the field of telecommunications, they have common spheres of usefulness. (This will require further reading.)

(b) A 50 c/s square wave voltage is applied to a silicon junction rectifier and a 10 ohm resistor in series. The rectifier has a forward voltage drop of 0·7 volt. Find the power dissipated in the rectifier and in the resistor, and hence the efficiency of the rectifier, if the peak-to-peak voltage is (i) 5 volts, and (ii) 50 volts. [Ans. (i) 150 mW, 925 mW, 86 per cent; (ii) 1·73 watts, 122·5 watts, 98·5 per cent.]

7.2 Explain the functions of the circuits of Figs. 7.3 and 7.4 using the concept of positive logic in which the more positive (i.e. less negative) of two voltage levels is taken as "1" and the less positive as "0". What effect does the choice of logical convention have on the actual performance of the circuit?

7.3 Contrast the performance of linear gradient and abrupt junction diodes as voltage-sensitive variable capacitances.

7.4 Using the characteristics of a 4D20–3 *pnpn* diode, design a monostable circuit capable of trigger by positive-going pulses. Estimate the amplitude of pulse necessary to operate the circuit. Discuss the factors limiting its switching time.

7.5 By considering an equivalent circuit for a tunnel diode, deduce an expression for its impedance, z. Consider the case when z is real, and hence deduce that the self-resonant frequency, f_r, is given by

$$f_r = \frac{1}{2\pi} \left(\frac{1}{LC} - \frac{1}{R^2 C^2} \right)^{1/2}$$

where L and C are the diode inductance and capacitance and R is its slope resistance. Find also an expression for z at this frequency.

BIBLIOGRAPHY

Adams: A Variable Semiconductor Capacitor, *Electronic Engng.*, 733, Nov. 1962.

Adler and Selikson: A Review of the Tunnel Diode, *Electronic Engng.*, 8, Jan. 1962.

Aleksander and Scarr: Tunnel Devices as Switching Circuits, *J.Brit.I.R.E.*, **23**, 177, 1962.

Carlson: Measurement of Tunnel Diode Parameters, *Electronic Components*, 633, June 1963.

Dean: "Counting Techniques and Transistor Circuit Logic", Chapman and Hall, 1964.

Esaki: Germanium *pn* Junctions, *Phys. Rev.*, **109**, 603, 1958.

Registrar: Silicon Junction Diodes as Variable Capacitors, *Electronic Engng.*, 783, Dec. 1961.

Young: Transistor-Diode Static Switching Units, *Electronic Engng.*, 595, Sept. 1962.

CHAPTER 8

Power Supplies

In this chapter constant voltage and constant current supplies will be considered together with some applications of silicon controlled rectifiers. In designing a power supply to give a constant direct voltage, it is important to know the output impedance and the degree of stabilization required, and to be able to measure them in practical circuits. The stabilization factor, S, is defined by:

$$S = \partial V_o / \partial V_i, \text{ with constant load resistance} \tag{8.1}$$

and the output resistance is defined by:

$$R_o = \partial V_o / \partial I_o, \text{ with } V_i \text{ constant} \tag{8.2}$$

There are two ways of regulating a voltage supply which is subject to fluctuation; these are known as series and shunt regulation. The shunt type of regulator is only of value when the power handled is small, but it is important here to discuss shunt regulators, since larger, series, regulators often employ shunt regulators to obtain reference voltages. Shunt regulation will, therefore, be considered first. The zener diode circuit of Fig. 8.1 is of this kind, fluctuations of input voltage falling across R.

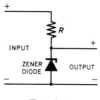

Fig. 8.1

Diode Shunt Regulators

R must be sufficiently small to keep the diode within the zener region, and since all the load current passes through this resistor it represents a voltage and power loss which should be kept as small as possible. However, if R is too small and the load is open-circuited the current through the zener diode will increase, perhaps excessively. Its maximum dissipation must not be exceeded. Some improvement on this circuit can be obtained when two stages of regulation are employed as in Fig. 8.2. The output impedance depends chiefly on the impedance of the zener diode on the output

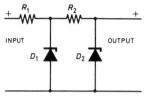

FIG. 8.2

side. D_1 will have a higher zener voltage than D_2. The stabilization factor, S, can be made very small with both series and shunt regulators by the use of multiple sections, as has been done here, although the improvement obtained seldom makes it worth while to use more than two sections in series.

Transistor Shunt Regulators

In the shunt regulator of Fig. 8.3, the current through the zener diode controls the base current of the *npn* transistor, and so does not have to vary as much as when the diode is the main current shunt, as in the circuits of Figs. 8.1 and 8.2. Since the diode has low impedance, variations in output voltage appear almost entirely across R_2, so that current through R_1 can be controlled by regulating the base current of T_1 thus keeping the output voltage constant.

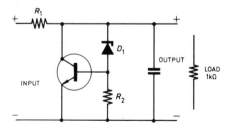

FIG. 8.3

If the circuit must handle an output current which changes within wide limits, the power which must be dissipated in both the diode and the transistor makes the system very inefficient and series regulation is to be preferred.

Series Regulators

The basic series regulator is the emitter follower, T_1 in Fig. 8.4, or a multiple stage of this kind consisting of a number of transistors in parallel. A phase inverting d.c. amplifier controls the base current of the series transistors. The error voltage fed to the d.c. amplifier,

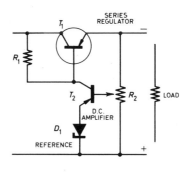

FIG. 8.4

T_2, is compared with a reference voltage, in practice always derived from a zener diode.

The bias on T_2 is adjusted by R_2 which in turn sets the base current for T_1 and so controls the load current. When the load potential tends to increase for any reason, the base current of T_2 tends to increase also, since its emitter is held at a constant potential by D_1. The increased collector current of T_2 decreases the base current available for T_1 and so opposes the increase of the output potential.

An alternative circuit is shown in Fig. 8.5, which should be compared with the shunt regulator of Fig. 8.3. In Fig. 8.5 the shunt transistor has become the d.c. amplifier operating at low current and controlling the base current of the series transistor. It is not, therefore, called upon to handle excessive current swings.

If the input impedance of T_2 in Fig. 8.5 is high compared with R_2, then

$$dV_{be} = \frac{R_2}{R_2 + R_z} dV_o \qquad (8.3)$$

where R_z is the impedance of the zener diode.
Also, if the mutual conductance of T_2 is given by $g_{m.2} = dI_c/dV_{be}$

then

$$dI_c = \frac{g_{m.2} R_2}{R_2 + R_z} dV_o \qquad (8.4)$$

And, since the base of T_1 is approximately at its emitter potential V_o,

$$dV_i = dI_c R_1 \qquad (8.5)$$

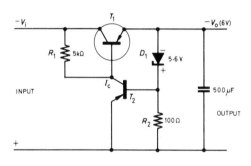

FIG. 8.5

Using equation (8.4) $dV_i = \dfrac{g_{m.2} R_1 R_2}{R_2 + R_z} dV_o$

Therefore $S = dV_o/dV_i = \dfrac{R_2 + R_z}{g_{m.2} R_1 R_2} \qquad (8.6)$

If $R_1 = 6$ kilohms, $R_2 = 100$ ohms, $R_z = 20$ ohms, $g_{m.2} = 40\,\text{mAV}^{-1}$, and $\alpha' = 50$, then $S = 0.03$.
Also, if $dI_o = \alpha_1'' \, dI_c$, from equation (8.5) $dV_i = dI_o R_1/\alpha_1''$
Then, from equation (8.6)

$$R_o = dV_o/dI_o = \frac{R_2 + R_z}{\alpha_1'' g_{m.2} R_2} \qquad (8.7)$$

and using the figures already stated, $R_o = 0.6$ ohm.

The d.c. amplifier which has just been described may have too high a stabilization factor, resulting from an amplifier with too small voltage gain, or it may have too high an output impedance. Some alternative circuits will be considered whose performance shows some improvement on that of Fig. 8.5. The amplifier can often be better controlled by a reference potential in the base-emitter circuit, either as an emitter follower regulator or as part of the d.c. amplifier. This is illustrated in Fig. 8.6.

In Fig. 8.6 the voltage divider has a total resistance, $R_2 + R_3$, of which a fraction, R_3, develops the voltage applied to the base of the d.c. amplifier.

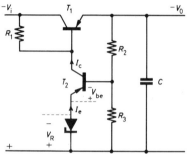

FIG. 8.6

If it is considered that the input impedance of T_2 is high compared with R_3, an approximate estimate of the stabilization factor can be found by a similar process to that which has just been described. (See Problem 8.1.)

To achieve a high degree of stabilization (low value of S), the gain of the amplifier should be high, since a decrease in S is brought about by an increase in $g_{m.2}$ (equation (8.6)). A higher gain amplifier may be used with a number of directly coupled stages. However, the more stages introduced between the reference voltage of the zener diode and the series transistor, the greater is the temperature drift of the output voltage likely to be. The temperature sensitivity is about 2·5 mV per degree C for each stage. The problems here are those of d.c. amplifier design, and a specific type of d.c. amplifier, the emitter coupled amplifier, is often used.

The shunt capacitors in Figs. 8.5 and 8.6 are to reduce oscillatory tendencies, and to reduce the output impedance at high frequencies.

The output resistance, R_o, can be reduced by increasing α_1'' (equation (8.7)). Therefore a multiple common collector stage will be used to replace the series transistor of simpler circuits. This means, that the series stage will be driven by one or more common collector driver stages having a high overall current gain. The number of driver stages required will depend on the output current and the load resistance of the d.c. amplifier. In practice, three stages are needed for output currents of the order of 1 amp or more, but only two stages are needed where the maximum load current is of the order of 100 mA. Power transistors, at present available, are capable of dissipating about 30 watts when mounted on a suitable heat sink without forced air cooling. To increase the maximum permissible power dissipation of the series transistors, they may be connected in parallel.

For power transistors in parallel, it is necessary to ensure that the power dissipations are matched at maximum power. The transistors should be matched, at maximum current, for current gains within 10 per cent. Resistors of about 1 ohm each are placed in the emitter leads to assist in maintaining matching. Thermal matching is also necessary to ensure that no transistor exceeds its maximum junction temperature. These problems become acute when the transistors are being operated close to their maximum power dissipation.

Temperature effects may be minimized by:

(a) Thermistors (having negative temperature coefficient of resistance) between base and emitter. As the temperature rises, the transistor requires less current, therefore, the thermistor as part of the bias divider draws the additional current no longer needed by the transistor, keeping the loading on the divider more nearly constant.

(b) A d.c. amplifier may be used which is designed for low thermal drift. The emitter coupled amplifier is an example of a circuit of this kind. The temperature variations in each transistor are similar and tend to balance out. One form of the amplifier is shown in Fig. 8.7.

The input transistor, T_1, is a common collector stage which drives the common base stage, T_2. It will be assumed that the two transistors used are matched for current gain and also for thermal characteristics. Equality of collector currents can be achieved by returning the emitter end of R_2 to the tap of a low resistance potentiometer, of the order of 20–50 ohms, which is connected between the two emitters. This can be used to compensate for unbalance in α' and

V_{be}. R_2 should be high compared with the input impedance of T_2 which it shunts, since this minimizes drift. On the assumption that

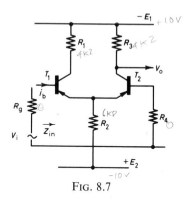

FIG. 8.7

R_2 is high, the equivalent circuit of Fig. 8.8 can be used to estimate the performance of the amplifier. In this simplified treatment, using T parameters, it is assumed that r_c and $r_c(1-\alpha)$ are large and can be ignored and that the two transistors have identical parameters.

$$V_i = \alpha' i_b (2r_e + r_b + R_4)$$
$$-\alpha i_e (r_b + R_4) + i_b r_b \tag{8.8}$$

$$V_o = \alpha i_e R_3 \tag{8.9}$$

$$i_e \doteqdot \alpha' i_b \tag{8.10}$$

From equations (8.8) and (8.9):

$$a_v = V_o/V_i$$

$$\doteqdot \frac{\alpha R_3}{2r_e + r_b + R_4 - \alpha(r_b + R_4)}$$

$$= \frac{\alpha R_3}{r_e + r_{ee} + R_4(1 - \alpha)} \tag{8.11}$$

Also $\qquad a_i = \alpha i_e / i_b = \alpha \alpha' \tag{8.12}$

From equations (8.8) and (8.10):

$$z_{in} = \alpha'(2r_e + r_b + R_4) - \alpha \alpha'(r_b + R_4) + r_b$$

$$= \alpha'[r_{ee} + r_e + R_4(1 - \alpha)] + r_b \tag{8.13}$$

If R_4 is small, it can be seen from equations (8.11), (8.12) and (8.13) that the voltage gain, current gain and input impedance approximate to those of a common emitter amplifier. When this type of amplifier is used as part of a stabilized power unit, it will be seen later that R_4 is the dynamic impedance of a zener diode, and

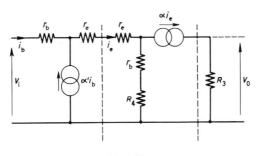

FIG. 8.8

so this condition is fulfilled. A circuit showing such an amplifier in a power unit is shown in Fig. 8.9. The use of this type of circuit has become common practice.

If the output potential momentarily increases, T_1 will be biased further into conduction and the current through R_1 and R_2 will increase. (This transistor corresponds to T_1 in Fig. 8.7.) Since the potential at the base of T_2 is constant, any increase in potential across R_2 will decrease the emitter current of T_2 which passes through it. Hence the potential across R_2 is maintained constant

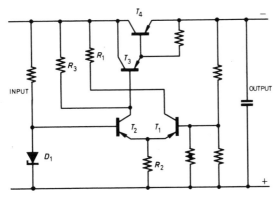

FIG. 8.9

and is the reference potential for T_1. This circuit is to be preferred to that of Fig. 8.6, since D_1 is used to control the small base current of T_2 rather than the emitter current of T_1. However, the reference potential across R_2 is one stage removed from that of the zener diode. A potentiometer across D_1 can provide initial setting of the output voltage by altering the potential across R_2.

Design of a Voltage Stabilizer

In a practical design, it is convenient to have the collector current of the transistors in the d.c. amplifier and the current flowing in the potential divider in the range 1–3 mA. The current through the zener diode should be such that its slope resistance is low; usually a current of 10–20 mA is suitable. If possible, the voltage of the diode used should be as near the zero temperature coefficient range as possible (5·6–6·0 volts).

The specification will determine the maximum output voltage and current. This will often be variable and by modifying the circuit of Fig. 8.9, it is possible to construct a high gain amplifier with a variable reference voltage.

Improved stabilization can be obtained, if the amplifier providing the correcting voltage is operated from a supply line whose potential is independent of the output voltage. This is illustrated in schematic form in Fig. 8.10.

As with high voltage stabilized supplies, using valves, the ripple voltage at the output can be reduced, if a.c. is purposely introduced into the d.c. amplifier and the amplifier has high gain. The injected

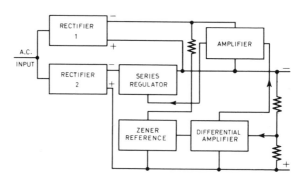

FIG. 8.10

voltage must have the correct amplitude and phase. A practical circuit based on Fig. 8.10 will be developed from Fig. 8.11.

T_1 and T_2 and their associated components, form the emitter coupled differential amplifier. It is here assumed that the output potential is controlled by the output of the amplifier. Since this potential is compared with the potential derived from the zener

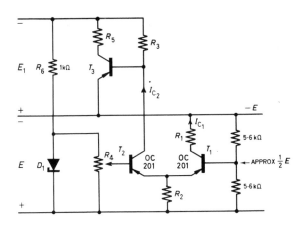

FIG. 8.11

diode D_1 by a 1:1 divider across the output terminals of the power unit, the zener potential must be $\frac{1}{2}E_{max}$. When the output of the power unit is E_{max}, T_1 will be subject to maximum dissipation and the potential across R_2 is approximately $\frac{1}{2}E_{max}$; R_2 must be high compared with the input impedance of the common base amplifier, T_2. Also the dissipation of T_1 must be limited to a safe level.

Suppose $E_{max} = 15$ volts. We have, due to the high value of R_3,

$$I_{c.2} \ll I_{c.1} \qquad (8.14)$$

For a maximum dissipation of 50 mW in T_1, when V_{ce} for T_1 is 7·5 volts:

$$I_{c.1} = \frac{50}{1,000 \times 7\cdot5} \doteqdot 6 \text{ mA},$$

and $$R_2 = 1\cdot2 \text{ kilohms}$$

A small resistor, R_1, about 50 ohms, may be included as a collector load for T_1 to limit its current.

The main amplifier uses an auxiliary power supply, E_1, which is not dependent on the output potential of the power unit.

If E_1 (approximately $\frac{1}{2}E_{max}$) $= 8$ volts, and if T_3 has a collector current of 0·5 mA, R_5 may have 4 volts dropped across it, and hence $R_5 = 8·2$ kilohms.

If $\alpha' = 25$, the base current of T_3 which corresponds to a collector current of 0·5 mA is 20 μA.

Hence the collector current of T_2 should be 200 μA, which is as low as possible since leakage current flows and this is consistent with equation (8.14).

It would be an advantage to use a silicon transistor for T_2, and also for T_1 since these should have similar characteristics.

Hence $$R_3 = \frac{8 \times 10^6}{200} = 40 \text{ kilohms}$$

The remainder of the amplifier is shown in Fig. 8.12.

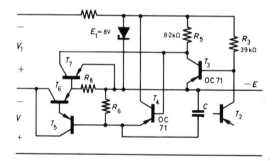

FIG. 8.12

T_4 and T_5 are emitter followers matching the voltage amplifier T_3 to the series regulator T_6. The dissipation of T_5, which provides the base current for T_6, will be high and so a small power transistor will be used here. The choice of T_5 and T_6 will depend on the current which the unit must be capable of supplying.

For a current of, say, 0·5 amp, a single regulator transistor, say 2N257 or OC 35, may be used but for higher currents a number of these will be paralleled each with its series emitter resistor. This resistor is necessary to give equitable distribution of this current between the regulator transistors.

Protection Circuits

Should the output of the power unit be shorted or called upon to supply an excess current, even for a very short time, the maximum dissipation of T_6 can easily be exceeded. Protection by fuses is too slow to safeguard the transistor.

Two methods which have been adopted are the use of (a) a bistable element operated by a schmitt trigger (see Chapter 10), and (b) a current limiting circuit. The first method necessitates resetting. Care should be taken not to attempt to reset the protection unit whilst the fault conditions causing the overload still exist.

Figure 8.12 illustrates the second method. T_7 and R_8 act as a current limiter. The output current passes through R_8, and a voltage is developed which is sufficient to drive T_7 into conduction. The current it takes robs the base of T_4 so reducing the drive on T_5 and T_6. For a 0·5 amp unit, R_8 is about 1 ohm and T_7 is a low gain silicon transistor, such as OC 200.

Constant Current Supplies

Constant current circuits are used, for example, for the field current of electromagnets, where control of the output current rather than the voltage is desired. It is possible to use a voltage supply with the protection circuit just described, for this turns the constant voltage supply into a constant current source for high current loads, where the protection circuit is operating. R_8 decides the magnitude of this current.

Figure 8.13 shows a circuit intended primarily as a constant current source. To stabilize the output current any change in the voltage across R_2 must be countered by changing the base current

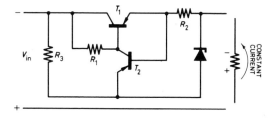

Fig. 8.13

of T_1. Therefore, the voltage drop across R_1 must be made independent of the output current. This is done by feeding the voltage developed across R_2 to the amplifier, T_2, and its reference diode.

The output resistance, R_o, is approximately equal to the product of R_2 and the gain of the feedback amplifier.

A practical constant current source is shown in Fig. 8.14. A constant current from 1 μA to 10 mA can be supplied. The internal resistance, which for a constant current source should be as high as possible, is 10 megohms at 25 μA and 50 kilohms at 10 mA.

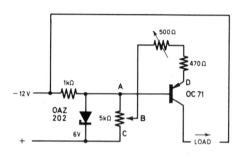

FIG. 8.14

A supposed increase in current through the load increases the voltage drop between B and C, and since the drop between A and C is constant due to the zener diode, the forward bias between A and B is reduced and the supposed increase reduced also. This has the effect of making the voltage drop between A and D largely independent of the output current.

Junction Diodes as Power Rectifiers

Stabilized voltage and current circuits may obtain their unregulated supplies from batteries, or from an alternating source with a power transformer and rectifier system. These rectifiers are very often germanium or silicon junction diodes as mentioned in Chapter 7. Amongst their advantages are their low forward voltage drop compared with older types, their small size and possible long life. However, many of these diodes are particularly sensitive to overload and can be destroyed by excessive reverse voltage transients or momentary current overloads. Some protection against voltage transients can be afforded if the diode has avalanche characteristics. In this case the transient brings about a reduction in impedance from which the diode is able to recover.

It is assumed that in the proper design of power supply circuits, the power rectifiers will have adequate heat sinks and be operated within their power dissipation ratings.

Four-Layer Diode With Gate

In the last chapter reference was made to the silicon four-layer diode. This diode, in a modified form, is known as the silicon controlled rectifier and is employed in power supply circuits as a rectifier or an inverter. This *pnpn* device is constructed as shown in Fig. 8.15. It consists of an *n*-type silicon wafer (A) with *p*-type layers

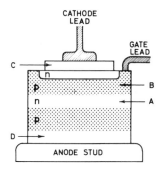

Fig. 8.15

above and below, formed by diffusion. An alloyed *pn* junction (B) is produced on this, the *n*-type material being connected via a molybdenum plate (C) to the cathode lead. This plate and another similar one (D) help eliminate the undesired results of thermal stresses. A gate electrode is also connected to the *p*-type material as shown.

With the anode positive, as shown in Fig. 8.16, only the leakage current flows due to the reverse biased diode formed by the two central sections. However, if now a positive current pulse arrives at the gate electrode, electrons from the cathode due to this pulse will be injected into the two left-hand sections of Fig. 8.16. The potential barrier of the reverse biased diode is thus broken down, and a high conduction current then flows typical of the forward biased diodes. The voltage across the conducting unit is of the order of 1 volt, even when a high current is flowing. The gate current required to initiate a current of about 50 amps may be of the order of 10 mA. In order to produce reliable firing the gate current should be, say, three times

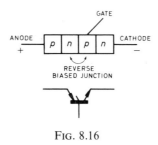

FIG. 8.16

this. If this is, for example, derived from a 10 volt peak pulse, then for a dissipation of a power of about 0·5 watt in the gate circuit, a peak power of the order of 10 kW may be switched in the anode circuit.

In Fig. 8.17, control pulses are used to fire two rectifiers. Once a rectifier has fired it continues to conduct until its anode voltage falls to almost zero. Hence the phasing of the control pulses can be used to vary the mean load current. Although the pulses are fed simultaneously to both rectifiers, only one of them fires, namely the one

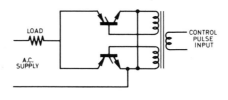

FIG. 8.17

with the positive anode to cathode voltage. The circuit of Fig. 8.17, together with its variable phase control circuits, could be used to vary the alternating current through a load. This is brought about with the dissipation of very little power in the rectifiers or control circuits. The control pulses could be derived from a sinusoidal oscillator (see Chapter 9), but for a precise firing phase, a pulse with a steep leading edge is to be preferred. Pulse generators of this type are described in Chapter 10.

PROBLEMS

8.1   Consider the circuit of Fig. 8.6 and deduce an expression for its stabilization factor, S. If $R_1 = 5$ kilohms, $R_2 = R_3 = 100$ ohms, $\alpha'' = 50$, $g_{m.2} = 40$ mAV^{-1}, $R_z = 20$ ohms, show that S is approximately 0·018. Find also the output impedance. [Ans. 1·8 ohms.]

8.2   Consider the emitter coupled amplifier of Fig. 8.7, with a push–pull input applied to the bases of the two transistors. Deduce an expression for the input impedance of the amplifier, and show that if $\alpha = 0·985$ and $r_{ee} = 95$ ohms the input impedance is approximately 12·5 kilohms.

8.3   Draw an equivalent circuit for Fig. 8.13, and so obtain an expression for the output resistance of this current generator.

8.4   (a) Sketch circuits showing how silicon controlled rectifiers may be used (i) as inverters, and (ii) as rectifiers of alternating voltage for half- and full-wave service. Discuss the gate pulses necessary for these applications.

(b) Assuming that the rectifier has a short rectangular gate pulse whose phase can be varied with regard to the anode voltage, sketch the anode current waveform you would expect for a number of phases of gate voltage.

8.5   Estimate the stabilization factor and output impedance of the voltage stabilizing circuit of Figs. 8.11 and 8.12. To what extent is the stabilization factor determined by T_1, T_2 and T_3? What is the purpose of the capacitor C in Fig. 8.12?

BIBLIOGRAPHY

Beneteau: The Design of High Stability D.C. Amplifiers, *Semiconductor Products*, 27, Feb. 1961.

Beneteau and Murai: D.C. Amplifiers Using Transistors, *Electronic Engng.*, 257, Apr. 1963.

Butler: Overload Protection of Transistor Regulated Power Supplies, *Wireless World*, 409, Aug. 1963.

13

Lowry: Industrial Applications of Silicon Controlled Rectifiers, *Proc.I.E.E.*, **106**, 1384, 1959.

Namibiar: Transistor Differential Amplifiers, *Electronic Tech.*, 147, Apr. 1962.

Nowicki: An Introduction to Transistor Transmitters, *Electronic Engng.*, 744, Nov. 1962.

Ritson and Foss: Transistor Power Supplies with Limited Overload Current, *Electronic Engng.*, 526, Aug. 1962.

Wenham: The Design of Direct Voltage and Current Stabilisers Using Semiconductor Devices, *Proc.I.E.E.*, **106**, 1384, 1959.

CHAPTER 9

Sinusoidal Oscillators

When a transistor amplifier has a portion of its output fed back to its input circuit its characteristics are modified. In Chapter 4, the case was considered where the voltage fed back had an important component in antiphase with the input signal, so causing the gain to be reduced. A more detailed analysis would show that the phase rotation of the signal was in every case partly due to the circuit used with the transistor and partly to the transistor itself. Both of these elements are frequency sensitive. In particular, the passive network connected to the transistor can easily be made frequency sensitive.

In this chapter, consideration will be given to circuits, called oscillators, in which the total loop phase shift is zero. A part of the output voltage is fed back to the input to provide the signal voltage without recourse to any external input. If the phase shift of the passive network is highly frequency sensitive, it is possible to control the frequency of oscillation by adjustment of the network. This frequency may also depend to some extent on the transistor parameters, but suitable circuit design can make it nearly independent of changes in the parameters brought about by changes in temperature. Since practicable realizable networks produce some attentuation, a further condition for oscillation is that the gain of the transistor must make up for this loss.

A suitable passive network is a three-terminal device connected to the transistor, so that the phase rotation and loop gain are correct. In this kind of circuit, it is a matter of opinion which of these three terminals is regarded as common to the input and output of the transistor. Therefore, transistor oscillators will not be classed as operating in the common base, common emitter or common collector modes, so far as their a.c. behaviour is concerned.

L–C Oscillators

Figure 9.1 shows a simplified circuit of a transistor oscillator, in which the bias components have been omitted. It is analogous to the tuned anode oscillator of valve electronics.

The currents which are assumed to flow are indicated in the figure, and the resistance r may be assumed to be the resistance of the inductance, L. The resistance R_1 represents power losses from the circuit. The analysis of Fig. 9.1 can be greatly simplified, if it is

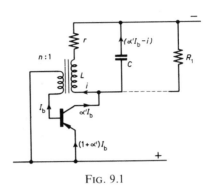

FIG. 9.1

assumed that the transistor is neither bottomed nor cut-off at any time. The transistor may be represented by the common emitter equivalent circuit using T parameters, with the simplifying assumption that $r_c(1-\alpha)$ is sufficiently large compared with all other impedances for the current through it to be neglected. The equivalent circuit of the oscillator is then as in Fig. 9.2, in which the currents are shown to correspond with Fig. 9.1.

These simplifications are satisfactory providing the frequency of operation is much less than f_1. The junction capacitances may be ignored at this stage. A more detailed treatment taking them into account may be justified at high frequencies.

Figure 9.2 is seen to consist of two meshes, and the analysis follows by application of Kirchhoff's laws to these meshes.

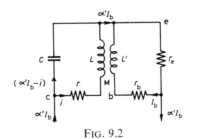

FIG. 9.2

Left-hand mesh:

$$(\alpha' I_b - i)\left(\frac{-j}{C\omega}\right) - i(r + j\omega L) = j\omega M I_b$$

i.e.
$$i\left[j\left(\frac{1}{C\omega}\right) - j\omega L - r\right] = I_b\left(j\omega M + \frac{j\alpha'}{C\omega}\right).$$

Right-hand mesh:

$$I_b(r_b + j\omega L') + (\alpha' + 1)I_b r_e = j\omega M i$$

i.e.
$$I_b[r_b + (\alpha' + 1)r_e + j\omega L'] = j\omega M i$$

Considering ratios $I_b : i$ in the two mesh equations we have:

$$\frac{j\left[\left(\frac{1}{C\omega}\right) - \omega L\right] - r}{j\omega M} = \frac{j\left(\omega M + \frac{\alpha'}{C\omega}\right)}{r_b + j\omega L' + (\alpha' + 1)r_e}$$

$$\therefore \quad \left[j\left(\frac{1}{C\omega} - \omega L\right) - r\right]\left[r_b + j\omega L' + (\alpha' + 1)r_e\right]$$
$$= -\omega M\left(\omega M + \frac{\alpha'}{C\omega}\right)$$

Equating imaginary terms:
$$\left[\frac{1}{C\omega} - \omega L\right]\left[r_b + (\alpha' + 1)r_e\right] - \omega L'r = 0$$

Then, putting $r_b + (\alpha' + 1)r_e = \alpha'' r_{ee}$

$$(1 - \omega^2 LC)\alpha'' r_{ee} - \omega^2 L'Cr = 0$$

or
$$\omega^2(LC\alpha'' r_{ee} + L'Cr) = \alpha'' r_{ee}$$

Therefore
$$\omega^2 = \left(\frac{1}{LC + CL'r/\alpha'' r_{ee}}\right) \qquad (9.1)$$

Equating real terms:

$$\alpha'' rr_{ee} + \omega L'\left(\frac{1}{C\omega} - \omega L\right) = \omega M\left(\omega M + \frac{\alpha'}{C\omega}\right)$$

or
$$\alpha'' Crr_{ee} + L' - \omega^2 LL'C = \omega^2 M^2 C + \alpha' M$$

and if $M^2 = LL'$ (if an iron core is not used $M^2 = k^2 LL'$)

$$\alpha'' rr_{ee} + L'/C - \alpha' M/C = 0$$

i.e.
$$M \geqslant Crr_{ee}/\alpha + L'/\alpha' \qquad (9.2)$$

Equation (9.1) enables the resonant frequency to be calculated and shows that it is dependent, not only on the L and C of the tuned circuit, but also on the loading and on $\alpha''r_{ee}$, i.e. on the transistor parameters. Now these are dependent on temperature, and hence so is the frequency.

For good frequency stability it may be necessary to stabilize the temperature. Also r should be small and $\alpha''r_{ee}$ should be high. Thus the Q of the tuned circuit and the transistor current gain should be high. The collector capacitance, so far neglected, is of the order of 50 pF for a collector voltage of about 3 volts and a germanium alloy transistor. Since this capacitance is a function of the collector voltage, this voltage should not vary, and the external tuning capacitance should be made much larger than the junction capacitance. The effect of changes in this capacitance and in r_e on frequency stability, can be reduced by using a tapped inductance.

The transformer turns ratio, n (Fig. 9.2), should be such that the reflected input resistance does not damp the tuned circuit. Oscillations build up and are limited by non-linearity. However, sinusoidal oscillations of good waveshape can be produced by increasing r_e by an external feedback resistor in the emitter circuit, R_E. The value of R_E can be found by experiment; it is often in the range 20–100 ohms. A fuller analysis shows that

$$R_E \doteqdot \frac{3r_b - \alpha'r_e}{\alpha' - 3} \text{ ohms} \tag{9.3}$$

The voltage loop gain after oscillation of constant amplitude has been achieved is of course unity, but a somewhat larger loop gain is desirable immediately before the build up of oscillations.

The loop gain, $a_v = ng_m R_L$ where n is the fractional turns ratio, and R_L is the effective load consisting of the dynamic impedance of the tuned circuit and R_1 in parallel with it. The choice of gain thus decides n.

But from equation (3.7), $g_m \doteqdot \alpha/r_e$ (when α tends to unity), $\doteqdot 1/r_e$. Hence loop gain $= nR_L/r_e$
or, if a feedback resistor, R_E, is used in the emitter lead

$$a_v = \frac{nR_L}{r_e + R_E} \tag{9.4}$$

Example. An $L - C$ oscillator will now be designed to provide an output of 50 mW into a load of 100 ohms. Twelve volt supplies are available. One possible circuit is shown in Fig. 9.3. Component values for this circuit will now be found, assuming that the oscillator is to operate at a frequency of 10 kc/s.

Figure 9.3 shows a transistor type OC 72 operating at a mean current of 10 mA. It is desirable to operate at 9 volts, so that V_{ce} is well within the ratings of the transistor, i.e., the voltage across $R_3 + R_4$ equals 3 volts.

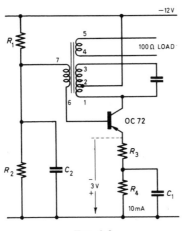

FIG. 9.3

If the power output is 50 mW, the voltage across the output terminals on load $= 2 \cdot 25$ volts.

It is desirable to operate the transistor in class B where the efficiency is higher than in class A. The collector peak swing will therefore correspond to a half-cycle of oscillation, and is approximately 8 volts assuming that it bottoms at $V_{ce} = 1$ volt. The impedance offered to it is $(8^2 \times 1,000)/(2 \times 50) = 640$ ohms, i.e. to match the load a turns ratio of $\sqrt{640/100}$, that is, $2 \cdot 55 : 1$ is needed.

If the frequency of oscillation is 10 kc/s and the impedance at the collector is $R = L/Cr$, where r is the effective series resistance of the tuned circuit, then, eliminating r, we have: $\omega^2 \doteqdot 1/LC$, whence $L\omega Q = R$ where $Q = \omega L/r$. Here $R = 640$ ohms and a working Q of about 10 is practicable.

Then $\omega L = 64$, and $L = 64/2\pi 10,000 \doteqdot 1 \cdot 0$ mH.

LA 1 ferroxcube specifies 53 turns per mH and here the output winding between points 1 and 2 in the figure has 53 turns. The tuning capacitance C for this frequency can now be found, since

$$C = 1/\omega^2 L = \frac{10^6}{4\pi^2 \times 10^8 \times 10^{-3}} \, \mu\text{F} \doteqdot 0.25 \, \mu\text{F}.$$

This may be reduced by a factor of 100, say, to 2,500 pF by a tapped coil where the appropriate turns ratio $n' = 100^{1/2} = 10:1$. This requires a total collector winding of 530 turns.

The input characteristics of the transistor show that a peak drive of about 0·35 volt is required, and if the output is 8 volts across 53 turns then $0.25 \times 53/8$ turns are required for the base winding, i.e. about three turns. In this example, the shunting effect of this feedback has been ignored (see problem 9.2).

For the OC 72, α' is about 70 and hence $I_b = 10/70$ mA.

A suitable bleed current is one order higher than this, i.e., about 1·5 mA. $\therefore R_2 = \dfrac{3 \times 1,000}{1.5} = 2$ kilohms, and $R_1 = 8$ kilohms. Also $R_3 + R_4 = \frac{1}{10}(3 \times 1,000) = 300$ ohms, and from equation (9.3) $R_3 \doteqdot 10$ ohms.

The complete circuit is illustrated in Fig. 9.4.

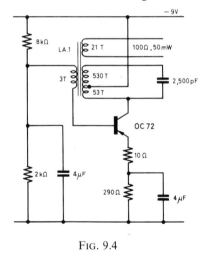

FIG. 9.4

L–C Oscillators at High Frequencies

Figure 9.5 shows a Colpitts oscillator, the two tuning capacitors being c_0 and c_1 in series across L. This oscillator is capable of operating at over 200 Mc/s with an output power of 40 mW. A further amplifier (not shown in the figure) might operate in common base and would use a transistor of the same type. It would probably

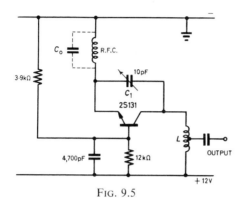

FIG. 9.5

operate in class B and deliver about 200 mW of power. Transistors are available to deliver several watts at this frequency.

The performance of oscillators at high frequencies can still be analysed by an equivalent circuit such as the T circuit, but it must be remembered that α and r_e must be considered as having imaginary as well as real components.

Frequency Modulated Oscillators

Frequency modulation of an L–C oscillator can be achieved by modulating either the base current or the emitter current of the

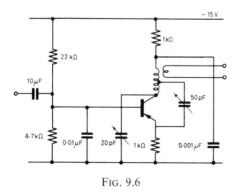

FIG. 9.6

transistor. The latter method requires a greater modulating power. Figure 9.6 shows a typical R.F. Hartley oscillator with base modulation.

The circuit produces a deviation characteristic of 30 mV r.m.s. for 100 kc/s deviation, which is substantially linear for modulating voltages up to about 100 mV. Some amplitude modulation is inevitably produced also. This can be removed with a suitable limiter.

R–C Oscillators

R–C phase shift networks and active devices such as valves or transistors may be used to construct either oscillators or selective amplifiers. The two types of circuit are similar, often differing only in the extent of the feedback current or voltage. There are special considerations in the case of transistor circuits.

(a) The phase shift network may have to operate into a low impedance, the transistor input impedance—about 50 ohms in common base or about 1,000 ohms in the common emitter mode. If multiple emitter followers are used in the feedback path, this drawback can be overcome.

(b) The gain of the transistor should be greater than the attenuation of the network.

(c) The transistor phase shift must be taken into account, and added to the network phase shift to obtain an accurate assessment of the conditions required for zero overall phase shift. This is of particular importance at frequencies only a little less than f_1.

The low input impedance of a transistor limits the use of those phase shifting networks which employ capacitors. Hence a C–R input circuit should be arranged, so that the resistor is in parallel with the input to the transistor rather than the capacity, unless special precautions are taken to ensure that the shunting effect of the transistor input has been kept small.

R–C Filter Networks

Oscillators with three similar stages of R–C filter require a gain from the amplifier of 29, and for four stages the minimum gain is 18·4. An example of this type of network is shown in Fig. 9.7. Since the attenuation of the network is rather high, it may be necessary to select transistors with high values of current gain for this par-

ticular application. Lower attenuation is obtained from networks
with more sections, or from using networks the sections of which
do not contain equal values of R and C. Hence, it can be shown,
that if the network contains C, nC and n^2C, and R, R/n and R/n^2
the attenuation is approximately 20 when n is 5 and is less for

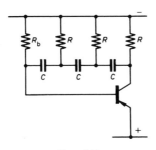

FIG. 9.7

higher values of n, provided the capacitors and resistors are
arranged, so that each section is not so severely shunted by the
previous section as when all the values of C and R are equal. The
attenuation tends to a theoretical minimum of less than 10 when
each section is not loaded by the following section.

In Fig. 9.7, the base current is determined by R_b and it is desirable
that this should be as large as possible consistent with a waveform
of high purity. For this reason, R_b is often variable. Variation of
frequency can be achieved by altering one of the networks or by

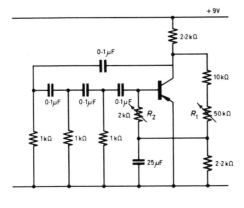

FIG. 9.8

using ganged potentiometers. A practical circuit taking these points into consideration is that of Fig. 9.8, where R_1 which sets the base current is preset for maximum gain consistent with a pure waveform. R_2 modifies the phase shift network and so is the frequency control. With these component values the frequency of oscillation is about 1 kc/s.

Twin-T Oscillators

The attenuation of twin-T networks is often lower than that of the phase shifting networks already described, so that even if a transistor with a lower gain is used the circuit will still oscillate. The conventional twin-T circuit of Fig. 9.9(a) should be operated from a low generator impedance between L and N, for example, and feed into a high output impedance across M and N. Although transistor oscillators can use twin-T networks of this kind if an emitter follower stage is used, this is not well suited to transistor impedances. However, a rearrangement of the component resistors and capacitors, whilst still a basic twin-T circuit, produces the network of Fig. 9.9(b). The input is now between L and M and the

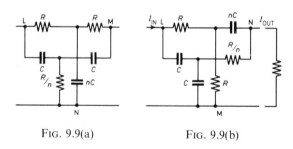

FIG. 9.9(a)   FIG. 9.9(b)

output is taken from M and N. This is suitable for termination by a low impedance and to be driven from a high impedance, and therefore lends itself more easily to transistor circuitry.

Analysis shows that for values of n between 3 and 8, the attenuation is less than 12, with a minimum at n just less than 5 (see problem 9.5). A circuit based on this network is shown in Fig. 9.10. The points L, M and N, already referred to, are shown in the figure. So far as alternating quantities are concerned, both supply lines are taken to the point M.

The oscillation frequency can be controlled by adjusting R_1. This has some effect on the minimum attenuation of the network. Alternatively, if C_1 is open-circuited at the point A and fed from an amplifier of low impedance, oscillation can be prevented by the 500 ohm resistor in series with C_1. The circuit then becomes that

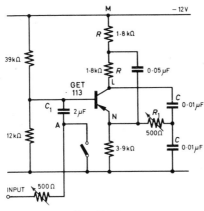

FIG. 9.10

of a selective amplifier, and this resistor controls its selectivity, while R_1 controls its centre frequency.

The frequency of operation, f, as an oscillator or selective amplifier, is given by $2\pi f = 1/CR$, when $R_1 = \frac{1}{5}R$ in the circuit.

However, the finite input resistance of the transistor lowers the resonant frequency and increases the minimum value of current gain required for oscillation. The output capacitance of the transistor also influences the resonant frequency and the minimum value of current gain.

Wien Bridge Oscillators

Wien bridge transistor oscillators can also be designed on similar principles. Their chief advantages are low attenuation and ease of adjustment when used in variable frequency oscillators. Only two components need be altered to change frequency independently of the attenuation introduced. Thermistors are often employed in the feedback loop to stabilize the load on the oscillator. Some precaution of this kind is necessary with most precision transistor R–C

oscillators, since changes made in the operating frequency often alter the loading on the R–C network. The wien bridge circuit of Fig. 9.11 balances when the real and imaginary components of voltage between P and Q are made to vanish simultaneously. Hence there is an in-phase relationship between input and output voltages of the wien bridge.

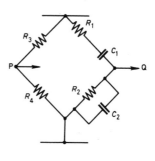

FIG. 9.11

The frequency of operation when $C_1 = C_2$, $R_1 = R_2$, $R_3 = R_4$ is given by

$$2\pi f = \frac{1}{\sqrt{C_1 C_2 R_1 R_2}} = \frac{1}{C_1 R_1}$$

A two-stage amplifier of very low gain is required, and there is thus much scope for circuits of high stability corrected against frequency drift.

Crystal Controlled Oscillators

The chief difficulty in crystal oscillator design is the high impedance of crystals. One common method employs two transistors to form a two-stage amplifier. Overall positive feedback is applied through the crystal and a tuned circuit resonating at the crystal frequency. A circuit of this kind could be used from low frequencies of the order of 10 kc/s upwards as a standard frequency oscillator. By using a crystal with a zero temperature coefficient centred on the operating temperature, for example a normal room temperature, a frequency standard can be produced which is accurate to three parts in 10^6, without resorting to oven control. Single transistor oscillators have also been designed. Two of these are shown in Figs. 9.12 and 9.13.

In Fig. 9.12, a 15 Mc/s crystal oscillates in a common emitter circuit which uses a diffused type transistor. A circuit of this kind is capable of giving a power output in excess of 20 mW at 25 per cent efficiency. It finds use as a local oscillator in communications

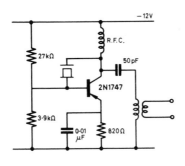

FIG. 9.12

receivers designed to operate at a number of preselected channel frequencies. When higher frequencies are necessary, frequency multiplication may be used, although less power will be obtained. Figure 9.13 shows a crystal oscillator in which the collector circuit is tuned to a harmonic of the crystal frequency. Such circuits extend the frequency of crystal oscillators by at least a factor of three before their low efficiency makes them impracticable.

Crystal oscillators can be designed using titanate ceramics of the kind used in I.F. filters (see Chapter 5). Although they have suitable impedances for transistor circuits they do not possess the stability

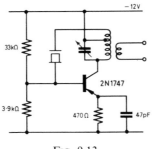

FIG. 9.13

of quartz. An example is shown in Fig. 9.14 of a typical circuit using silicon transistors and a voltage stabilized supply line. The frequency stability of the oscillator is 20 parts in 10^6 per degree C change in ambient temperature, and 75 parts in 10^6 per volt change in the operating supply potential. The output is taken from across the titanate filter using an emitter follower. Although this provides the relatively small output of 0·5 volt peak-to-peak the waveform is of good quality.

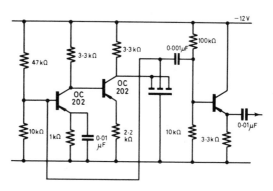

FIG. 9.14

Oscillators at Very Low Frequencies

Oscillators have been designed which are capable of providing a good sinusoidal output at frequencies down to the order of 1 cycle in five minutes. However, the difficulties of these circuits has led to the development of light-operated function generators, in which a rotating transparent disc carries an opaque section, the shape of which, together with the optical system, is responsible for producing the desired output waveform.

Electronic oscillators, however, as distinct from these photo-mechanical types, are usually based on $C–R$ filters. An example is shown in Fig. 9.15 where a $C–R$ phase shifting network is used. The 10 kilohm preset potentiometer is used as a feedback control, and is set so that oscillation has commenced, but is not limited by extreme non-linearity. When the frequency is very low, the leakage of the first transistor and of the capacitors in the network becomes very important. The circuit shown oscillates at approximately 1 cycle per minute with $C = 80 \ \mu F$, or 11 c/s with $C = 0·1 \ \mu F$.

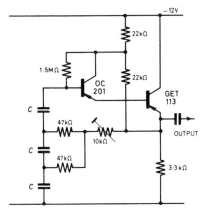

FIG. 9.15

PROBLEMS

9.1   It has been stated that $g_m = \alpha/r_e$. Examine this approximation and find a more accurate equation for g_m and hence for the loop gain of an L–C oscillator.

9.2   Design an L–C oscillator capable of operating at 50 kc/s and using 9 volt supplies. Use the characteristics of a small power transistor to deliver 1 watt to a 75 ohm load. Consider the effect of the power dissipated in the input impedance of the transistor by the feedback winding, shunting the output, and so find the extent of the inaccuracy introduced by ignoring this in the design.

9.3   Deduce a value for the loop gain of the L–C oscillator designed as an example in this chapter. If this pre-oscillation loop gain should be readjusted to about 3, how should the design be modified to bring this about?

9.4   Deduce expressions for 180° phase shift, and the associated attenuation of a three-stage R–C filter network whose elements are R, R/n and R/n^2, and C, nC and n^2C. Hence, by putting $n = 1$ show that the corresponding attenuation is 29. (The method suggested is not the quickest for obtaining this result, but it enables the effect of changes in n to be clearly seen.)

9.5   Find the ratio I_{in}/I_{out} for the circuit of Fig. 9.9(a), and hence show that the frequency at which I_{in} and I_{out} are in phase is independent of n. Find the attenuation of the network when $n = 5$. [Ans. 10·7.]

14

9.6   Figure 9.11 shows a wien bridge network. Use this in the design of a 1,000 c/s oscillator. Find also the attenuation of the wien network. How may the gain of the active elements be matched to the attenuation of the network? [Ans. 3.]

BIBLIOGRAPHY

Baxandall: Transistor Sine Wave Oscillators, *Proc.I.E.E.*, **106**, 748, 1959.

Lambden: Network Tuned Amplifiers with Variable Bandwidth, *Electronic Engng.*, 109, Feb. 1963.

Stott: Transistor *RC* Oscillator, *Wireless World*, 91, Feb. 1962.

CHAPTER 10

Switching and Pulse Circuitry

Figure 10.1 shows a family of output characteristics and a super-imposed load line **AB**. There are three possible states of operation as shown.

These states are (i) cut-off, both junctions reverse biased, (ii) normal operation for amplifiers, and (iii) saturation, both junctions being forward biased.

Depending on how the extreme regions are reached in a switching operation, the transistor may be under-driven or over-driven. The extent of the drive affects the response time of the transistor to changes of level at its input terminals. If over-driven, for example,

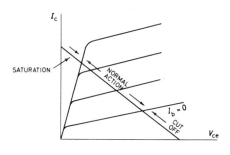

FIG. 10.1

both junctions must be cleared of carriers before it can become cut-off, the stored carriers having recombined or been swept away.

Switching characteristics include rise time, storage time, and fall time. These are found by examination of the output for a given input pulse. Manufacturers quote these times and the turn-on and turn-off times as measured in test circuits using mercury-wetted relays. These times may be understood with reference to Fig. 10.2.

The turn-on time, t_{on}, is the sum of the delay time, t_D, and the rise time, t_R, where the delay time is measured from the commencement

199

of the input pulse until the output has reached 10 per cent of its full amplitude. The rise time is measured as the time taken to rise from 10 per cent to 90 per cent of the full amplitude. The turn-off time, t_{off}, is the sum of the storage time, t_S, and the fall time, t_F. Typical times for alloy transistors are of the order of 0·3 microsec, whereas for alloy-diffused transistors they are of the order of 20 nanosec. The delay time is always somewhat less than the storage and fall times, while the rise time is usually slightly greater than any of the others.

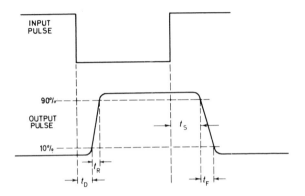

Fig. 10.2

For current drive, the turn-on and turn-off times are equal, and may be reduced by reducing R_1 in Fig. 10.3. Further reduction can be achieved by the introduction of a small emitter-resistor, R_2, of the order of 10–100 ohms. Also, for a short switching time a transistor with a high cut-off frequency is required. If f_1 is the frequency for unity current gain, and the charge injected into the base circuit by a pulse is δq, then

$$\delta q = I_b\,\delta t, \text{ in time } \delta t \tag{10.1}$$

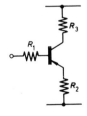

Fig. 10.3

But this charge δq must be sufficient to establish the emitter current at the frequency f_1

Therefore $$I_e = 2\pi f_1 \, \delta q \qquad (10.2)$$

and $$I_b = I_e/(1+\alpha') \qquad (10.3)$$

Then, from equations (10.1) and (10.2), eliminating δq:

$$I_e = I_b 2\pi f_1 \, \delta t$$

and from equation (10.3) $\quad \delta t = \dfrac{1+\alpha'}{2\pi f_1} \qquad (10.4)$

This is a simplified approximate relationship, a better result being that the turn-on and turn-off times are approximately $2 \cdot 2 \, \delta t$.

If, for example, $\alpha' = 80$ and $f_1 = 40$ Mc/s, $\delta t =$ approximately $0 \cdot 7$ microsec.

In Fig. 10.3, the switching times may be reduced by a low value of R_3; also the turn-on time may be reduced by overdriving, although this also increases the turn-off time.

However, if the transistor is bottomed, the turn-on time is increased by a quantity representing the time taken to overcome the excess base charge brought about by bottoming. In the design of pulse circuits, a useful compromise between heavy bottoming and underdriving is to take the value of α' as that of the lowest expected value of the range quoted by the manufacturer.

Charge Parameters

Attempts to predict the behaviour of a given transistor in any particular circuit along these lines have not been particularly successful. With the introduction of charge parameters a new method has become available. The transistor is here regarded as a charge operated device, a finite input current being required, only in order to counter the effects of recombination of carriers.

For an emitter with unity efficiency, an injection of charge into the base, not subject to loss, will cause a current to flow in the collector circuit until the charge is removed. However, in practice, a sustained base current, I_b, will be needed to maintain the level of the base charge, Q_b. Now I_b is proportional to Q_b and so all currents can be expressed in terms of Q_b.

First, consider the case where the transistor is turned off. The shaded area in Fig. 10.4 shows the electron charge which must be supplied to maintain the equilibrium with donors in the *n*-type base of a *pnp* transistor.

Now, if the transistor is turned on, but has a short-circuited load,

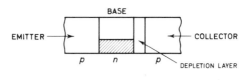

FIG. 10.4

so that V_{cb} is constant, the additional injected charge, Q_b (Fig. 10.5), will be distributed across the base, as shown, causing a collector current, I_c. It might be noted here that the distribution of charge follows the dotted line in a graded base transistor, while in a linear alloy junction it follows the solid line. Now I_c is proportional to Q_b

Therefore $$T_c = Q_b/I_c \qquad (10.5)$$

where T_c is the collector time constant. T_c depends on base width, a narrower base needing a smaller charge to set up a given gradient.

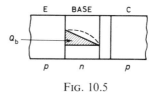

FIG. 10.5

Now base width depends on collector voltage since this controls the width of the depletion layer. In this elementary treatment, it will be assumed that when a transistor is bottomed, $V_{cb}=0$, and T_c can therefore be conveniently defined for this condition,

i.e. $$T_{co} = Q_b/I_c, \qquad V_{cb} = 0 \qquad (10.6)$$

This assumption is a valid approximation for most types of alloy transistors.

Next, consider the transistor turned on with a finite collector load. Here V_{cb} changes at turn-on but then becomes approximately zero. A charge Q_v is needed to charge the collector depletion layer capacitance, C_{tc}, as shown in Fig. 10.6. The total charge Q_{on} is given by equation (10.7). A similar charge is required to turn the transistor off:

$$Q_{on} = Q_b + Q_v = Q_{off} \tag{10.7}$$

$$= I_c T_{co} + Q_v \tag{10.8}$$

where $$Q_v = K C_{tc} \, \delta V_{cb} \tag{10.9}$$

K is a constant, 1–1·5 for diffused base and 1–2 for alloy junctions.

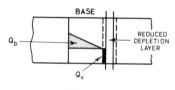

FIG. 10.6

So far, the transistor has been assumed to be operating in the active region, and T_{co} and Q_v together with the current gain, α'_o (defined in equation (10.10)) are sufficient to describe its performance:

$$\alpha'_o = I_c/I_b, \qquad V_{cb} = 0 \tag{10.10}$$

Saturation Region

However, if the base current is sufficient to drive the transistor into saturation, a charge Q_{bs}, additional to Q_{on}, must be given to the base so that the corresponding saturation base current, I_{bs}, may be greater than I_c/α'_o. This extra charge, Q_{bs}, is illustrated in Fig. 10.7.

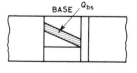

FIG. 10.7

The saturation time constant, T_s, is given by equation (10.11):

$$T_s = Q_{bs}/I_{bs} \qquad (10.11)$$

To turn the transistor off the total charge which must now be removed, Q_{off}, is given by equation (10.12):

$$Q_{off} = Q_b + Q_v + Q_{bs} = I_c T_{co} + Q_v + I_{bs} T_s \qquad (10.12)$$

The "On Demand" Current Gain

In the transistor–resistor logic circuits which will be described later, it may often be the case that when a transistor has been turned on, only a small collector current flows. However, a larger collector current may be demanded when diode gates connected to its output are subsequently opened, thus lowering the collector load. This must not cause the transistor to leave the saturated state. Hence, the base charge must be capable of allowing a current, $I_{c.max}$, to flow on demand. The base current, $I_{c.max}/\alpha_o'$, is not sufficient for this. In this new situation, the collector current, in an extreme case, may be zero, so that a base charge with a current $I_{c.max}$ will then be $Q_{bs}(= I_{c.max} Q_b/I_c)$.

But
$$\frac{I_{c.max}}{I_c} Q_b = I_{c.max} T_c \quad \text{(from equation (10.5))}$$

The base charge present under these conditions must be set up by a base current, I_{bs}, where the charge is:

$$I_{bs} T_s = Q_{bs} \qquad \text{(from equation (10.11))}$$

Therefore
$$I_{bs} T_s = Q_{bs} = I_{c.max} T_c$$

or
$$T_s = \frac{I_{c.max}}{I_{bs}} T_c = \alpha_s' T_c \qquad (10.13)$$

where α_s' is the "on demand" current gain.

$$\alpha_s' = \frac{\text{available transient collector current}}{\text{base current}}$$

Some typical figures for the charge parameters are given in Table 10.1.

Then, from equation (10.10) $\quad \alpha_o' = I_c/I_b, \qquad V_{cb} = 0$

Therefore $\quad\quad I_b = I_c/\alpha_o', \quad\quad V_{cb} = 0$

and the difference between the steady I_b and this value is I_{bs},

i.e. $\quad\quad\quad\quad\quad\quad I_{bs} = I_b - I_c/\alpha_o',$

when, from equation (10.12) $\quad Q_{off} = I_c T_{co} + Q_v + T_s(I_b - I_c/\alpha_o')$

$$= Q_v + T_s I_b + I_c(T_{co} - T_s/\alpha_o')$$

Hence, using equation (10.13)

$$Q_{off} = Q_v + T_s I_b + T_c I_c(1 - \alpha_s'/\alpha_o') \quad\quad (10.14)$$

Table 10.1

Charge Parameters

	T_c (μsec)	T_s (μsec)	α_o'	α_s'	Q_v (pC)	$\alpha_o' T_c$ (μsec)	α_o'/α_s'
TK 20	0·05	1·5	40	30	250	2	1·33
NKT 101	0·02	2·0	50	25	220	1	2
NKT 109	0·06	2·0	50	25	220	3	2

Equation (10.14) is important, since the maximum values of T_s, T_{co} and $(1 - \alpha_s'/\alpha_o')$ tend to occur together and hence may be used to find a likely value for Q_{off}.

This theory has been found to account for the behaviour of alloy transistors. It can be modified to extend it to the newer types. Methods of measurement of the charge parameters and their use will be found in some of the papers listed in the bibliography.

As an example, consider the case of a transistor which has a 12 volts supply and a 1·2 kilohms collector load, and has f_T equal to 5 Mc/s. If the collector depletion layer capacitance is 10 pF, then, assuming K to be 2 (in equation (10.9)), Q_{on} can be found from equation (10.7).

$$\omega_T = 2\pi \times 5 \times 10^6$$

Therefore $\quad\quad T_{co} = \dfrac{1}{10^7\pi}$ (since $T_{co} = 1/\omega_T$)

Therefore, if $I_c = 10$ mA, $I_c T_{co} = 10^3/\pi$ picocoulombs, and

$$Q_{on} = \dfrac{10^3}{\pi} + 2 \times 10 \times 12 \text{ pC} \fallingdotseq (315 + 240) \text{ pC} = 555 \text{ pC}.$$

If the input potential also swings through 12 volts, for a square wave output the input charge of 555 pC must be supplied from the charge stored in the capacitor C_1 in Fig. 10.8. Therefore $C_1 = 555/12$ pF $\fallingdotseq 47$ pF.

R_1 is then designed to supply the current needed to make up for the charge lost due to recombination, so that the base current

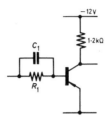

Fig. 10.8

remains constant at the desired value whilst the transistor is turned on. If the transistor is driven into saturation (see Fig. 10.9) the saturation base current can be found from equation (10.11). Therefore, $I_{bs} = I_b - I_c/\alpha'$, where α' is the lowest current gain which can be expected from the manufacturing "spread".

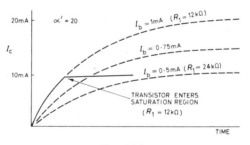

Fig. 10.9

If $\alpha' = 20$ and $R = 18$ $k\Omega$, so that $I_b = 0.75$ mA, $I_{bs} = 0.75 - 0.5 = 0.25$ mA.

The base current is often designed to be the least which the transistor with the lowest gain needs, so that it is just saturated. If the "on demand" current gain, α_s', is known, the "turn-off" time can be calculated. In this example it can be seen that $Q_{bs} = 0$ for $I_b = 0.5$ mA.

If here, $I_{bs} = 0.25$ mA, and $\alpha'_s = 15$ (which is likely for $\alpha' = 20$), $T_s = 15/10^7\pi$ (from equation (10.13)), and $Q_{off} = (555 + 350)$ pC = 905 pC.

Q_{on} is supplied, and Q_{off} is extracted in an exponential manner, so that the turn-on and turn-off times defined from the 10 per cent and 90 per cent levels can be estimated from the geometry of the waveforms. In the case of current drive, an approximation based on this and on equation (10.5) leads to the following result for t_{on}, when the transistor is not saturated:

$$t_{on} = t_{off} = \frac{T_{co}Q_{on}}{Q_b} \log_e 9$$

$$= 0.055 \log 9 = 0.12 \ \mu\text{sec}$$

Static Switching Circuits

One example of transistor switching circuits is that known as static switching. Here, the logical function of gating is carried out by resistor networks, and transistors invert the gated output and maintain the voltage levels which correspond to the switch being opened or closed. In diode gating circuits (Chapter 7), these levels deteriorated due to the finite potential drop across each diode, even when conducting. For this reason, amongst others, inverting amplifiers are often used between each "and-or" combination. With static switching the basic element is that of Fig. 10.10.

The number of inputs which may be used to drive the transistor is called the "fan-in". The number of outputs which may be taken

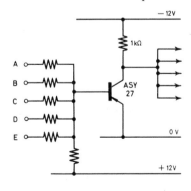

Fig. 10.10

from the transistor to drive other similar circuits is called the "fan-out". Commercial circuits commonly have a fan-in and fan-out of about five. The object of design technique is to obtain high fan-in and fan-out with a small signal propagation time.

In order to describe the function of a circuit of this kind, it is usual to define two voltage levels which correspond to the two states "transistor on" and "transistor off". These levels are written as "1" and "0". If the circuit is used with a negative voltage convention, that is, when the more negative of the input levels represents a "1", then it carries out the function "not-or" often abbreviated to "nor". When one or more of the inputs is made negative, i.e. is a "1", the transistor is switched on and the output is at nearly the same level as that of the common line, the more positive of its two possible states, i.e. it is a "0". The gating function is thus A or B or C or D or E. It is more usual to write this as $A + B + C +.D + E$. The transistor inverts this to $\text{not}(A + B + C + D + E)$, more usually written as $\overline{A + B + C + D + E}$.

Simple combinations of these circuits can be used to provide the functions "and" and "or" comparable with those obtained at lower impedance than with simple diode circuits. The higher fan-out of these transistor–resistor elements is one of their advantages compared with the diode circuits. However, the maximum speed of operation which can be predicted from a knowledge of the charge parameters is frequently less than that of the diode networks.

An example of the combination of transistor–resistor elements is shown in Fig. 10.11 in block diagram form. Three transistors are used to invert the inputs A, B and C and are all connected to a further element. It will be seen that only when all the inputs are "1", are the outputs $\overline{A}$, $\overline{B}$ and $\overline{C}$ all at the "0" level. Thus the output transistor is turned off and (in the negative convention) its output is

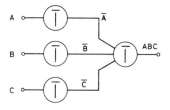

FIG. 10.11

also "1". The complete circuit thus performs the function "and". The same principles can easily be extended to other functions.

Phototransistor Pulse Circuits

Carriers can be injected into a semiconductor junction by photons of light falling on the junction, and giving up their energy to the impurity carriers. One example of a pulse circuit, using a phototransistor, in which the junctions are exposed to light, is that of a slave flash unit in which a photographic flash bulb is to be fired automatically when a master bulb fires, so momentarily illuminating the phototransistor. Two typical circuits are shown in Figs. 10.12 and 10.13.

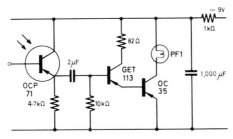

FIG. 10.12

In Fig. 10.12, the charge stored in the 1,000 μF capacitor is discharged by the power transistor through the flash bulb causing it to be ignited. The time taken for this to happen is chiefly due to the time taken after the commencement of current flow for the light output of the master bulb to reach its peak, a delay of about 16

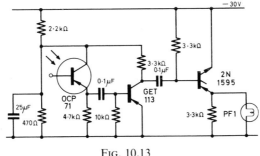

FIG. 10.13

msec. In Fig. 10.13, a small controlled rectifier is used for the same purpose.

Pulse Generators

Figure 6.1, which showed the output characteristics of a power transistor, included the region of avalanche multiplication. If a transistor is operated in this region, a very rapid multiplicative formation of electron-hole pairs takes place which, if not controlled, may result in the destruction of the transistor. If the multiplication factor is large, then the minority collector current may exceed the emitter current and the current gain is thus greater than unity.

Figure 10.14 shows a typical avalanche circuit, in which E_1 is sufficiently high for the transistor to enter the avalanche region, and E_2 causes reverse base current to flow. The characteristic in this

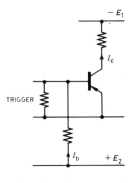

Fig. 10.14

region has a negative slope, and this leads to two stable points of operation at the extremes of this slope. These are (a) with a high V_{ce} and low I_c, typically about 100 μA, and (b) a high current and lower voltage where α is approximately unity (α' tending to infinity, as shown by the vertical slope of the characteristic). Transition between these levels results in pulses with a rise time of a few nanoseconds.

The Astable Pulse Generator

Another pulse generator is the multivibrator or astable circuit. This is often used as a "square wave" generator. An example is shown in Fig. 10.15, in which T_1 and T_2 are the active elements of the multivibrator. The transistors switch on alternately. The effect of switching on initiates a cumulative action which switches off the other transistor of the pair. Since capacitive coupling is used, this state of affairs cannot be maintained, and when the coupling

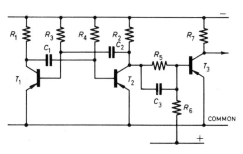

FIG. 10.15

capacitor has partly discharged, a second cumulative action commences to reverse the situation. This gives output voltages at the collectors which are approximately rectangular and are in anti-phase.

Typical waveforms are shown in Fig. 10.16. In the operation of this circuit, the time for which the cumulative action persists is very

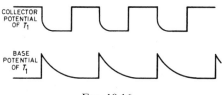

FIG. 10.16

short, so that providing the pulse recurrence time is long compared with the turn-on time, the time for which both transistors are actively acting as amplifiers is negligible. Also, if the circuit is designed so that the transistors T_1 and T_2 saturate, there will be a delay, t_D, between one of these transistors starting to conduct and the collector current of the other transistor starting to fall. This is because the excess charge, Q_{bs}, is first removed from the base region of the transistor which is switched off, and this has no effect on its collector potential.

If the circuit is symmetrical, $C_1 = C_2 = C$; $R_1 = R_2 = R_L$; $R_3 = R_4 = R$.

Consider the case when T_2 is on and is being switched off.

$$C \frac{dV_{c.2}}{dt} = -I_{c.2} \tag{10.15}$$

$$I_{b.2} = E/R = T_c \frac{dI_{c.2}}{dt}$$

Therefore
$$I_{c.2} = \frac{1}{T_c} \int_0^{t_D} \frac{E}{R} \, dt$$

or
$$I_{c.2} = \frac{Et_D}{T_c R} \tag{10.16}$$

$$I_{b.1} = E/R + C \frac{dV_{c.2}}{dt} \tag{10.17}$$

$$Q_{bs} = \int_0^{t_D} -I_{b.1} \, dt$$

$$= -\int_0^{t_D} \left(E/R + C \frac{dV_{c.2}}{dt} \right) dt \qquad \text{(from equation (10.17))}$$

$$= \int_0^{t_D} \left(-E/R + \frac{Et_D}{T_c R} \right) dt \quad \text{(from equations (10.15) and (10.16))}$$

Therefore
$$Q_{bs} = \frac{Et_D}{R} \left(\frac{t_D}{2T_c} - 1 \right) \tag{10.18}$$

This assumes that t_D is much less than $R_L C$.

When T_2 has been turned off, its collector potential rises exponentially with a time constant $R_L C$ as C charges. This charging current is a component of the base current, $I_{b.1}$, of T_1 which is being switched on, so that $I_{b.1} \doteqdot E(1/R + 1/R_L)$. The collector potential of T_1 rises from the supply potential, $-E$, to nearly zero. If t_R is the rise time for this change in potential, and for the associated increase in $I_{c.1}$ to E/R_L, then since $I_{c.1} = Q_{b.1}/T_c$ (from equation (10.5)), $I_{c.1} = I_{b.1} t_R/T_c$, if t_R is small.

Therefore
$$t_R \doteqdot \frac{T_c}{1 + R_L/R} \tag{10.19}$$

If C has started to charge at the commencement of the rise time, then the actual rise time will be longer than that calculated from equation (10.19).

The base potential of T_2 which has been driven positive by this action now starts to recover, C charging through R.

Thus
$$V_{b.1} = E - (E - V_{b(off)})e^{-t/RC}$$

where $V_{b(off)}$ is the value of V_b when T_2 is off, just before the commencement of this change.

Hence
$$t = RC \log_e(1 + V_{b(off)}/E) \qquad (10.20)$$

It can be assumed that it is a good approximation that the *change of voltage* at a collector is transmitted unattenuated to the base of the opposite transistor, so that $V_{b(off)}$ is approximately equal to E and equation (10.20) reduces to $t = RC \log_e 2$.

If the transient times given by equations (10.18) and (10.19) are short compared with t, the time for one complete cycle is $2t$, i.e., approximately $1.38\, RC$, so that the recurrence frequency, f, is given by $f = 1/(1.38\, RC)$ (to a first order of approximation). If required, a more accurate value can be deduced from equations (10.18)–(10.20).

A modification of Fig. 10.15 is to use a complementary circuit of *pnp* and *npn* transistors. A circuit of this kind can produce a faster switching time, because the low impedance of each transistor is capable of supplying the high drive current which is required by the other, but has not found much favour in the past, since well matched *pnp–npn* transistors were not available. This is no longer the position and this type of circuit is likely to become more commonly used in future.

There are some interesting circuits which are similar to the multivibrator, but which use direct coupling between the transistors. In these circuits, a small rapid change in current or voltage level brings about a change in the state of the circuit. The circuit may automatically revert after some given time, when it is termed "monostable" or it may require a second change to bring this about, when it is termed "bistable".

Monostable Circuits

These are regenerative circuits which have one stable and one unstable or quasi-stable state. Such circuits have been used to produce a rectangular pulse of known duration from a given, shorter,

15

pulse, and also to introduce a predetermined time delay between an input pulse and an output. A typical circuit is shown in Fig. 10.17. This circuit is capable of producing delays of the order of a few milliseconds by a suitable choice of components. To obtain

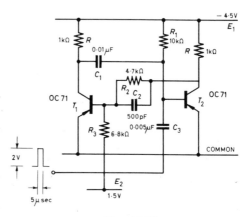

FIG. 10.17

delays of the order of 1 minute, the value of R_1 must be raised in order to increase the time constant. Often silicon transistors are used and the capacitor C_1 connected between the base of T_2 and the collector of T_1 via an emitter follower.

The output pulse length depends on the time constant, C_1R_1, and finally decays exponentially as set by C_1R. The method of analysis is similar to that already described for the astable circuit. On a positive pulse arriving at the base of T_2, differentiated by C_3, T_2 cuts off and T_1 is driven heavily into conduction. C_1 charges through R_1 until T_2 conducts again. T_1 is then rapidly cut off and C_1 discharges through R, while C_2 controls the recovery time of the circuit as a whole.

The quasi-stable state can be shown to persist for a time, t, where

$$t = R_1 C_1 \log\left(\frac{E + V_{b(off)}}{E}\right)$$

The Emitter Coupled Monostable Circuit

The emitter-coupled monostable circuit is illustrated in Fig. 10.18. In its stable state, T_2 is conducting and T_1 is off. A positive-going edge at the input is differentiated by C_1 and routed through the diode (which prevents negative-going pulses being applied) to the collector of T_1 and the base of T_2. T_2 is turned off and the collector potential of T_1 rises to near zero, driving the base of T_2 further

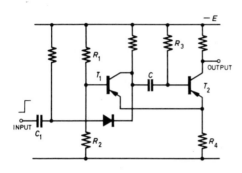

FIG. 10.18

positive. The circuit reverts to its stable state as C charges through R_3. The coupling from T_2 to T_1 is through the common emitter resistance, R_4. Because of this, it is not necessary for T_2 to be taken out of the saturation region, unlike the astable circuit already described, before the regenerative transient can commence. This is because the removal of the charge, Q_{bs}, from T_2 causes a current flow in its emitter resistance, so initiating the feedback to T_1 even before Q_{bs} has been completely removed. One application of this circuit is as a pulse-width modulator, since the base of T_1 is easily accessible and variation of the base potential varies the pulse width. The calculation of the duration of the negative-going monostable pulse output follows the same lines as in the previous circuits.

The Blocking Oscillator

Figure 10.19 shows a blocking oscillator. This device produces an approximately rectangular output pulse at the collector, and an approximately linear ramp voltage at its base. When the potentials are applied, the collector current rises nearly linearly due to the inductance in the collector lead, until the collector potential is nearly zero. This induces a voltage, E/n, into the base circuit, so that the base current, I_b, is given by

$$I_b = [E(1+1/n)-V]1/R \qquad (10.21)$$

Now, as C charges, V increases, causing I_b to fall, while I_c is still increasing. Thus, eventually, I_c/I_b becomes equal to α' and it is no longer saturated. Any further increase in I_c cannot take place, and so the voltage E/n ceases, causing the base current to fall rapidly and the transistor to be turned off. This reverses the sign of the voltage injected into the base circuit, which makes the effect cumulative, so

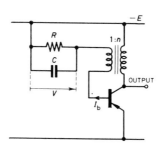

FIG. 10.19

that a large reverse bias is applied to the transistor. When this dies away the cycle can start again.

Conduction ceases when $V = E(1 + 1/n)$ (from equation (10.21)), and C discharges through R so that $V = E(1 + 1/n)e^{-t/RC}$.

When the feedback voltage, E/n, equals zero the transistor conducts again, when $t = RC \log(1 + 1/n)$.

This is the time for which the transistor is turned off. The calculation of this time assumes that the transformer does not "ring" after this time, and that the duration of the switching transients is small compared with it.

When the transistor is turned on, the equations defining its behaviour can be deduced, if the transformer is considered as an ideal transformer shunted by its leakage inductance, L, and having series resistance, r, as shown in Fig. 10.20.

$$E = i_c r + L \, di/dt \qquad (10.22)$$

$$L \, di/dt = (i_c - i)n^2 R \qquad (10.23)$$

A differential equation can be formed from these equations in which i_c is eliminated.

Thus $$-L \, di/dt(1 + r/n^2 R) = ir - E$$

The solution of this yields a value for i:

$$i = \frac{E}{r}\left\{1 - \exp\left(\frac{-n^2 R r t_1}{(r + n^2 R)L}\right)\right\} \qquad (10.24)$$

where i is the current at any time, t_1.

If now, $L\, di/dt$ is eliminated between equations (10.22) and (10.23), and i substituted from equation (10.24), expressions can be

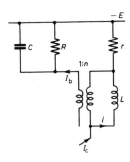

FIG. 10.20

found for i_c and, knowing the transformer ratio, n, for i_b. Then, putting $i_c = \alpha' i_b$, yields an approximate value for the time for which the transistor conducts.

Thus
$$t_1 = \frac{L}{n^2 R}(\alpha' n - 1)$$

This assumes that r is small and that $\int i_b\, dt_1$ equals the charge lost by C during the time t. Hence the recurrence frequency, f, is given by $f = 1/(t + t_1)$.

Bistable Circuits

The third of the family of cross coupled generators is the Eccles–Jordan bistable circuit. A typical circuit is shown in Fig. 10.21.

There are two stable states, in each of which one transistor is cut off and the other is bottomed. Simplified design formulae are:

$$R_c = E_1/I_{c.on} \qquad (10.25)$$

$$R_f = \frac{\alpha' R_B E_1}{R_B I_{c.on} + \alpha' E_2} \qquad (10.26)$$

where α' is the bottom of the spread so that the poorest transistor just bottoms.

The design procedure commences with a choice of supply potential and $I_{c.on}$. A transistor is then chosen which can operate at the potentials concerned, perhaps limited by the use of a diode clamp which prevents the transistor becoming saturated. Also, the

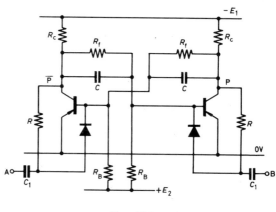

FIG. 10.21

transistor must be capable of switching at the desired rate. This leads to the value of α' and so to R_f and R_B.

The speed-up capacitors C assist in the switching between the two stable states. The pulses to the circuit may be derived from separate sources A and B. Alternatively, these points may be joined together when the input pulses are routed to the transistors by two diodes. Only one of these is able to conduct at a time, due to the bias with which they are supplied from the collectors via the resistors R in the figure. The output can be taken from either collector, and in some cases outputs are used from both of them. These are labelled P and $\overline{P}$ in the figure, since if one of them is at a voltage level designated "1" the other must be at the "0" level.

In common with the astable and monostable circuits, complementary transistor arrangements are possible. In such cases, in the "on" state both transistors are conducting, and in the "off" state both are cut off. Since both transistors switch together and conduct at the same time, the low input impedance of each is here also capable of supplying the high drive current required by the other.

One disadvantage of this mode of operation is that a better regulated power supply is required due to the more irregular current drain.

One application of the bistable circuit is for binary stores and for binary and modified binary decade counting systems. For example, three binary stages in tandem can be used to divide a train of pulses by eight (n stages divide by 2^n), and hence can bring the counting of rapid pulse trains within the capabilities of other slower, but perhaps economically desirable counting systems. They are used in nuclear instrumentation, frequency division, process control and pattern generators. Figure 10.22 shows diagrammatically three bistable stages used in a pattern generator which produces groups of four pulses. When the level at D is negative, the "nor" element is

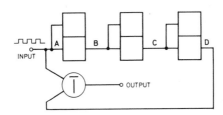

Fig. 10.22

held with its output at its more positive level. When D is positive the "nor" element is controlled by the input pulse train. Circuits of this kind can be made very flexible and have many applications.

In describing these and similar circuits using bistable elements, it will be noticed that their outputs follow the binary code. Thus, in Fig. 10.22, two input pulses at A are needed for every change in level at B, four for a change at C and eight for a change at D. The weighting of D, C, B and A is said to be 8421.

A train of four bistable elements of this kind can easily be modified to give scales of ten, for example, by resetting on the tenth pulse, or by resetting to the state which would have been reached after six pulses, or by omitting some of the sixteen possible counts. An example of this last kind is shown in Fig. 10.23 where the eighth pulse causes the fourth bistable element to change state. The pulse this produces is used to set the second and third bistable elements, so that the count jumps from seven to fourteen. An output is obtained from the fourth bistable element after two more input pulses, that is, after ten pulses in all.

The capacitors in the feedback loop provide sufficient delay, so that the resetting of the second and third bistable elements due to

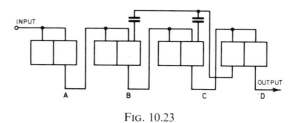

INPUT

OUTPUT

A   B   C   D

FIG. 10.23

the feedback takes place just after the eighth pulse. Using the concept of negative logic, the state of the collectors labelled A, B, C and D in the figure after each count is shown in Table 10.2.

Table 10.2

Modified Binary Counting using Feedback

Count	D	C	B	A	
0	0	0	0	0	
1	0	0	0	1	
2	0	0	1	0	
3	0	0	1	1	
4	0	1	0	0	
5	0	1	0	1	
6	0	1	1	0	
7	0	1	1	1	
8	1	0	0	0	before feedback (transitory state)
	1	1	1	0	after feedback
9	1	1	1	1	

From this table, it can be seen that the output of each element is no longer representing the binary code, i.e. 8421, but now the weighting of the elements can be seen by inspection to be 2421. The whole unit is said to be a 2421 binary coded decimal counter. It is clearly possible to connect a number of 2421 BCD decades in tandem as a decimal counter.

The Schmitt Trigger

Another similar circuit is the schmitt trigger, an example of which is shown in Fig. 10.24. The operation of the circuit depends on the d.c. level of the input. When it is below triggering level, T_1 is shut off and T_2 is conducting. As the triggering voltage rises, it rapidly changes the circuit to the "on" state with T_1 conducting and

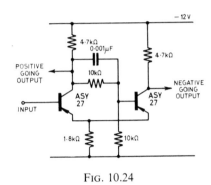

Fig. 10.24

T_2 shut off. It will do this even when the input level changes extremely slowly. It will maintain this state until the input level falls again, when it will rapidly revert. It is not necessarily the case that the "on" and the "off" input levels are identical, and circuits have been devised which make use of the backlash obtainable in this way. The circuit finds use as a pulse shaper, and as a discriminator or gate

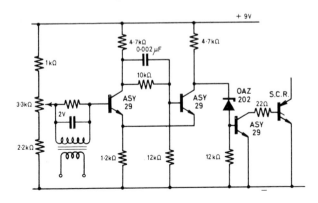

Fig. 10.25

selector. It is not desirable to load the positive-going output from
T_1, and if a positive-going output is required which has a good
switching performance, an inverting amplifier similar to that used
in Fig. 10.12 should be employed.

As an example of one application of a schmitt trigger, it will be
remembered that the control circuits for firing silicon controlled
rectifiers operate with greater precision if the pulses used have steep
leading edges. This is shown in Fig. 10.25, where an a.c. supply
derived from the mains is used as input to a schmitt trigger. In this
way the precise phase of firing can be controlled.

Photoschmitt Trigger

It might seem that if the first transistor of a schmitt trigger be
replaced by a phototransistor, it would still operate as a trigger with
fast switching times. However, problems of temperature and incident light level make it difficult to design a reliable circuit. It is better
to use a separate phototransistor directly coupled to the schmitt
trigger. A circuit of this kind is shown in Fig. 10.26.

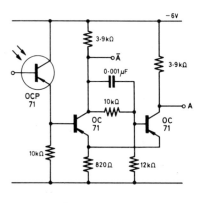

FIG. 10.26

Outputs of A and $\overline{A}$ can be obtained as shown in the figure.
Despite previous comments on the loading of $\overline{A}$, which applied
chiefly if rapid switching must be maintained, $\overline{A}$ can be loaded by
diode "and–or" logic networks such as might be employed in a
card sorter.

Biased Amplifier

Used in conjunction with the output from a calibrated biased amplifier, the schmitt trigger can be used as a pulse height discriminator. Carrier storage affects the response of circuits of this kind. A typical case, using germanium alloy transistors with $f_1 = 10$ Mc/s, might be that after a 3 volt peak 1 microsec pulse, the trigger level would be reduced by about 10 per cent for the order of a further 500 nanosec. Hence, for a fast discriminator, high frequency transistors would be used to keep this effect to a minimum.

A biased amplifier is shown in Fig. 10.27. In this circuit, when the input is driven sufficiently negative, the common collector stage conducts, and an in-phase output is produced across the 4·7 kilohm

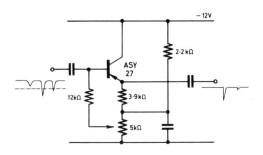

FIG. 10.27

load. When the potentiometer is calibrated, the stage may be employed as a simple pulse height discriminator. Often pulses within a given height range only are required. Then two such amplifiers are used, and only when an output is available from the lesser and not from the greater level, is the pulse within the range. If these outputs are A and B where A is greater than B, and are coupled to schmitt triggers capable of supplying $\overline{A}$ and $\overline{B}$ also, the trigger outputs then supply diode gates capable of operating in the condition $B\overline{A}$. Only pulses satisfying this condition then operate the following counter. Pulse height discriminators used in nuclear instrumentation may have as many as fifty adjacent channels, and the circuitry just described or some modification of it could be used in each of them.

Unijunction Transistors

The unijunction transistor is a semiconductor junction device, the action of which is in some ways similar to the four-layer diode described in Chapter 7. It is included here, since it finds application as a pulse generator and frequency divider. It is becoming increasingly common to find the unijunction transistor used to fire silicon controlled rectifiers.

The device consists of a slab of n-type silicon to the ends of which are connected two contacts. These are called the base contacts. A typical interbase resistance is 5,000 ohms. An aluminium wire is used to form a pn junction between the bases and near to one of them. This is base 2 in Fig. 10.28. An emitter contact is brought out

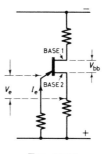

FIG. 10.28

by this wire from the junction. By means of a suitable potential at the emitter lead the junction is reverse biased. This may be brought about by the current through the transistor itself. If this junction is now biased into conduction, holes are injected into the silicon slab, and, due to the internal field produced by the current flow through the slab, these carriers are swept towards the further base terminal (base 1 in the figure).

The interbase resistance falls rapidly as the hole density increases, and so the potential drop between the emitter and base 1 falls also. This in turn causes an increase in emitter current. This effect is cumulative, the emitter current being limited only by the external resistances of the circuit and of the power supply.

The emitter characteristic of the device is shown in Fig. 10.29. When the junction is reverse biased the emitter current is small. A voltage V_{bb} is developed between the base contacts, and a fraction of it, ηV_{bb}, where η is called the intrinsic stand-off ratio, is developed between the emitter and base 2. η is typically about 0·5. When the external voltage exceeds ηV_{bb}, holes are injected into the base material and the consequent increase in I_e produces the negative characteristic shown in the figure.

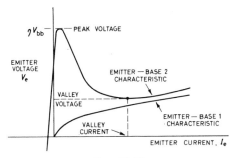

FIG. 10.29

The emitter current which corresponds to the peak voltage is only a few microamps, but the valley current is often of the order of 10 mA and the maximum continuous emitter current of the order of 50 mA.

Figure 10.30 shows a typical pulse generator. C charges through R_3 until the charging current becomes sufficiently small to lift the

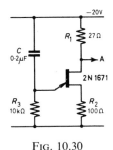

FIG. 10.30

reverse bias due to the voltage across R_3. Then it is rapidly discharged until the voltage falls below the valley voltage. The output at the point A in the figure consists of a train of positive-going pulses of short duration, and is directly suitable for operating a silicon controlled rectifier.

Conclusion

Most of the circuits described in this chapter lend themselves to modular construction. For example, transistor–resistor logic modules are available from a wide variety of manufacturers in the United Kingdom and in America. A similar state of affairs exists regarding binary stages and modified binary decades. Along with this is the tendency, which is undoubtedly growing at the present time, to limit the work of a designer either to circuit design or to systems design. With the introduction of solid state devices and circuits, it appears that this trend is bound to continue. This situation sometimes involves the engineer in a precise determination of the performance of a circuit, and more often in an estimate of known but lesser accuracy. It is the author's hope that, as stated in the preface, this book has been of some assistance in introducing students to the theory of transistors and allied devices with their applications, and in helping engineers to make the right approximations in the situations in which they find themselves.

PROBLEMS

10.1   (a) Contrast diode logic with transistor–resistor logic.

(b) Show how the functions "nor" and "nand"* can be carried out by diode circuits and inverters and the function "or" can be carried out by transistor–resistor logical elements. Use negative logic throughout.

10.2   Sketch a typical transistor–resistor logical element, using an *npn* transistor. Explain what are its functions using (a) negative, and (b) positive logical conventions.

10.3   Design a schmitt trigger to operate between supplies of $+6$ and -6 volt and using germanium *pnp* transistors. The voltage levels which may be applied are to be taken as -5 volts and $+0.5$ volts and the collector current when conducting is to be 4 mA.

10.4   Show how it is possible to produce trains of two, three or four pulses (a) spaced at known intervals, and (b) only when a "start" button is pressed. A second group of pulses should only occur in case (b) when the button is pressed a second time. What type of circuit may be used to avoid the uncertainty of contact bounce on the push button?

* Common abbreviation for "not-and".

10.5 Given that two matched *pnp* transistors are available to be operated between supplies of $+6$ and -6 volt, design a bistable circuit assuming that the collector current in the conducting transistor is 6 mA, and that the current gain is 25. Assume also that the transistors bottom at 0·1 volt, V_{be} when cut off is $+2$ volts, and that when conducting, V_{be} is $-0·2$ volt. Deduce values for the collector load and other resistors. [Ans. 1 kilohm, 12 kilohms, 22 kilohms.]

BIBLIOGRAPHY

Beaufoy: Transistor Switching Circuit Design Using Charge Control Parameters, *Proc.I.E.E.*, **106**, 1085, 1959.

Beaufoy and Sparkes: The Junction Transistor as a Charge Controlled Device, *A.T.E. Journal*, 310, 1957.

Chaplin: Pulse Circuits, *Proc.I.E.E.*, **106**, 1208, 1959.

Dean: "Counting Techniques and Transistor Circuit Logic", Chapman and Hall, 1964.

den Brinker, Fairbairn and Norris: An Analysis of the Switching Behaviour of Graded Base Transistors, *Electronic Engng.*, 500, Aug. 1963.

Ebers and Moll: Large Signal Behaviour of Junction Transistors, *Proc.I.R.E.*, **42**, 1761, 1954.

Hamilton, Griffith and Shaver: Avalanche Transistor Circuits for Generating Rectangular Pulses, *Electronic Engng.*, 808, Dec. 1962.

Haskard: Computer Logic Circuits, *Proc.I.R.E.(Aust.)*, **23**, 183, 1962.

Hawker: Transistor-Resistor Logical Circuits, *Mullard Tech. Comm.*, **45**, 174, 1960.

Hooper and Turnbull: Applications of Charge Control Concept to Transistor Characterisation, *Proc.I.R.E.(Aust.)*, **23**, 132, 1962.

Sparkes: Measurement of Transistor Transient Switching Parameters, *Proc.I.E.E.*, **106**, 562, 1959.

Tomlinson: Switching Circuits Using Bi-Directional Non-Linear Impedances, *J.Brit.I.R.E.*, **19**, 571, 1959.

Wells and Page: Pulse Counting and Fast Scaling Transistor Circuits, *J.Brit.I.R.E.*, **23**, 231, 1962.

Formulae for Conversion between Parameters

The h Parameters

The general equations which define the h parameters are equations (A.1) and (A.2). It should be noted that the treatment employed in Chapter 2, and, in particular, in equations (2.5a) and (2.6a) are specific examples of these equations.

$$v_i = h_i i_i + h_r v_o \tag{A.1}$$

$$i_o = h_f i_i + h_o v_o \tag{A.2}$$

These equations lead to the equivalent circuit of Fig. A.1. In this circuit, the generator resistance, R_g, and the load, R_L, are also shown.

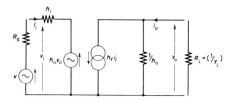

Fig. A.1

From this circuit, when R_g and R_L are taken into account

$$v = i_i(R_g + h_i) + h_r v_o \tag{A.3}$$

$$i_o(R_L + 1/h_o) = (h_f/h_o)i_i \tag{A.4}$$

Input Impedance, z_{in}

From equations (A.3) and (A.4)

$$v = i_i \left[(R_g + h_i) - \frac{h_r h_f R_L}{h_o(R_L + 1/h_o)} \right], \quad \text{since } i_o R_L = -v_o$$

But $v = i_i(R_g + z_{in})$

228

Therefore
$$z_{in} = h_i - \frac{h_r h_f R_L}{(R_L h_o + 1)}$$

or
$$z_{in} = h_i - \frac{h_r h_f}{h_o + Y_L} \qquad (A.5)$$

Current Gain, a_i

From equation (A.4)

$$a_i = i_o/i_i = \frac{h_f}{h_o(R_L + 1/h_o)} = \frac{h_f}{R_L h_o + 1}$$

or
$$a_i = \frac{h_f Y_L}{h_o + Y_L} \qquad (A.6)$$

Voltage Gain, a_v

Hence we obtain:

$$a_v = -\frac{a_i}{Y_L z_{in}} = -\frac{h_f Y_L}{(h_o + Y_L) Y_L} \frac{h_o + Y_L}{(h_i h_o + h_i Y_L - h_r h_f)}$$

$$= -\frac{h_f}{h_i(h_o + Y_L) - h_r h_f} \qquad (A.7)$$

Output Admittance, Y_o

The method here is to put equations (A.3) and (A.4) in the form $f(v) = i_o(1/Y_L + 1/Y_o)$ and hence deduce Y_o.
Substituting for i_i in equation (A.3):

$$v = i_o \left[(1/Y_L + 1/h_o) \frac{h_o}{h_f} (R_g + h_i) - \frac{h_r}{Y_L} \right]$$

$$= i_o \left\{ \frac{1}{Y_L} \left[\frac{h_o}{h_f} (R_g + h_i) - h_r \right] + \frac{R_g + h_i}{h_f} \right\}$$

Therefore
$$\frac{v}{\frac{h_o}{h_f}(R_g + h_i) - h_r} = i_o \left[\frac{1}{Y_L} + \frac{R_g + h_i}{h_o(R_g + h_i) - h_r h_f} \right]$$

Hence
$$Y_L = h_o - \frac{h_r h_f}{R_g + h_i} \qquad (A.8)$$

16

Table A.1

Conversion from T Parameters to h Parameters

	common base	common emitter	common collector
h_i	$r_e + r_b/\alpha''$	$\alpha'' h_{ib}$	$\alpha'' h_{ib}$
h_r	r_b/r_c	$\dfrac{\alpha'' r_e}{r_c}$	$\dfrac{r_c}{r_c + \alpha'' r_e}$
h_f	$-\alpha$	α'	$-\alpha''$
h_o	$1/r_c$	$\alpha'' h_{ob}$	$\alpha'' h_{ob}$

Table A.2

Conversion of h Parameters between Common Base, Common Emitter and Common Collector Circuits

common base	common emitter	common collector
h_{ib}	$h_{ib} = \dfrac{h_{ie}}{1 + h_{fe}}$	$h_{ic} = h_{ie}$
h_{rb}	$h_{rb} = \dfrac{h_{ie} h_{oe}}{1 + h_{fe}}$	$h_{rc} = \dfrac{1}{1 + h_{re}}$
h_{fb}	$h_{fb} = \dfrac{-h_{fe}}{1 + h_{fe}}$	$h_{fc} = -(1 + h_{fe})$
h_{ob}	$h_{ob} = \dfrac{h_{oe}}{1 + h_{fe}}$	$h_{oc} = h_{oe}$

Table A.3

Conversion between h and y Parameters

$$h_i = 1/y_i \qquad\qquad y_i = 1/h_i$$

$$h_r = -y_r/y_i \qquad\qquad y_r = -h_r/h_i$$

$$h_f = y_f/y_i \qquad\qquad y_f = -h_f/h_i$$

$$h_o = -\frac{y_r y_f}{y_i} + y_o \qquad\qquad y_o = -\frac{h_r h_f}{h_i} + h_o$$

Table A.4

Conversion of y Parameters between Common Base, Common Emitter and Common Collector Circuits

$$y_{ib} = y_{ie} + y_{re} + y_{fe} + y_{oe} \qquad y_{ic} = y_{ie}$$

$$y_{rb} = -(y_{re} + y_{oe}) \qquad\qquad y_{rc} = -(y_{ie} + y_{re})$$

$$y_{fb} = -(y_{fe} + y_{oe}) \qquad\qquad y_{fc} = -(y_{ie} + y_{fe})$$

$$y_{ob} = y_{oe} \qquad\qquad\qquad\quad y_{oc} = y_{ie} + y_{re} + y_{fe} + y_{oe}$$

Table A.5

Performance of a Transistor Amplifier in Terms of the y Parameters

Input admittance, y_{in}	$y_i - \dfrac{y_r y_f}{Y_L + y_o}$
Output admittance, y_{out}	$y_o - \dfrac{y_r y_f}{Y_g + y_i}$
Voltage gain, a_v	$\dfrac{-y_f}{Y_L + y_o}$
Current gain, a_i	$Y_L \left\{ \dfrac{y_f}{y_i(y_o + Y_L) - y_r y_f} \right\}$

Derivation of the Input Impedance, Output Impedance, Current Gain and Voltage Gain of Amplifiers in the Three Modes of Working

COMMON BASE CIRCUIT

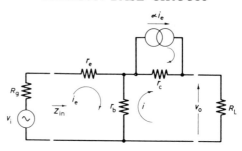

FIG. B.1

Input Impedance, z_{in}

$$v_i = (R_g + r_e)i_e + (i_e - i)r_b \tag{B.1}$$

$$0 = iR_L + r_c(i - \alpha i_e) + r_b(i - i_e) \tag{B.2}$$

$$\therefore \quad 0 = i(R_L + r_c + r_b) - r_b i_e - \alpha i_e r_c \tag{B.3}$$

$$\therefore \quad i(R_L + r_b + r_c) = i_e(r_b + \alpha r_c) \tag{B.4}$$

$$\text{and} \quad v_i = (R_g + r_e + r_b)i_e - \frac{r_b(r_b + \alpha r_c)}{R_L + r_b + r_c} i_e \tag{B.5}$$

$$\text{and} \quad z_{in} = v_i/i_e = r_e + r_b - \frac{r_b(r_b + \alpha r_c)}{R_L + r_b + r_c} \tag{B.6}$$

(1) When $R_L = \infty$

$$z_{in}, \text{ with open-circuited load, } = r_e + r_b \tag{B.7}$$

232

(2) When $R_L = 0$

z_{in}, with short-circuited load, $= r_e + r_b(1 - \alpha) = r_{ee}$ (B.8)

since $r_b \ll r_c$

(3) When R_L, $r_b \ll r_c$

$$z_{in} = r_{ee} \qquad (B.9)$$

Current Gain, a_i

From equation (B.4) $a_i = i/i_e = \dfrac{r_b + \alpha r_c}{R_L + r_b + r_c}$ (B.10)

and, if R_L and $r_b \ll r_c$ $a_i = \alpha$

Output Impedance, z_o

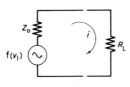

FIG. B.2

If an expression can be put into the form $f(v_i) = i(z_o + R_L)$, then z_o can be found.

From equation (B.1)

$$v_i = (R_g + r_e + r_b)i_e - ir_b \qquad (B.11)$$

And from equation (B.4)

$$v_i = \left[(R_g + r_e + r_b)\frac{(R_L + r_b + r_c)}{r_b + \alpha r_c} - r_b \right] i \qquad (B.12)$$

$\therefore$ $\dfrac{(r_b + \alpha r_c)v_i}{R_g + r_e + r_b} = \left[R_L + r_b + r_c - \dfrac{r_b(r_b + \alpha r_c)}{R_g + r_e + r_b} \right] i$ (B.13)

and $z_o = r_b + r_c - \dfrac{r_b(r_b + \alpha r_c)}{R_g + r_e + r_b}$ (B.14)

(1) When $R_g = \infty$, i.e. for current drive, $z_o \fallingdotseq r_c$

(2) When $R_g = 0$, i.e. for voltage drive

$$z_o = r_b + r_c - \frac{r_b(r_b + \alpha r_c)}{r_e + r_b} \tag{B.15}$$

$$= \frac{r_b[r_c(1 - \alpha)] + r_e(r_b + r_c)}{r_{eb}} \tag{B.16}$$

$$\doteq \frac{r_c r_{ee}}{r_{eb}}, \text{ if } r_b \ll r_c \tag{B.17}$$

Voltage Gain, a_v

(1) When $R_L = \infty$
From equation (B.13)

$$a_v = \frac{r_b + \alpha r_c}{R_g + r_e + r_b} \tag{B.18}$$

and, if also $R_g = 0$, so that the maximum theoretical voltage gain is achieved

$$a_v = \alpha r_c / r_{eb} \qquad\qquad \text{assuming that } r_b \ll r_c \tag{B.19}$$

(2) For R_L finite and much less than r_c

$$a_v = iR_L / v_i \tag{B.20}$$

From equation (B.12)

$$a_v = R_L \div \left[\frac{(R_g + r_e + r_b)(R_L + r_b + r_c)}{r_b + \alpha r_c} - r_b \right] \tag{B.21}$$

and, if also R_g is zero

$$a_v = R_L \div \left[\frac{(r_e + r_b)}{\alpha} - r_b \right] \tag{B.22}$$

$$= \frac{\alpha R_L}{r_{ee}} \tag{B.23}$$

COMMON EMITTER CIRCUIT

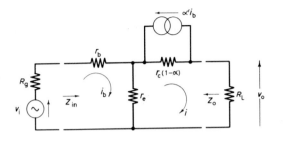

FIG. B.3

Input Impedance

$$v_i = i_b(R_g + r_b + r_e) - i r_e \tag{B.24}$$

$$i[R_L + r_e + r_c(1-\alpha)] + \alpha' i_b r_c(1-\alpha) = i_b r_e$$

$$\therefore \qquad i[R_L + r_e + r_c(1-\alpha)] = i_b(r_e - \alpha r_c) \tag{B.25}$$

since $\alpha' = \alpha/(1-\alpha)$

From equations (B.24) and (B.25)

$$R_g + z_{in} = v_i/i_b = R_g + r_b + r_e - \frac{r_e(r_e - \alpha r_c)}{R_L + r_e + r_c(1-\alpha)} \tag{B.26}$$

(1) When $R_L = \infty$

$$z_{in} = r_{eb} \tag{B.27}$$

(2) When $R_L = 0$

$$z_{in} \fallingdotseq r_e + r_b + \alpha r_e/(1-\alpha)$$

$$= \alpha'' r_{ee}, \text{ since } \alpha'' = 1/(1-\alpha) \tag{B.28}$$

(3) When $R_L \ll r_c(1-\alpha)$

$$z_{in} = \alpha'' r_{ee} \tag{B.29}$$

Current Gain

$$a_i = i/i_b$$

From equation (B.25)

$$a_i = \frac{r_e - \alpha r_c}{R_L + r_e + r_c(1-\alpha)} \tag{B.30}$$

If $R_L \ll r_c(1-\alpha)$,

$$a_i = -\alpha/(1-\alpha) = -\alpha' \tag{B.31}$$

(The sign shows that the incorrect phase has been assumed for the output current.)

Output Impedance

Proceeding as in the case of the common base circuit, from equations (B.24) and (B.25)

$$v_i = \left\{ \frac{[R_L+r_e+r_c(1-\alpha)](R_g+r_b+r_e)}{r_e-\alpha r_c} - r_e \right\} i \tag{B.32}$$

$$\therefore \quad \frac{(r_e-\alpha r_c)v_i}{R_g+r_b+r_e} = \left[R_L+r_e+r_c(1-\alpha)-\frac{r_e(r_e-\alpha r_c)}{R_g+r_b+r_e} \right] i \tag{B.33}$$

$$= (R_L+z_o)i$$

$$\therefore \quad z_o = r_e+r_c(1-\alpha)-\frac{r_e(r_e-\alpha r_c)}{R_g+r_b+r_e} \tag{B.34}$$

(1) When $R_g=\infty$, i.e. for current drive

$$z_o \fallingdotseq r_c(1-\alpha) = r_c/\alpha'' \tag{B.35}$$

(2) When $R_g=0$, i.e. for voltage drive

$$z_o = \frac{r_c(1-\alpha)(r_b+r_e)+\alpha r_c r_e}{r_e+r_b} \tag{B.36}$$

$$= \frac{r_c r_{ee}}{r_{eb}} \tag{B.37}$$

Voltage Gain

(1) When $R_L=\infty$
From equation (B.33)

$$a_v = \frac{r_e-\alpha r_c}{R_g+r_b+r_e} \tag{B.38}$$

If also, $R_g=0$, so that maximum theoretical voltage gain is achieved

$$a_v = -\alpha r_c/r_{eb} \tag{B.39}$$

(2) For R_L finite and much less than $r_c(1-\alpha)$, $a_v = iR_L/v_i$

From equation (B.32)

$$a_v = R_L \div \left\{ \frac{[R_L + r_e + r_c(1-\alpha)](R_g + r_b + r_e)}{r_e - \alpha r_c} - r_e \right\} \qquad \text{(B.40)}$$

If also, R_g is zero

$$a_v = R_L \div \frac{(1-\alpha)(r_b + r_e) - \alpha r_e}{\alpha} \qquad \text{(B.41)}$$

$$= \frac{\alpha R_L}{r_{ee}} \qquad \text{(B.42)}$$

COMMON COLLECTOR CIRCUIT

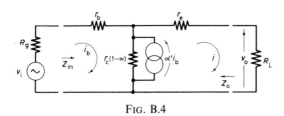

FIG. B.4

Input Impedance

$$v_i = i_b(R_g + r_b) + i(r_e + R_L) \qquad \text{(B.43)}$$

$$i[r_e + R_L + r_c(1-\alpha)] = r_c(1-\alpha)(1+\alpha')i_b = r_c i_b \qquad \text{(B.44)}$$

$$\therefore \qquad v_i/i_b = R_g + r_b + \frac{(r_e + R_L)r_c}{r_e + R_L + r_c(1-\alpha)} \qquad \text{(B.45)}$$

$$\therefore \qquad z_{in} = r_b + \frac{(r_e + R_L)r_c}{r_e + R_L + r_c(1-\alpha)} \qquad \text{(B.46)}$$

(1) When $R_L \gg r_c$

$$z_{in} \fallingdotseq r_c \qquad \text{(B.47)}$$

(2) When $R_L = 0$

$$z_{in} = r_b + \frac{r_e r_c}{r_e + r_c(1-\alpha)} \tag{B.48}$$

$$= \alpha'' r_{ee} \tag{B.49}$$

(3) When $R_L \ll r_c(1-\alpha)$

$$z_i = r_b + \frac{(r_e + R_L)r_c}{r_e + R_L + r_c(1-\alpha)} \tag{B.50}$$

$$\doteqdot r_b + (r_e + R_L)/(1-\alpha) \tag{B.51}$$

$$= \alpha''(r_{ee} + R_L) \tag{B.52}$$

Current Gain

$$a_i = i/i_b$$

From equation (B.44)

$$a_i = \frac{r_c}{r_e + R_L + r_c(1-\alpha)} \tag{B.53}$$

If $r_c(1-\alpha) \gg R_L$

$$a_i = \alpha'' \tag{B.54}$$

Output Impedance

Proceeding as in the previous two cases
From equations (B.43) and (B.44)

$$v_i = i\left\{\frac{[r_e + R_L + r_c(1-\alpha)](R_g + r_b)}{r_c} + r_e + R_L\right\} \tag{B.55}$$

$$\frac{v_i r_c}{R_g + r_b} = i\left\{[r_e + R_L + r_c(1-\alpha)] + \frac{r_c(r_e + R_L)}{R_g + r_b}\right\} \tag{B.56}$$

$$= i\left[R_L\left(1 + \frac{r_c}{R_g + r_b}\right) + r_e + r_c(1-\alpha) + \frac{r_c r_e}{R_g + r_b}\right] \tag{B.57}$$

$$\frac{v_i r_c}{R_g + r_b + r_c} = i\left\{R_L + \frac{[r_e + r_c(1-\alpha)](R_g + r_b) + r_c r_e}{R_g + r_b + r_c}\right\} \tag{B.58}$$

Hence
$$z_0 = \frac{[r_e + r_c(1-\alpha)](R_g + r_b) + r_c r_e}{R_g + r_b + r_c}$$
(B.59)

(1) When $R_g \gg r_c(1-\alpha)$, i.e. for current drive

$$z_0 = r_c(1-\alpha) = r_c/\alpha''$$
(B.60)

(2) When $R_g = 0$, i.e. for voltage drive

$$z_0 = \frac{[r_e + r_c(1-\alpha)]r_b + r_e}{r_b + r_c}$$
(B.61)

$$\doteqdot r_{ee}$$
(B.62)

(3) When R_g is finite and small

$$z_0 \doteqdot (1-\alpha)(R_g + r_b) + r_e$$
(B.63)

$$= r_{ee} + R_g/\alpha''$$
(B.64)

Voltage Gain

(1) When $R_L = \infty$
From equation (B.58)

$$a_v = r_c/(R_g + r_b + r_c)$$
(B.65)

and, if also R_g is zero
$$a_v \doteqdot 1$$
(B.66)

(2) When R_L is finite and much less than $r_c(1-\alpha)$
From equation (B.55)

$$a_v = R_L \div \left\{ \frac{[r_e + R_L + r_c(1-\alpha)](R_g + r_b)}{r_c} + r_e + R_L \right\}$$
(B.67)

$$\doteqdot R_L \div [(1-\alpha)(R_g + r_b) + R_L]$$

and, if $R_L \gg R_g$, $a_v \doteqdot 1$.

Analysis of the Four Principal Systems of Negative Feedback

FEEDBACK IN SERIES AT BOTH INPUT AND OUTPUT

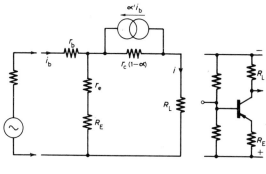

FIG. C.1

Input Impedance

From equations (B.8) and (B.29) replacing r_e by $r_e + R_E$

$$z_{in} = \alpha''(r_{ee} + R_E) \tag{C.1}$$

Hence the input impedance is increased.

Output Impedance

From equation (B.34)

$$z_o \doteqdot r_e + R_E + r_c(1 - \alpha) \tag{C.2}$$

Thus the output impedance is barely altered by feedback, since $r_c(1 - \alpha)$ is the most important term.

Current Gain

From equation (B.30)

$$a_i = \frac{r_e + R_E - \alpha r_c}{R_L + r_e + R_E + r_c(1 - \alpha)}$$

and with typical values, $a_i \doteq \alpha'$, and hence is barely altered by feedback.

Voltage Gain

From equation (B.42)

$$a_v = \frac{\alpha R_L}{r_{ee} + R_E} \tag{C.3}$$

and since R_E can easily be greater than r_{ee}, the voltage gain is reduced.

Transconductance

The transconductance or mutual conductance of the stage, g_m, is defined as

$$\left(\frac{\partial I_o}{\partial V_i}\right)_{V_o} = \frac{i}{i_b z_{in}} = \frac{\alpha'}{\alpha''(r_{ee} + R_E)}$$

Therefore
$$g_m = \frac{\alpha}{r_{ee} + R_E} \tag{C.3a}$$

FEEDBACK IN PARALLEL AT BOTH INPUT AND OUTPUT

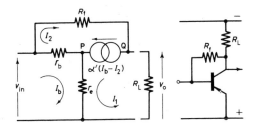

FIG. C.2

In Fig. C.2, it is assumed that $r_c(1-\alpha)$ is large compared with the parallel path $r_e + R_L$. Also, since the current through $r_b = I_b - I_2$ where these are mesh currents, the current generator in the equivalent circuit is $\alpha'(I_b - I_2)$:

$$V_{in} = (I_b - I_2)r_b + (I_b + I_1)r_e \qquad (C.4)$$

Applying Kirchhoff's laws at P:

$$I_1 + I_2 = \alpha'(I_b - I_2)$$

$$\therefore \qquad I_1 + \alpha'' I_2 = \alpha' I_b$$

$$\therefore \qquad I_2/I_b = \alpha - I_1/\alpha'' I_b \qquad (C.5)$$

Equating the potential differences between P and Q

$$(I_2 - I_b)r_b + I_2 R_f = (I_b + I_1)r_e + I_1 R_L \qquad (C.6)$$

From equation (C.4)

$$z_{in} = V_{in}/I_b = (1 - I_2/I_b)r_b + (1 + I_1/I_b)r_e \qquad (C.7)$$

and from equation (C.5)

$$z_{in} = \frac{r_b}{\alpha''}(1 + I_1/I_b) + (1 + I_1/I_b)r_e \qquad (C.8)$$

From equations (C.5) and (C.6)

$$I_b(\alpha R_f - r_b/\alpha'' - r_e) = I_1(R_f/\alpha'' + R_L + r_b/\alpha'' + r_e)$$

where, since $r_{ee} = r_e + r_b/\alpha''$

$$I_b(\alpha R_f - r_{ee}) = I_1(R_f/\alpha'' + R_L + r_{ee}) \qquad (C.9)$$

Input Impedance

From equations (C.8) and (C.9)

$$z_{in} = r_{ee}\left(1 + \frac{\alpha R_f - r_{ee}}{r_{ee} + R_L + R_f/\alpha''}\right)$$

$$= r_{ee}\frac{R_L + R_f}{r_{ee} + R_L + R_f/\alpha''} \qquad (C.10)$$

$$= \alpha'' r_{ee}\left(1 - \frac{\alpha'' r_{ee} + \alpha' R_L}{\alpha'' r_{ee} + \alpha'' R_L + R_f}\right) \qquad (C.10a)$$

As R_f tends to infinity, z_{in} tends to $\alpha'' r_{ee}$, but for finite values of R_f as shown in equation (C.10a) the input impedance is reduced.

Output Impedance

From equations (C.4) and (C.5)

$$V_{in} = (I_b + I_1) r_{ee}$$

Hence from equation (C.9)

$$V_{in} \frac{(\alpha R_f - r_{ee})}{r_{ee}} = I_1(R_L + R_f)$$

This is in the form $f(V_{in}) = I_1(R_L + z_0)$

so that
$$z_0 = R_f \tag{C.11}$$

As R_f tends to zero z_0 tends to zero also. It must be remembered that $r_c(1 - \alpha)$ has been ignored in this analysis, but this treatment does show that the effect of feedback is to reduce the output impedance.

Current Gain

From equation (C.9)

$$a_i = I_1/I_b = \frac{\alpha R_f - r_{ee}}{R_f/\alpha'' + R_L + r_{ee}} \tag{C.12}$$

$$\fallingdotseq \alpha'' \left(1 - \frac{R_f/\alpha'' + \alpha'' R_L + \alpha' r_{ee}}{R_f + \alpha'' R_L + \alpha'' r_{ee}} \right)$$

which tends almost to zero as R_f tends to zero. Hence the current gain is reduced with a finite load. However, if R_L is very small it is seen that the short-circuit current gain is not reduced.

Voltage Gain

$$a_v = I_1 R_L / I_b z_{in}$$

From equations (C.9) and (C.10)

$$a_v = \frac{(\alpha R_f - r_{ee}) R_L}{r_{ee}(R_L + R_f)}$$

$$= \frac{\alpha R_L}{r_{ee}} \left(\frac{R_f - r_{ee}/\alpha}{R_f + R_L} \right) \tag{C.13}$$

which tends to unity as R_f tends to zero. Hence the voltage gain is reduced.

From equation (C.12) the transresistance of the stage, R_T, defined as

$$\left(\frac{\partial V_o}{\partial I_i}\right)_{V_i} = v_o/i_b = I_1 R_L/I_b = \frac{\alpha R_f R_L}{R_f/\alpha'' + R_L}$$

if r_{ee} is ignored as small.

Therefore $$R_T = \frac{R_f}{1 + (R_f + R_L)/\alpha' R_L}$$ (C.14)

FEEDBACK IN PARALLEL AT THE INPUT AND IN SERIES AT THE OUTPUT

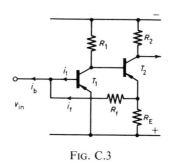

FIG. C.3

Output Impedance

Suppose that R_2 is small compared with z_o for T_2 (see Fig. C.1 and equation (C.2)). Hence, since z_{in} for T_2 is large (see equation (C.1)), T_1 is a voltage amplifier and T_2 acts as (a) a current amplifier for the output, and (b) an emitter follower for the feedback.

Input Impedance

The input impedance of T_1 is low (see equations (C.10) and (C.10a), for, as far as this input impedance is affected, the circuit is similar to that of Fig. C.2)

Hence $$z_{in} = r_{ee}\left(\frac{R_E + R_f}{r_{ee} + R_E + R_f/\alpha''}\right)$$ (C.15)

Current Gain

If the transistors have similar characteristics, the current gain of T_2 is approximately $\alpha'\alpha''I_1$, and hence the overall current gain, a_i, is given by:

$$a_i = \alpha'\alpha''I_1/I_b = \alpha'\alpha''I_1/(I_1+I_f) \qquad (C.16)$$

Now

$$V_{in} = I_1\alpha''r_{ee}$$

$$\doteqdot I_f(R_f+R_E)+\alpha'\alpha''I_1R_E \qquad (C.17)$$

$$\therefore \qquad I_1(\alpha''r_{ee}-\alpha'\alpha''R_E) = I_f(R_f+R_E) \qquad (C.17a)$$

Hence from equations (C.16) and (C.17a)

$$a_i = \frac{\alpha'\alpha''(R_f+R_E)}{R_f+R_E+\alpha''r_{ee}-\alpha'\alpha''R_E}$$

$$\doteqdot (R_f+R_E)/R_E \qquad (C.18)$$

$$\doteqdot R_f/R_E \qquad (C.18a)$$

Voltage Gain

If the stage is driven by a voltage source there can be no feedback and the gain is unaffected.

Generally, $a_v = a_iR_2/z_{in}$, where both a_i and z_{in} have been reduced. The percentage reduction in a_i is often greater than that in z_{in}, so that a_v is somewhat reduced.

FEEDBACK IN SERIES AT THE INPUT AND IN PARALLEL AT THE OUTPUT

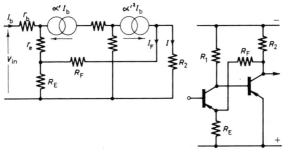

Fig. C.4

An analysis of this type of feedback circuit can only be attempted here if certain assumptions are made so as to simplify the circuit. In Fig. C.4, an approximate equivalent circuit is shown. From this the input impedance and voltage gain can be deduced.

Input Impedance

$$I_F = \frac{\alpha'^2 R_2 I_b}{R_2 + R_F + R_E} \tag{C.19}$$

$$I = \frac{\alpha'^2 (R_F + R_E) I_b}{R_2 + R_F + R_E} \tag{C.20}$$

$$V_{in} = I_b \left(r_b + \alpha'' r_{ee} + \alpha'' R_E + \frac{\alpha'^2 R_2 R_E}{R_2 + R_F + R_E} \right)$$

$$\therefore \qquad z_{in} = \alpha''(r_{ee} + R_E) + \frac{\alpha'^2 R_2 R_E}{R_2 + R_F + R_E} \tag{C.21}$$

Hence the input impedance is increased and often the second term is larger than the first. This is assumed to be the case in finding an expression for the voltage gain.

Voltage Gain

$$a_v = I R_2 / I_b z_{in}$$

and from equations (C.20) and (C.21)

$$a_v = \frac{\alpha'^2 (R_F + R_E) R_2}{(R_2 + R_F + R_E)} \cdot \frac{(R_2 + R_F + R_E)}{\alpha'^2 R_2 R_E}$$

$$= (R_F + R_E) / R_E$$

$$\doteqdot R_F / R_E \tag{C.22}$$

which is generally much less than without feedback.

Current Gain

When $R_2 = 0$, there is no feedback and hence the gain is unaltered. Generally, however, the current gain is somewhat reduced as given by equation (C.20).

Output Impedance

The output impedance is reduced due to the shunting effect of R_F and R_E.

Index